**NATIONAL GEOGRAPHIC**

U.S. HISTORY
AMERICAN STORIES

California Knowledge, Concepts, and Skills
Every Day for Every Student

BEGINNINGS TO WORLD WAR I

- Social Studies Skills Reading and Writing Lessons

- Reading and Note-Taking

- Vocabulary Practice

- Biographies

- Document-Based Question Templates

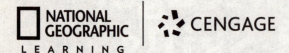

Acknowledgments

Grateful acknowledgment is given to the authors, artists, photographers, museums, publishers, and agents for permission to reprint copyrighted material. Every effort has been made to secure the appropriate permission. If any omissions have been made or if corrections are required, please contact the Publisher.

Photographic Credits

Wrap Cover: Mark Summers/National Geographic Learning

For product information and technology assistance, contact us at Customer & Sales Support, 888-915-3276

For permission to use material from this text or product, submit all requests online at **www.cengage.com/permissions**

Further permissions questions can be emailed to **permissionrequest@cengage.com**

National Geographic Learning | Cengage
1 N. State Street, Suite 900
Chicago, IL 60602

Cengage is a leading provider of customized learning solutions with employees residing in nearly 40 different countries and sales in more than 125 countries around the world. Find your local representative at **www.cengage.com**.

Visit National Geographic Learning
online at **NGL.Cengage.com/school**

ISBN: 978-133-7700-078

Printed in the United States of America

Print number: 10
Print year: 2021

U.S. History Knowledge and Concepts

U.S. History Knowledge and Concepts

UNIT 1

CHAPTER 1 SECTION 1
Societies of the Americas

NATIONAL GEOGRAPHIC LEARNING

READING AND NOTE-TAKING

ORGANIZE INFORMATION   Use the table below to organize information about the early American civilizations after you read Section 1.

CULTURE'S LOCATION	PEOPLE WHO LIVED THERE	CHARACTERISTICS
Mesoamerica	Olmec, Maya, and Aztec	The fertile landscape of Mesoamerica consisted of two areas, the highlands and lowlands. The highlands are in the mountains of the Sierra Madre. The Lowlands are along the coast of the Gulf of Mexico and in the jungles of the Yucatán Peninsula.
South America		
The Far North and Pacific Coast		
The Southwest and Great Plains		

UNIT **1**

CHAPTER 1 SECTION 1

Societies of the Americas *continued*

CULTURE'S LOCATION	PEOPLE WHO LIVED THERE	CHARACTERISTICS
The Midwest and Eastern States (Mound Builders)		
The Southeastern Woodlands		
The Eastern Woodlands		

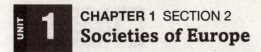

UNIT 1

CHAPTER 1 SECTION 2
Societies of Europe

NATIONAL GEOGRAPHIC LEARNING

READING AND NOTE-TAKING

OUTLINE AND TAKE NOTES As you read Section 2, use the headings and subheadings of each lesson to create an outline. Summarize each lesson as you finish taking notes.

2.1 The Middle Ages

A. A Feudal Society

- Feudalism achieved security by keeping a strict social hierarchy.

- _____

- _____

- _____

B. Wars, Trade, and Towns

- _____

- _____

- _____

Summarize

_____

_____

_____

2.2 Renaissance and Reformation

A.

- _____

- _____

- _____

B.

- _____

- _____

- _____

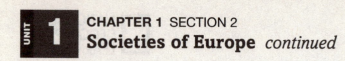

UNIT 1 | **CHAPTER 1** SECTION 2
Societies of Europe *continued*

Summarize

_____
_____
_____

2.3 Trade Expands

A.

- _____
- _____
- _____

B.

- _____
- _____
- _____

Summarize

_____
_____
_____

Write a summary paragraph of Section 2. Include a topic sentence, 3 to 5 sentences, and a concluding sentence.

_____
_____
_____
_____
_____
_____
_____

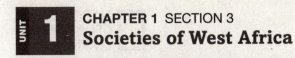

UNIT 1 CHAPTER 1 SECTION 3
Societies of West Africa

NATIONAL GEOGRAPHIC LEARNING

READING AND NOTE-TAKING

SUMMARIZE INFORMATION   Summarize details about the kingdom of Ghana as you read Section 3. Complete the Idea Web with notes about the rise and fall of Ghana. Add extra spokes and circles as needed.

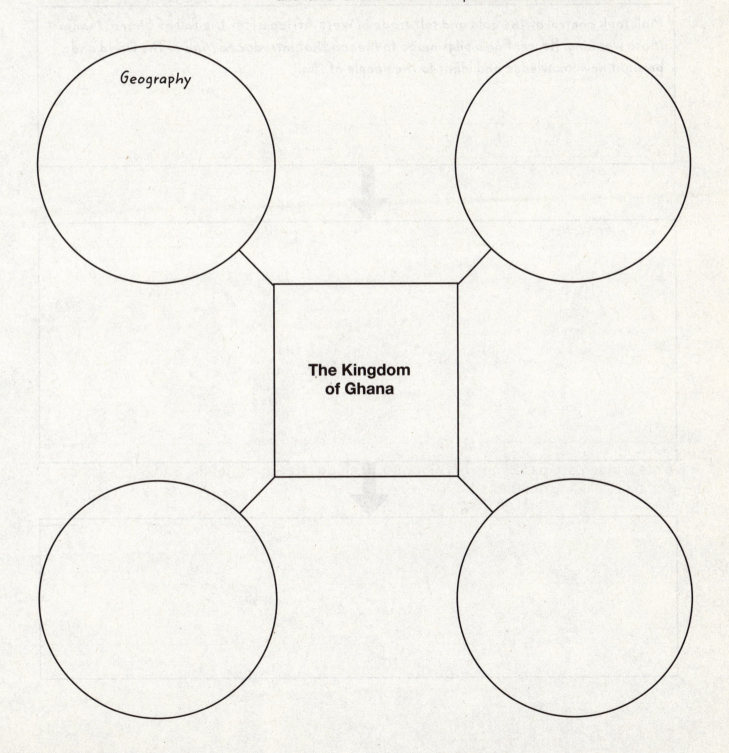

Geography

The Kingdom
of Ghana

UNIT 1

CHAPTER 1 SECTION 3
Societies of West Africa

NATIONAL GEOGRAPHIC LEARNING

READING AND NOTE-TAKING

SEQUENCE EVENTS   As you read Section 3, take notes on the cultures of West Africa after Ghana's decline.

Mali took control of the gold and salt trade in West Africa after the fall of Ghana. Mansa Musa was king. He went on a pilgrimage to Mecca that introduced Mali to the world and brought new knowledge and ideas to the people of Mali.

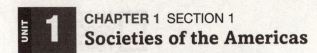

UNIT 1

CHAPTER 1 SECTION 1
Societies of the Americas

VOCABULARY PRACTICE

KEY VOCABULARY

- **civilization** (sih-vuhl-ih-ZAY-shun) *n.* a society with a highly developed culture and technology

- **domesticate** (doh-MEHS-tih-kayt) *v.* to raise plants and animals for human benefit and consumption

- **geographic perspective** *n.* the examination of how geography affects people and culture

- **human geography** *n.* the study of how people and their cultures are affected by physical geography and how human activities affect the environment

- **Iroquois League** (EER-uh-koy leeg) *n.* the confederation of five Iroquois-speaking nations: the Mohawk, Oneida, Onondaga, Cayuga, and Seneca; later joined by the Tuscarora

- **irrigation** (eer-uh-GAY-shun) *n.* the supply of water to fields using human made systems

DEFINITION CHART   Complete a Definition Chart for the Key Vocabulary words.

WORD	DEFINITION	IN MY OWN WORDS
civilization		

UNIT 1 | **CHAPTER 1 SECTION 1**
Societies of the Americas

NATIONAL
GEOGRAPHIC
LEARNING

VOCABULARY PRACTICE

KEY VOCABULARY

- **kayak** (KAI-yak) *n.* a canoe with a light frame and a small opening on top in which to sit

- **matrilineal** (ma-truh-LIN-ee-uhl) *adj.* relating to descendants traced through the mother

- **migrate** (MY-grayt) *v.* to move from one place to another

- **physical geography** *n.* the study of Earth's exterior physical features

- **potlatch** *n.* a gift-giving ceremony practiced by the Kwakiutl and Haida Native American tribes

- **slash-and-burn-agriculture** *n.* a method of clearing fields for planting that involves cutting and setting fire to existing trees and plants

- **tepee** (TEE-pee) *n.* a cone-shaped tent made of bison hides

- **tundra** *n.* the flat treeless land found in arctic and subarctic regions

WRITE A SUMMARY   Reread Section 1. Then write a summary of the section using the Key Vocabulary words. Underline the vocabulary words when they appear in your summary. Use the words in a way that defines and explains them.

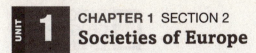

UNIT 1

CHAPTER 1 SECTION 2
Societies of Europe

NATIONAL
GEOGRAPHIC
LEARNING

VOCABULARY PRACTICE

KEY VOCABULARY

- **feudalism** (FEW-dahl-izm) *n.* a political and social system in which a vassal receives protection from a lord in exchange for obedience and service

- **hierarchy** (HY-ur-ayrk-ee) *n.* the classification of a group of people according to ability or to economic, social, or professional standing

- **manor system** *n.* an economic system in which peasants are bound to a lord and work his land, or manor, in exchange for food and shelter

- **serf** *n.* a person who lived and worked on the private land of a landowner, such as a noble or medieval lord

- **vassal** (VAS-ehl) *n.* in the midieval European feudal system, a person, usually a lesser nobleman, who received land and protection from a feudal lord in exchange for obedience and service

EXPOSITORY PARAGRAPH

Write a paragraph that explains feudalism. Use all of the Key Vocabulary words. Start with a strong topic sentence, and then write three to six sentences describing the structure of feudal society and what happened as a result. Be sure to include a summarizing sentence at the end of your paragraph.

Topic Sentence:

_____

_____

_____

_____

_____

_____

_____

Summarizing Sentence:

_____

_____

_____

UNIT 1

CHAPTER 1 SECTION 2

Societies of Europe

NATIONAL
GEOGRAPHIC
LEARNING

VOCABULARY PRACTICE

KEY VOCABULARY

- **caravel** (KEHR-ah-vehl) *n.* a small, fast ship used by Spanish and Portuguese explorers

- **humanism** (HYOO-man-izm) *n.* a movement that focuses on the importance of the individual

- **navigation** (nav-ih-GAY-shun) *n.* the science of finding position and planning routes, often used in relation to seafaring

- **printing press** *n.* an invention that used movable metal type to print pages

- **profit** *n.* the amount of money left after expenses are deducted

- **Protestant** (PRAH-teh-stant) *n.* a follower of the Reformation in Christianity

THREE-COLUMN CHART

Complete the chart for each of the six Key Vocabulary words. Write each word's definition, and then provide a definition in your own words.

WORD	DEFINITION	IN MY OWN WORDS
caravel		

UNIT 1 CHAPTER 1 SECTION 3
Societies of West Africa

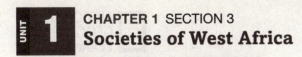

NATIONAL GEOGRAPHIC LEARNING

VOCABULARY PRACTICE

KEY VOCABULARY

- **caravan** (KARE-uh-van) *n.* a group of people and animals traveling together, usually for trade

- **trans-Saharan** (tran-suh-HAHR-uhn) *adj.* across the Sahara

COMPARISON CHART Complete the chart below for both Key Vocabulary words from Section 3. Write the definition and details for each word, and then explain how the two words are related.

TRANS-SAHARAN	CARAVAN
across the Sahara	

HOW ARE THE WORDS RELATED?

UNIT 1

CHAPTER 1 SECTION 3
Societies of West Africa

VOCABULARY PRACTICE

KEY VOCABULARY

- **convert** (kuhn-VERT) *v.* to persuade to change one's religious beliefs

- **oasis** (oh-AY-sihs) *n.* a fertile place with water in a desert

- **pilgrimage** (PILL-gruhm-ij) *n.* a religious journey

- **steppe** (step) *n.* a vast, grassy plain

WDS CHART Complete a Word-Definition-Sentence (WDS) Chart for each Key Vocabulary word.

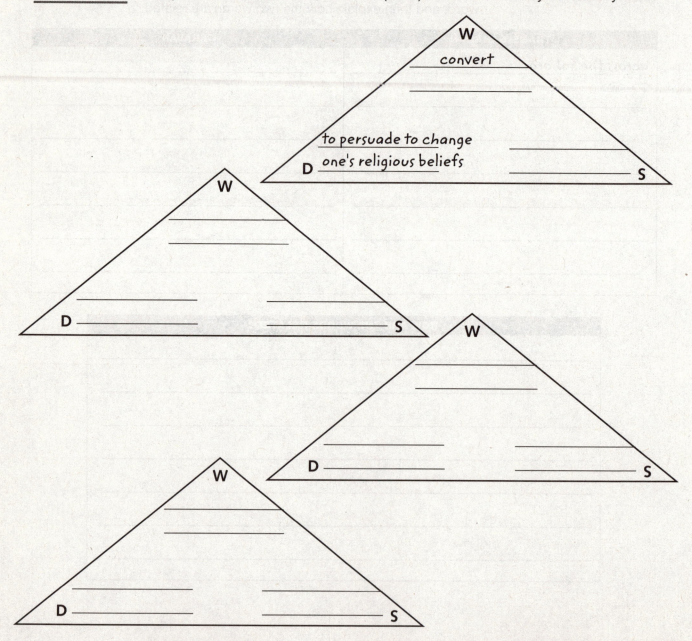

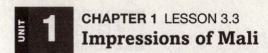

UNIT 1 CHAPTER 1 LESSON 3.3
Impressions of Mali

NATIONAL GEOGRAPHIC LEARNING

DOCUMENT-BASED QUESTION

Use the questions here to help you analyze the sources and write your paragraph.

DOCUMENT ONE: from the *Catalan Atlas, c. 1375*

1A Why do you think Mansa Musa would be included on the map?

_____

_____

1B Constructed Response What does this image suggest about the impression Mansa Musa made on people outside of Mali?

_____

DOCUMENT TWO: from *Travels in Asia and Africa 1325–1354*, by Ibn Battuta

2A What detail about the sultan and his actions most impressed you?

_____

_____

2B Constructed Response What impression do you think the sultan made on his audience?

_____

DOCUMENT THREE: from *Travels in Asia and Africa 1325–1354*, by Ibn Battuta

3A Why do you think the culture was so determined to have the children memorize the Koran?

_____

_____

3B Constructed Response What does this description tell you about the importance of Islam in Mali?

_____

SYNTHESIZE & WRITE

What impressions did Mali make on those who traveled there?

Topic Sentence: _____

_____

Your Paragraph: _____

_____

_____

_____

_____

UNIT 1

CHAPTER 2 SECTION 1
Spain Claims an Empire

NATIONAL GEOGRAPHIC LEARNING

READING AND NOTE-TAKING

BUILD A TIME LINE After reading Section 1, use the Time Line below to keep track of key events in the age of exploration.

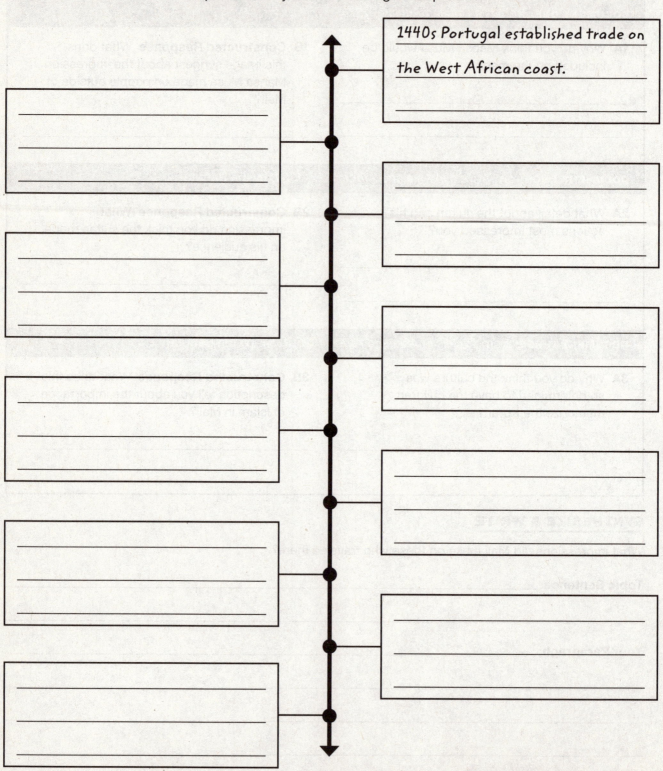

1440s Portugal established trade on the West African coast.

UNIT 1

CHAPTER 2 SECTION 1
Spain Claims an Empire

NATIONAL GEOGRAPHIC LEARNING

READING AND NOTE-TAKING

IDENTIFY CAUSES AND EFFECTS Use the chart below to record what caused the Spanish to defeat the Aztecs and the Incas. Write 3 causes for each effect.

Causes

1. Some Native American tribes join Hernando Cortes because they were dissatisfied with the Aztecs. **2.** **3.** **1.** **2.** **3.**

Effects

Cortes defeats the Aztecs in Mexico. Pizarro defeats the Incas in South America.

CHAPTER 2 SECTION 2
Europe Fights Over North America

READING AND NOTE-TAKING

SEQUENCE EVENTS   In the Sequence Chain below, list the major events addressed in Section 2. Start your Sequence Chain with the Northwest Passage and end with Spain losing its position as the dominant world power.

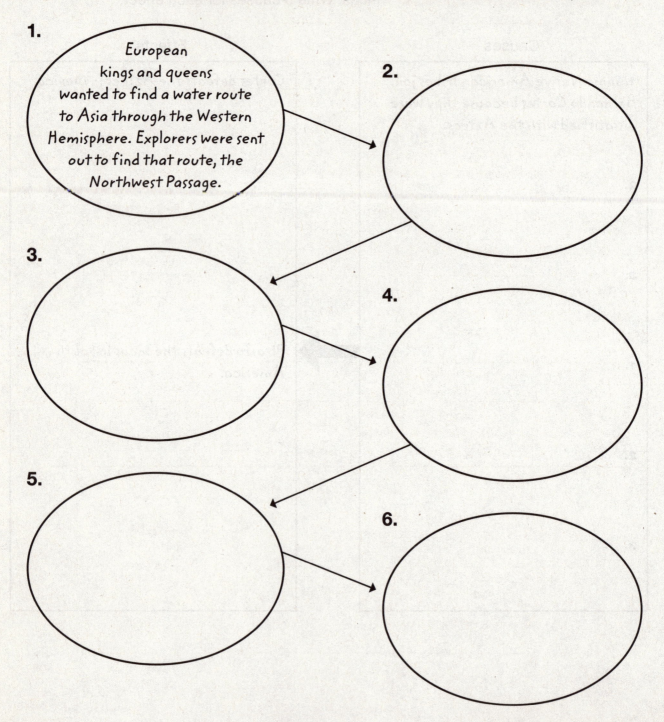

1.

European kings and queens wanted to find a water route to Asia through the Western Hemisphere. Explorers were sent out to find that route, the Northwest Passage.

2.

3.

4.

5.

6.

UNIT **1** CHAPTER 2 SECTION 2
Europe Fights Over North America

NATIONAL GEOGRAPHIC LEARNING

READING AND NOTE-TAKING

IDENTIFY MAIN IDEA AND DETAILS Use a Main Idea Diagram to keep track of the main ideas and details about New France and New Netherland featured in Section 2.

Main Idea
New France

Detail
Samuel de Champlain established a fur-trading post along the St. Lawrence River. He explored the watershed around his post for years and strengthened ties with the Huron, the Algonquian, and the Montagnai—all against the Iroquois.

Detail

Detail

Main Idea

Detail

Detail

Detail

UNIT 1

CHAPTER 2 SECTION 3
Spanish Rule in the Americas

NATIONAL GEOGRAPHIC LEARNING

READING AND NOTE-TAKING

CATEGORIZE INFORMATION   After reading Section 3, complete a Concept Cluster with information about Spanish rule in the Americas.

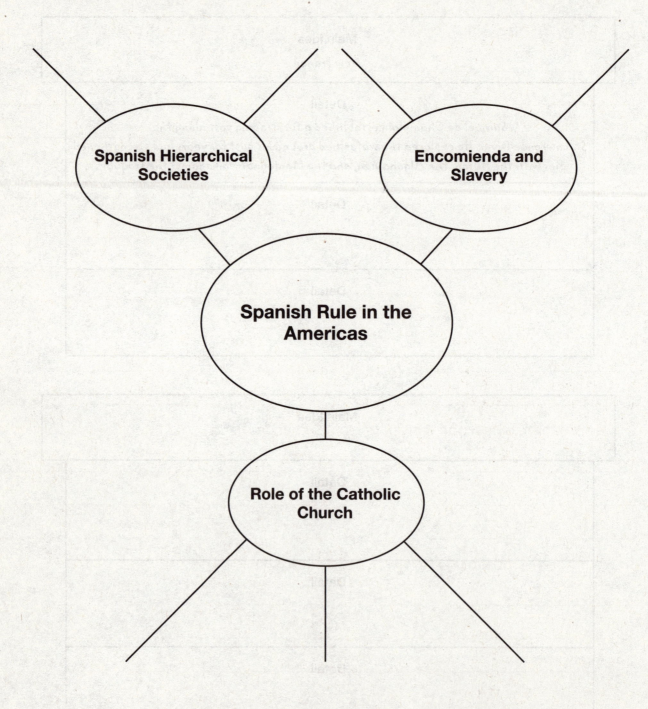

UNIT 1

CHAPTER 2 SECTION 3
Spanish Rule in the Americas

NATIONAL GEOGRAPHIC LEARNING

READING AND NOTE-TAKING

SYNTHESIZE VISUAL AND TEXTUAL INFORMATION   Read Section 3, Lesson 3 and study the map. Use the textual and visual information to answer the questions below.

1. How did Europe, Africa, North America, and South America develop so differently?

_____

_____

_____

2. How did the two hemispheres begin to interact?

_____

_____

_____

3. What happened when Europeans crossed the Atlantic in 1492?

_____

_____

_____

4. Use the map to describe the Columbian Exchange.

_____

_____

_____

5. How did the Columbian Exchange affect Native Americans?

_____

_____

_____

UNIT 1

CHAPTER 2 SECTION 4
Slavery Begins in the Americas

NATIONAL GEOGRAPHIC LEARNING

READING AND NOTE-TAKING

OUTLINE AND TAKE NOTES   Use the Section Map below to outline and take notes as you read Section 4.

What is the title of this section? _____

_____

Explain the meaning of this section title. _____

_____

_____

Explain the broad definition of slavery. _____	Give details about the types of slavery that did not
_____	involve a lifetime of bondage. _____
_____	_____
_____	_____
What was the new kind of slavery called? Give details.	Describe what happened to a person who became a slave in the 1400s in the Portuguese trade with West Africa.
_____	_____
_____	_____
_____	

Describe what the Middle Passage was like for a slave. _____

_____

_____

_____

_____

_____

UNIT 1

CHAPTER 2 SECTION 4
Slavery Begins in the Americas *Continued*

NATIONAL GEOGRAPHIC LEARNING

READING AND NOTE-TAKING

How was the stage set for the growth of slavery in North America? _____ _____ _____ _____	What happened to the Native Americans as the Spanish forced them to work in the sugarcane fields? _____ _____ _____

How did 75,000 enslaved Africans end up working on Spanish plantations by the end of the 1500s? _____

_____

_____

_____

What was the African diaspora? _____ _____ _____ _____	How long did slavery exist in the United States before it was abolished? _____ _____ _____

Describe the many ways that slavery has had an impact on people around the world. _____

_____

_____

_____

_____

What are the Key Vocabulary words for this section? Define them briefly in your own words. _____

_____

_____

_____

_____

_____

_____

_____

UNIT **1**

CHAPTER 2 SECTION 1
Spain Claims an Empire

NATIONAL GEOGRAPHIC LEARNING

VOCABULARY PRACTICE

KEY VOCABULARY

- **conquistador** (kahn-KEES-tah-dohr) *n.* a Spanish conqueror who sought gold and other riches in the Americas

- **mercantilism** (MUHR-kuhn-teel-ih-zuhm) *n.* an economic policy that gives a country sole ownership of the trade occurring in its colonies

- **missionary** (MIH-shih-nair-ee) *n.* a person who tries to spread Christianity to others

DEFINITION TREE For each Key Vocabulary word in the Definition Tree below, write the definition on the top branch and then use each word in a sentence.

conquistador

Definition
a Spanish conqueror who sought gold and other riches in the Americas
_____

Sentence
_____
_____

mercantilism

Definition
_____
_____

Sentence
_____
_____

missionary

Definition
_____
_____

Sentence
_____
_____

UNIT 1
CHAPTER 2 SECTION 1
Spain Claims an Empire

**NATIONAL
GEOGRAPHIC
LEARNING**

VOCABULARY PRACTICE

KEY VOCABULARY

- **smallpox** (SMAWL-poks) *n.* a deadly virus that causes a high fever and small blisters on the skin

- **viceroy** (VY-suh-roy) *n.* a governor of Spain's colonies in the Americas who represented the Spanish king and queen

- **viceroyalty** (vyce-ROHY-ahl-tee) *n.* a territory governed by a viceroy

WORDS IN CONTEXT   Follow the directions for using the Key Vocabulary words in context.

1. Explain how *smallpox* affected the Aztec.

_____

_____

_____

_____

_____

2. What is a *viceroy*?

_____

_____

_____

_____

3. How is a *viceroyalty* governed?

_____

_____

_____

_____

_____

CHAPTER 2 SECTION 2
Europe Fights Over North America

NATIONAL GEOGRAPHIC LEARNING

VOCABULARY PRACTICE

KEY VOCABULARY

- **circumnavigate** (sur-cuhm-NAV-ih-gayt) *v.* to travel completely around Earth

- **galleon** (GAL-eeahn) *n.* a large sailing ship used especially by the Spanish in the 16th and 17th centuries

- **heretic** (HAYR-eh-tik) *n.* a person who holds beliefs different from the teachings of the Catholic Church

- **Northwest Passage** *n.* a passage by water between the Atlantic and Pacific oceans along the northern coast of North America

FOUR-COLUMN CHART Complete the chart below for each Key Vocabulary word.

WORD	DEFINITION	ILLUSTRATION	SENTENCE
circumnavigate	to travel completely around Earth		

UNIT 1

CHAPTER 2 SECTION 2
Europe Fights Over North America

NATIONAL GEOGRAPHIC LEARNING

VOCABULARY PRACTICE

KEY VOCABULARY

- **persecute** (PUR-seh-kyoot) *v.* to punish, particularly because of beliefs or background
- **privateer** (PRY-vah-teer) *n.* a ship or sailor on a ship licensed by an individual or government to attack enemy ships

- **watershed** (WAH-tuhr-shed) *n.* an area of land that includes a particular river or lake and all the bodies of water that flow into it

WORDS IN CONTEXT   Complete a Word Square for the Key Vocabulary words *persecute*, *privateer*, and *watershed*.

Definition	Characteristics
persecute	
Examples	Non-Examples

Definition	Characteristics
Examples	Non-Examples

Definition	Characteristics
Examples	Non-Examples

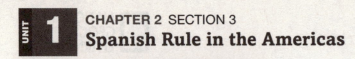

UNIT 1

CHAPTER 2 SECTION 3
Spanish Rule in the Americas

VOCABULARY PRACTICE

KEY VOCABULARY

- **Columbian Exchange** (kuh-LUM-bee-uhn ehks-CHAYNJ) *n.* the exchange of plants, animals, microbes, people, and ideas between Europe and the Americas following Columbus's first voyage to the Western Hemisphere

- **encomienda** (en-coh-mee-EHN-dah) *n.* a system in Spain's American colonies in which wealthy settlers were given plots of land and allowed to enslave the people who lived there

- **hacienda** (hah-see-EHN-dah) *n.* a large plantation in a Spanish-speaking colony

- **immunity** (ih-MYOO-nih-tee) *n.* a protection against disease, either natural or induced by vaccination

DESCRIPTIVE PARAGRAPH

Using each of the four Key Vocabulary words, write a paragraph describing the Spanish rule in the Americas. Be sure to write a clear topic sentence as your first sentence. Then write at least four to six sentences with supporting details. Conclude your paragraph with a summarizing sentence.

Topic Sentence:

_____

_____

_____

_____

_____

_____

_____

Summarizing Sentence:

_____

_____

_____

UNIT 1

CHAPTER 2 SECTION 3
Spanish Rule in the Americas

NATIONAL GEOGRAPHIC LEARNING

VOCABULARY PRACTICE

KEY VOCABULARY

- **mestizo** (mehs-TEE-zoh) *n.* a person who has mixed Spanish and Native American ancestry

- **mission** *n.* a Christian church settlement established to convert native peoples

- **plantation** *n.* a large farm; on southern plantations, slaves worked to grow and harvest crops

- **quinine** (KWHY-nyn) *n.* a substance made from the bark of a tree that is an effective remedy for malaria

THREE-COLUMN CHART   Complete the chart for each of the four Key Vocabulary words. Write the word's definition, and then provide a definition in your own words.

WORD	DEFINITION	IN MY OWN WORDS
mestizo		

UNIT 1

CHAPTER 2 SECTION 4
Slavery Begins in the Americas

NATIONAL GEOGRAPHIC LEARNING

VOCABULARY PRACTICE

KEY VOCABULARY

- **African diaspora** (DY-as-poh-rah) *n.* the removal of Africans from their homelands to the Americas

- **chattel slavery** (shah-TEL) *n.* a system in which enslaved people have no human rights and are classified as goods

- **institution** (in-stuh-TOO-shuhn) *n.* an established and accepted practice in a society or culture

SUMMARY PARAGRAPH   Write a summary paragraph explaining the relationship among the three Key Vocabulary words. Use all of the Key Vocabulary words in your summary.

_____

_____

_____

_____

_____

_____

_____

_____

_____

_____

_____

_____

_____

_____

_____

_____

U.S. HISTORY   Chapter 2 SECTION 4 **Activity A**

UNIT 1

CHAPTER 2 SECTION 4
Slavery Begins in the Americas

NATIONAL GEOGRAPHIC LEARNING

VOCABULARY PRACTICE

KEY VOCABULARY

- **Middle Passage** *n.* the long trip across the Atlantic Ocean in which enslaved Africans were brought to the Americas; the second leg of the triangular trade route

- **slavery** *n.* a social system in which human beings take complete control of others

- **triangular trade** *n.* a transatlantic trade network formed by Europe, West Africa, and the Americas

INFORMATIVE PARAGRAPH

Write a paragraph describing the institution of slavery. Use the Key Vocabulary words to describe the slave trade and the Middle Passage.

_____

_____

_____

_____

_____

_____

_____

_____

_____

_____

_____

_____

_____

_____

_____

UNIT 2

CHAPTER 3 SECTION 1
Early Colonies Have Mixed Success

READING AND NOTE-TAKING

SEQUENCE EVENTS In the Sequence Chain below, list the major events addressed in Section 1. Start your Sequence Chain with the first English settlement at Jamestown and end with the establishment of the House of Burgesses.

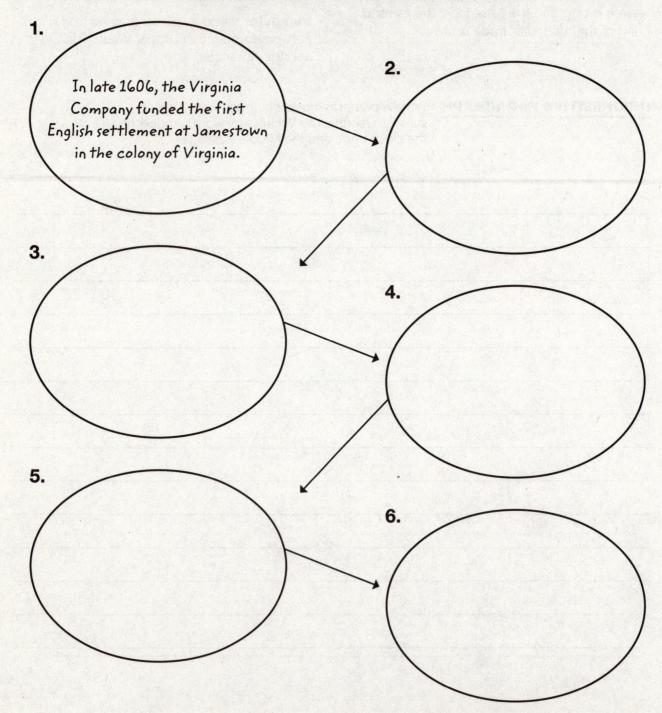

1. In late 1606, the Virginia Company funded the first English settlement at Jamestown in the colony of Virginia.

2.

3.

4.

5.

6.

UNIT 2

CHAPTER 3 SECTION 1
Early Colonies Have Mixed Success

READING AND NOTE-TAKING

POSE AND ANSWER QUESTIONS Use a Pose and Answer Questions Chart to ask any questions that arise before or while you read about Bacon's Rebellion.

Questions	Answers
By 1670, what was the main source of tension between the colonists and the Powhatan?	

READING AND NOTE-TAKING

SUMMARIZE DETAILS As you read Section 2, keep track of details about the Pilgrims and Puritans in a Summary Diagram. Add spokes if needed. Then, summarize the information in the box provided below.

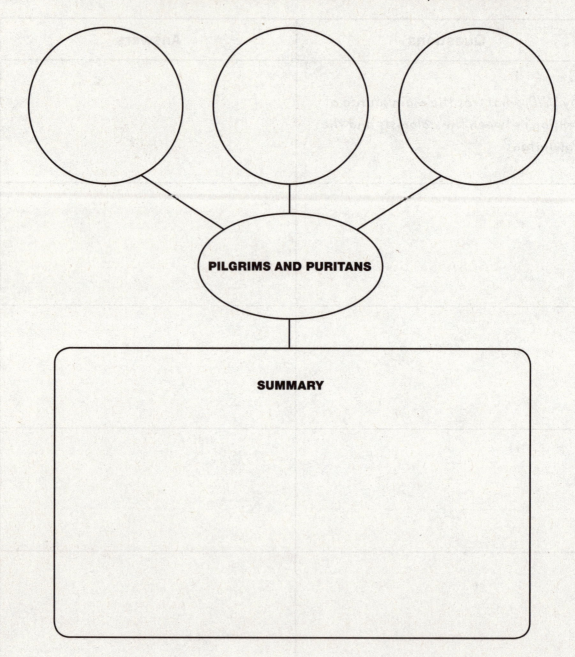

PILGRIMS AND PURITANS

SUMMARY

UNIT 2

CHAPTER 3 SECTION 2
New England Colonies

NATIONAL GEOGRAPHIC LEARNING

READING AND NOTE-TAKING

CAUSE-AND-EFFECT CHART After you read Section 2, write down several effects of the accusation of the three women in Salem. Then summarize the information in the box provided below.

Cause   **Effect**

In February 1692, authorities in the village of Salem, Massachusetts, accused three women of witchraft.

SUMMARY

UNIT 2

CHAPTER 3 SECTION 3
Middle and Southern Colonies

NATIONAL GEOGRAPHIC LEARNING

READING AND NOTE-TAKING

OUTLINE AND TAKE NOTES As you read Section 3, take notes using the headings and subheading of Sections 3.1-3.3. Then write a few sentences to summarize the content.

3.1 The Middle Colonies

A. *New Netherland to New York*

- *Settlers from many different countries came to the Middle Colonies for many reasons.*
- _____
- _____
- _____

B. *Penn's Woods*

- _____
- _____
- _____
- _____

3.2 Forming Alliances

A. _____

- _____
- _____
- _____
- _____

B. _____

- _____
- _____
- _____
- _____

UNIT 2

CHAPTER 3 SECTION 3
Middle and Southern Colonies *continued*

3.3 The Southern Colonies

A. _____

- _____
- _____
- _____
- _____

B. _____

- _____
- _____
- _____
- _____

Summary: _____

_____

_____

_____

_____

_____

_____

_____

_____

_____

_____

UNIT 2

CHAPTER 3 SECTION 1
Early Colonies Have Mixed Success

VOCABULARY PRACTICE

KEY VOCABULARY

- **charter** *n.* a written grant establishing an institution and detailing members' rights and privileges

- **indentured servant** *n.* a person under contract to work, usually without pay, in exchange for free passage to the colonies

I READ, I KNOW, AND SO   Complete the charts below for the Key Vocabulary words *charter* and *indentured servant*. Write down the sentence in which the word appears. Then write down what else you read about the word. Finally, draw a conclusion about the word based on what you have learned.

I Read

King James I had provided a charter, or written grant detailing rights and privileges, to the company to settle the colonies.

| **I Know** | **charter** | **And So** |

I Read

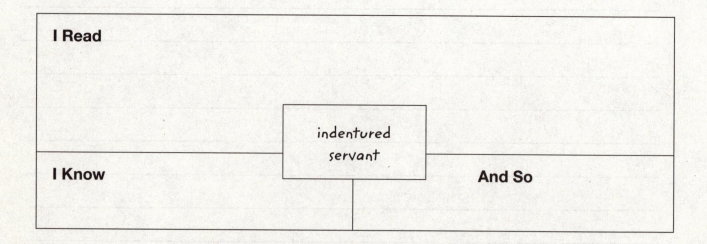

| **I Know** | **indentured servant** | **And So** |

UNIT 2 CHAPTER 3 SECTION 1
Early Colonies Have Mixed Success

NATIONAL GEOGRAPHIC LEARNING

VOCABULARY PRACTICE

KEY VOCABULARY
- **joint-stock company** *n.* a company whose shareholders own stock in the company
- **traitor** (TRAY-tohr) *n.* a person who betrays his or her own people, nation, or cause

WORD MAP Complete a Word Map for the word *traitor*.

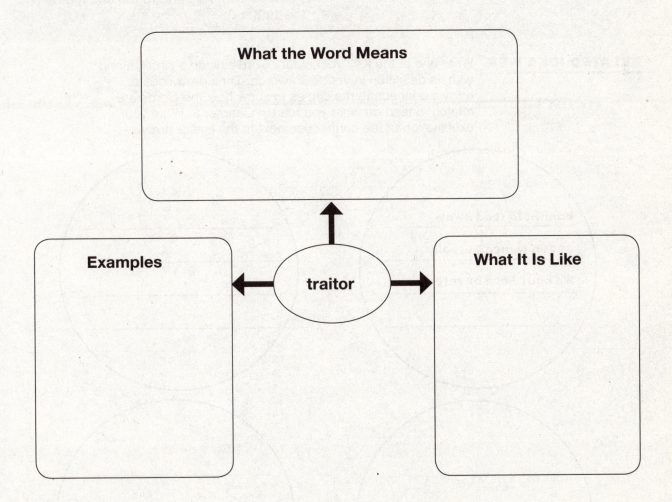

Write a sentence using both vocabulary words, based on what you learned in Chapter 3.

_____

_____

UNIT 2 CHAPTER 3 SECTION 2
New England Colonies

VOCABULARY PRACTICE

KEY VOCABULARY

- **banish** (BA-nish) *v.* to send away as punishment, usually without hope of return

- **dissenter** (dih-SEHN-tur) *n.* a person who disagrees with a majority belief or position

- **Fundamental Orders of Connecticut** *n.* a founding document of the Connecticut colony that listed 11 laws and stood as the framework for governing the colony

- **Great Migration** *n.* the movement of Puritans from England to the colonies in the 1600s

RELATED IDEA WEB
Write one of the Key Vocabulary words inside a circle, along with its definition in your own words. Then draw lines or arrows connecting the circles to show how the words are related, based on what you read in Chapter 3. Write your explanation of the connection next to the line or arrow..

banish: to send away
as punishment, usually
without hope of return

2 UNIT

CHAPTER 3 SECTION 2
New England Colonies

NATIONAL GEOGRAPHIC LEARNING

VOCABULARY PRACTICE

KEY VOCABULARY

- **King Philip's War** *n.* a violent conflict between Native Americans and English colonists from New England, aided by their Native American allies

- **levy** (LEH-vee) *v.* to require the payment of a tax

- **Mayflower Compact** *n.* a shipboard contract signed by the Pilgrims on the *Mayflower* before they landed in North America, binding them to abide by their own laws and establish a civil society

- **self-governance** *n.* the control of one's own affairs; the control of community affairs and laws by those who live there rather than by an outside ruler or monarch

- **separatist** (SEH-prah-tihst) *n.* a person who wished to leave the Church of England

KWL CHART   Fill in the KWL Chart for the Key Vocabulary words.

WORD	WHAT I KNOW	WHAT I WANT TO KNOW	WHAT I LEARNED
King Philip's War			

UNIT 2

CHAPTER 3 SECTION 3
Middle and Southern Colonies

NATIONAL GEOGRAPHIC LEARNING

VOCABULARY PRACTICE

KEY VOCABULARY

- **alliance** (ah-LY-ans) *n.* an agreement between nations to fight each other's enemies or otherwise collaborate; a partnership

VOCABULARY PYRAMID   Complete a Vocabulary Pyramid for the Key Vocabulary word *alliance*.

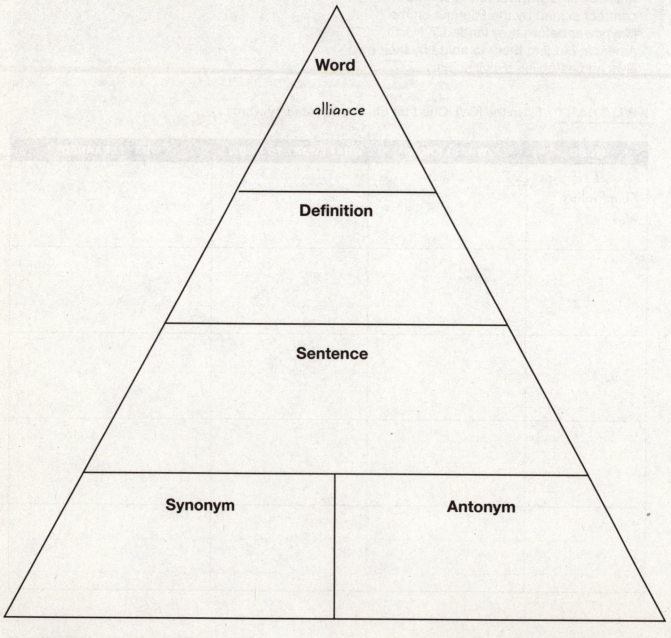

Word

alliance

Definition

Sentence

Synonym   Antonym

UNIT 2

CHAPTER 3 SECTION 3
Middle and Southern Colonies

VOCABULARY PRACTICE

KEY VOCABULARY

- **confederacy** (kon-FED-ur-uh-see) *n.* an agreement among several groups, states, or governments to protect and support one another in battle or other endeavors

- **doctrine** (DOK-truhn) *n.* a principle or set of beliefs accepted by a group

- **economic activity** *n.* actions that involve the production, distribution, and consumption of goods and services

- **natural resource** *n.* material or substance found in nature that can be used to sustain a society or exploited for economic gain, such as minerals, water, living things

- **neutrality** (noo-TRA-luh-tee) *n.* the refusal to take sides or become involved

- **proprietor** (pruh-PRY-uh-tuhr) *n.* a person with ownership of a colony, including the right to manage and distribute land and to establish government

- **raw material** *n.* the basic substances and elements used to make products

- **royal colony** *n.* a colony ruled by a monarch through an appointed governor

- **tributary** (TRIH-byoo-tair-ee) *n.* a creek, stream, or river that flows into a larger river or other body of water

SUMMARY PARAGRAPH Use all of the Key Vocabulary words to write a paragraph summarizing Section 3.

_____

_____

_____

_____

_____

_____

_____

_____

_____

_____

_____

_____

AMERICAN VOICES
John Smith
1580–1631

Early 17th century engraving of John Smith

"... you must obey this now for a Law, that he that will not work shall not eat: ... for the labors of 30 or 40 honest and industrious men shall not be consumed to maintain 150 idle loiterers." — John Smith

John Smith loved adventure—of every kind. Explorer, soldier, adventurer, and author, Captain John Smith led the first permanent English settlement in colonial Virginia through a rocky beginning.

Born in Willoughby, England, in 1580 on the family farm, John Smith yearned for adventures at sea. After his father died, Smith left home at age 16 and traveled to the European continent. In France, he joined volunteer soldiers who were helping the Dutch fight for independence from Spain. He eventually returned to England to study military strategy from books and to learn horsemanship. His next adventure was to set sail on a merchant ship for the Mediterranean Sea, where he acted as both a legitimate trader and a pirate. Then, in 1600, he led the Austrians in liberating the Hungarian capital from the Turks. Smith was wounded in battle and sold as a slave to a Turk. After being passed from person to person, Smith murdered his last captor and escaped to England in 1604.

He soon became involved with the Virginia Company, which chose him to lead the 1606 expedition to establish the Jamestown colony in Virginia for financial profit. Three ships set off from England in December, but after weeks of sailing in stormy seas, they had only reached the Canary Islands off the coast of Africa. Following accusations that he wanted to make himself king, Smith was chained for the final 13 weeks of the journey. Once in Virginia, Reverend Hunt helped Smith regain his council position.

In Jamestown, the settlers faced illness, starvation, and contaminated water. Many settlers considered themselves "gentlemen" and refused to plant and tend crops like common farmers. To save the colony, Smith began trading with Native Americans for food. He was captured, but befriended Pocahontas, the daughter of the Powhatan chief. The two worked together to ensure the colonists' survival. When Smith became council president in 1608, he ordered everyone to work or go hungry.

Smith returned to England in 1609. With his appetite for adventure still strong, he sailed back to North America in 1614, to a place farther north, which he called "New England." Smith returned to England to write about his adventures. He died in 1631 at the age of 51.

HISTORICAL THINKING

DRAW CONCLUSIONS What made John Smith a good choice as a leader for the new settlement?

_____

_____

AMERICAN VOICES
Anne Hutchinson
c.1591–1643

John Winthrop
1588–1649

"We must be knitt together in this worke as one man." — John Winthrop (from "City Upon a Hill, 1630")

"Now if you do condemn me for speaking what in my conscience I know to be truth I must commit myself unto the Lord." — Anne Hutchinson

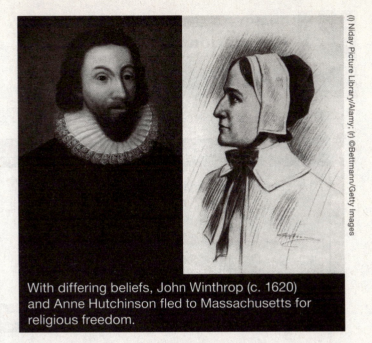

With differing beliefs, John Winthrop (c. 1620) and Anne Hutchinson fled to Massachusetts for religious freedom.

Both John Winthrop and Anne Hutchinson fled England for religious freedom—but clashed over what such freedom should mean in Massachusetts.

John Winthrop was born in Suffolk, England, on January 12, 1588. He attended Trinity College, pursued law, and earned a government office. His religious studies had persuaded him to convert to Puritanism. This denomination strictly adhered to specific Biblical interpretations, including gaining salvation by following rules set by ministers, or "saints." Facing persecution in England, Winthrop and other Puritans set sail for New England in 1630 to establish a new colony. On the journey, Winthrop wrote a sermon describing how the colonists should work together. Part of that sermon is now known as "City Upon a Hill, 1630."

The colony struggled—and succeeded—in the Massachusetts wilderness, electing Winthrop to serve as governor 12 times. He guided the colonists in laying out a network of towns ruled by "saints." Winthrop made his home in Boston, which became Massachusetts's main port and capital.

Anne Hutchinson also left England to seek religious freedom. While the year of her birth is unknown, Hutchinson was baptized July 20, 1591, in Lincolnshire, England. In 1634, Hutchinson and her husband William joined Winthrop's young colony. There, she bristled at the narrow views of salvation, believing that salvation came from personal intuition rather than from obeying rules set by ministers. She began holding meetings for the community's women, sharing personal theological views that differed from strict Puritan doctrine. Her meetings drew in some male members of the clergy as well.

Hutchinson's behavior outraged Winthrop. Preaching against Puritan beliefs was heresy, and in his view, women were not meant to preach. Tried and found guilty of slander, Hutchinson was excommunicated, or cast out of the faith, and banished from Massachusetts. She and some followers settled what is now the town of Portsmouth, Rhode Island. Native Americans attacked and killed Hutchinson and her family in 1643. Winthrop died of fever on April 5, 1649.

HISTORICAL THINKING

MAKE INFERENCES Why might some of the Massachusetts colonists have attended the "heretical" meetings of Anne Hutchinson?

_____

_____

(l) Niday Picture Library/Alamy; (r) ©Bettmann/Getty Images

Foundations Of Democracy

NATIONAL GEOGRAPHIC LEARNING

DOCUMENT-BASED QUESTION

Use the questions here to help you analyze the sources and write your paragraph.

DOCUMENT ONE: from the Magna Carta, 1215

1A Restate the passage in your own words.

_____

_____

1B Constructed Response Why is it significant that the Magna Carta includes the phrase "lawful judgment of his equals"?

_____

DOCUMENT TWO: from the Mayflower Compact, 1620

2A What kind of government do the signers hope to put in place?

_____

_____

2B Constructed Response What reasons do the Mayflower Compact signers give for working together as a "civil body politic"?

_____

DOCUMENT THREE: from the Fundamental Orders of Connecticut, 1639

3A What were the requirements for serving as a representative in Connecticut?

_____

_____

3B Constructed Response Why do you think it was important to the colony founders that the representatives lived in the towns they represented?

_____

SYNTHESIZE & WRITE

How is the Magna Carta, written in 1215, similar to the Mayflower Compact and the Fundamental Orders of Connecticut?

Topic Sentence: _____

_____

Your Paragraph: _____

_____

_____

UNIT 2

CHAPTER 4 SECTION 1
New England: Commerce and Religion

NATIONAL GEOGRAPHIC LEARNING

READING AND NOTE-TAKING

POSE AND ANSWER QUESTIONS Use a Pose and Answer Questions Chart for Section 1. Answer the questions after you have finished reading.

Questions	Answers
Why did New England farmers rely on large families?	

UNIT 2 CHAPTER 4 SECTION 1
New England: Commerce and Religion

READING AND NOTE-TAKING

SUMMARIZE After you read Section 1, complete the boxes below with notes on slavery, Puritanism, and early education. Add at least three details for each.

Slavery:

Puritanism:

Early Education:

UNIT 2

CHAPTER 4 SECTION 2
The Southern Colonies

NATIONAL GEOGRAPHIC LEARNING

READING AND NOTE-TAKING

OUTLINE AND TAKE NOTES   As you read Section 2, use the headings and subheadings of each lesson to create an outline. Summarize each lesson as you finish taking notes.

2.1 Slavery Expands

A. Plantation Crops

- The fertile land and mild climate in the Southern Colonies made it possible to grow cash crops.

- _____

- _____

B. New Slave Trading

- _____

- _____

- _____

Summarize

_____

_____

_____

2.2 From Plantations to the Backcountry

A. _____

- _____

- _____

- _____

B. _____

- _____

- _____

- _____

Summarize

_____

_____

_____

2.3 Life Under Slavery

A. _____

- _____

- _____

- _____

B. _____

- _____

- _____

- _____

Summarize

_____

_____

_____

Use your notes from each lesson to write a summary paragraph of Section 2.

_____

_____

_____

_____

_____

_____

_____

_____

UNIT 2

CHAPTER 4 SECTION 3
The Middle Colonies

NATIONAL
GEOGRAPHIC
LEARNING

READING AND NOTE-TAKING

MAKE GENERALIZATIONS Complete an Idea Diagram about the information in Section 3.1. Rewrite the Introduction to the Lesson in your own words. Then take notes on specific details under each subheading. After you finish reading, write a generalization about the resourcefulness of the people who settled in the Middle Colonies.

Agricultural Production

INTRODUCTION _____
_____
_____

Farmland and Freedom

Grist for the Mill

DETAILS:
_____
_____
_____
_____
_____
_____

DETAILS:
_____
_____
_____
_____
_____
_____

GENERALIZATION: _____
_____
_____

UNIT 2

CHAPTER 4 SECTION 3
The Middle Colonies

READING AND NOTE-TAKING

IDENTIFY CAUSES AND EFFECTS   Use the chart below to record causes and effects that relate to the diversity that came with the stream of settlers to the Atlantic coast.

Causes	Effect
The colonies produced more and more goods.	Trade from the ports in New York City and Philadelphia grew.

UNIT 2 CHAPTER 4 SECTION 4
Roots of American Democracy

NATIONAL GEOGRAPHIC LEARNING

READING AND NOTE-TAKING

CATEGORIZE INFORMATION Complete a Concept Cluster to organize information about rights and wealth as discussed in Section 4.1.

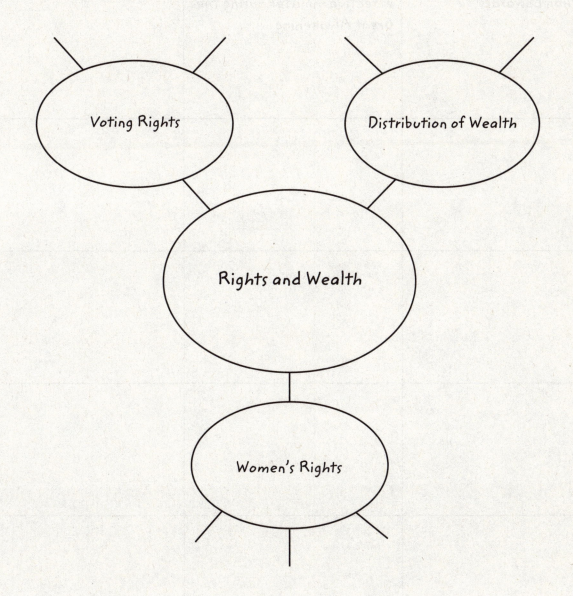

Voting Rights

Distribution of Wealth

Rights and Wealth

Women's Rights

CHAPTER 4 SECTION 4
Roots of American Democracy

NATIONAL GEOGRAPHIC LEARNING

READING AND NOTE-TAKING

IDENTIFY SIGNIFICANCE   As you read Section 4, take notes about the actions of historical figures mentioned in the text. Then in the third column, identify why each historical figure's actions are significant.

HISTORICAL FIGURE	ACTIONS	SIGNIFICANCE
Jonathan Edwards	effective minister during the Great Awakening	

UNIT 2

CHAPTER 4 SECTION 5
The French and Indian War

NATIONAL GEOGRAPHIC LEARNING

READING AND NOTE-TAKING

ANNOTATE A TIME LINE After you read Section 5, consider the dates listed below. Review the text and identify one event for each year listed. Write a description of the event in the box provided.

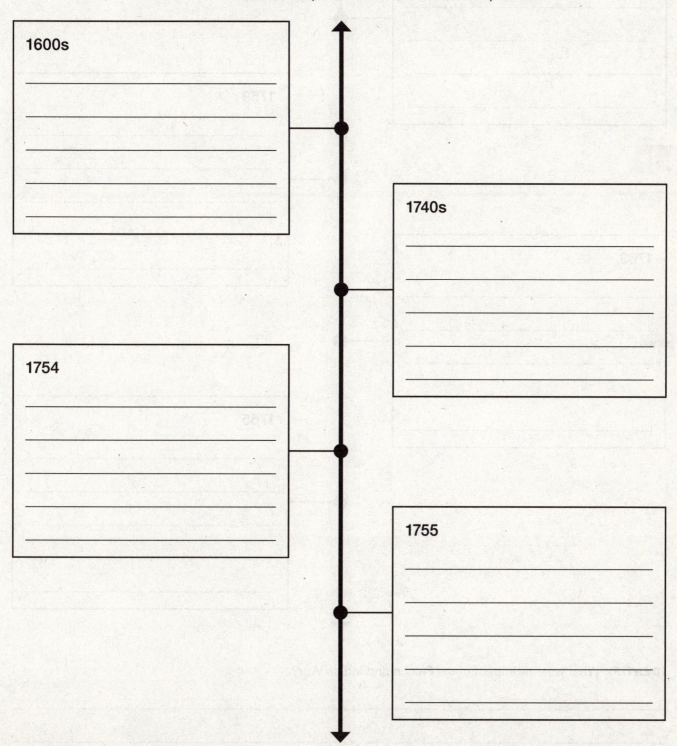

1600s

_____

_____

_____

_____

1740s

_____

_____

_____

_____

1754

_____

_____

_____

_____

1755

_____

_____

_____

_____

UNIT 2 | CHAPTER 4 SECTION 5
The French and Indian War *continued*

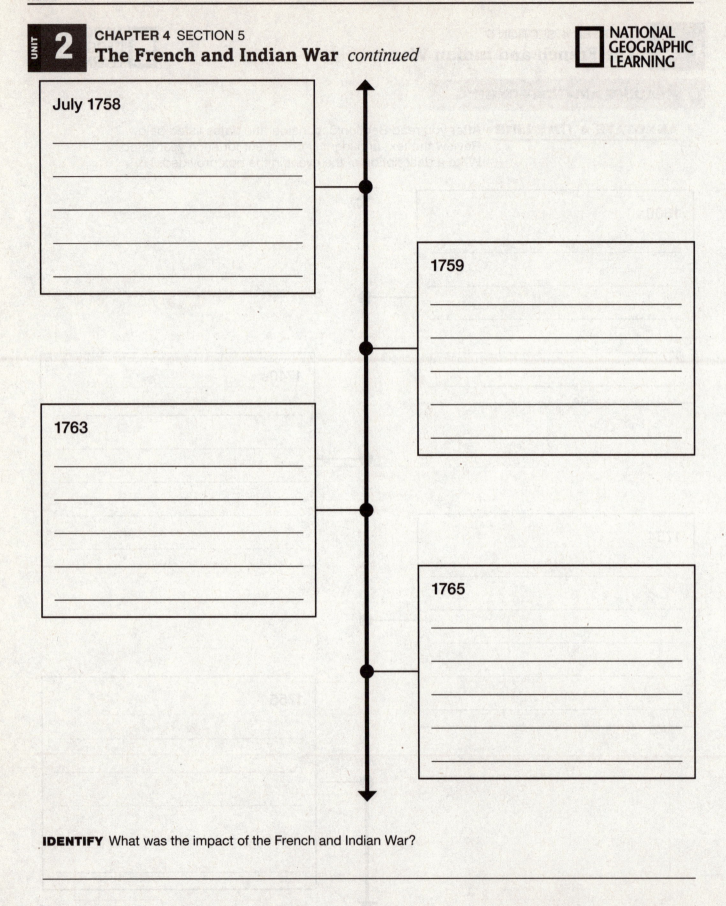

July 1758

_____

_____

_____

_____

1759

_____

_____

_____

_____

1763

_____

_____

_____

_____

1765

_____

_____

_____

_____

_____

IDENTIFY What was the impact of the French and Indian War?

_____

UNIT 2

CHAPTER 4 SECTION 1

New England: Commerce and Religion

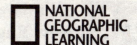

NATIONAL GEOGRAPHIC LEARNING

VOCABULARY PRACTICE

KEY VOCABULARY

- **apprentice** (ah-PREHN-tis) *n.* a person who learns a craft or trade by working with a skilled member of that craft or trade

- **common school** *n.* a colonial elementary school

MEANING MAP   Complete a Meaning Map for each Key Vocabulary word.

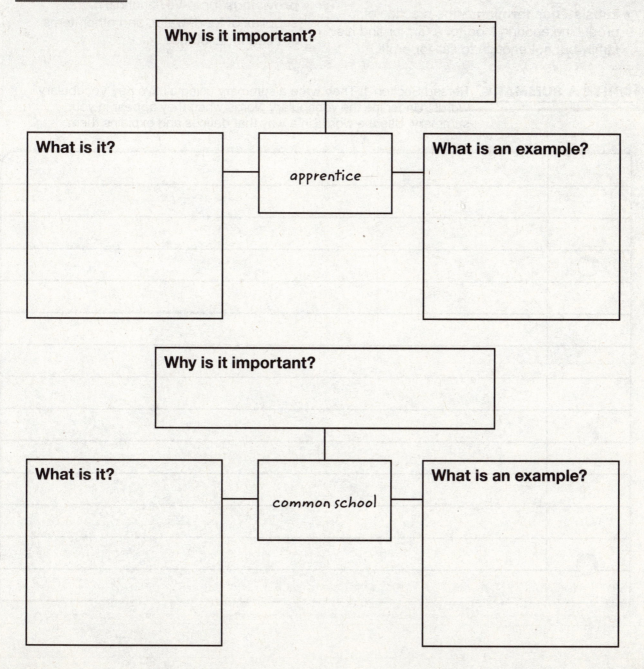

Why is it important?

What is it?

apprentice

What is an example?

Why is it important?

What is it?

common school

What is an example?

UNIT **2** CHAPTER 4 SECTION 1
New England: Commerce and Religion

NATIONAL GEOGRAPHIC LEARNING

VOCABULARY PRACTICE

KEY VOCABULARY

- **religious freedom** *n.* the right to practice the religion of one's choosing without government interference

- **smuggle** *v.* to import or export goods illegally

- **subsistence farming** *n.* the practice of producing enough food for a farmer and his family but not enough to sell for profit

- **Navigation Acts** *n.* a series of laws passed by the English Parliament to protect English shipping by restricting the transport of goods to and from the English colonies

- **provisions** (pruh-VIH-zhuhnz) *n.* the supplies of food, water, and other items needed for a journey

WRITE A SUMMARY   Reread Section 1. Then write a summary using all five Key Vocabulary words. Underline the vocabulary words when they appear in your summary. Use the words in a way that defines and explains them.

UNIT 2

CHAPTER 4 SECTION 2
The Southern Colonies

NATIONAL GEOGRAPHIC LEARNING

VOCABULARY PRACTICE

KEY VOCABULARY

- **artisan** (AR-tih-san) *n.* a person skilled at making things by hand
- **backcountry** *n.* the western part of the Southern Colonies just east of the Appalachian Mountains
- **cash crop** *n.* a crop grown for sale rather than for use by farmers
- **indigo** (IHN-dih-goh) *n.* a plant that produces a blue dye for cloth

- **overseer** (OH-vur-see-ur) *n.* a supervisor
- **Piedmont** (PEED-mont) *n.* a relatively flat area between the Appalachian Mountains and the coastal plain
- **Stono Rebellion** *n.* a 1739 revolt by enslaved Africans against their owners

DEFINITION TREE   For each Key Vocabulary word in the Tree Diagrams below, write the definition on the top branch and then use each word in a sentence.

artisan ———

Definition _____

Sentence _____

backcountry ———

Definition _____

Sentence _____

cash crop ———

Definition _____

Sentence _____

indigo

Definition

Sentence

overseer

Definition

Sentence

Piedmont

Definition

Definition

Stono Rebellion

Definition

Sentence

UNIT 2

CHAPTER 4 SECTION 3
The Middle Colonies

NATIONAL GEOGRAPHIC LEARNING

VOCABULARY PRACTICE

KEY VOCABULARY

- **arable** (AIR-ah-bl) *adj.* able to grow crops; fertile
- **commodity** (kuh-MAH-duh-tee) *n.* a trade good
- **Conestoga wagon** (kah-nuh-STOH-guh) *n.* a kind of wagon made by German settlers in North America that could carry heavy loads

RELATED IDEA WEB   Write one of the Key Vocabulary words inside each circle, along with its definition in your own words. Then draw lines or arrows connecting the circles to show how the words are related, based on what you read in Section 3. Write your explanation of the connection next to the line or arrow.

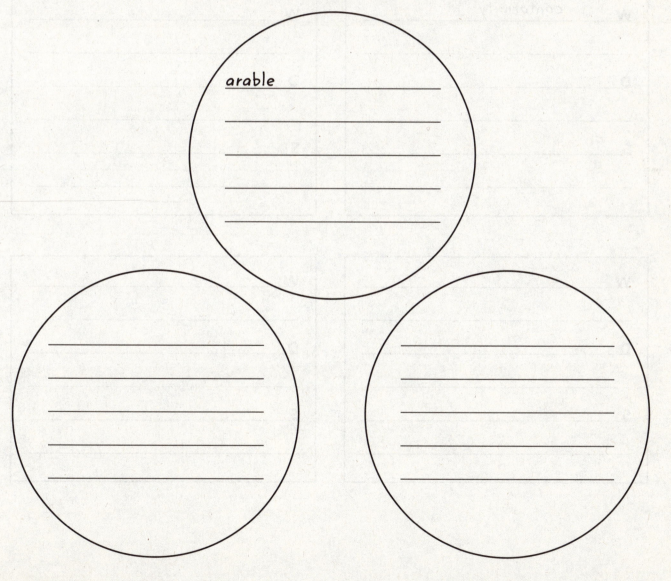

arable

© National Geographic Learning, a part of Cengage Learning

UNIT 2

CHAPTER 4 SECTION 3
The Middle Colonies

NATIONAL GEOGRAPHIC LEARNING

VOCABULARY PRACTICE

KEY VOCABULARY

- **conformity** (kuhn-FAWR-mih-tee) *n.* an obedience to a set of beliefs

- **diversity** (duh-VUR-suh-tee) *n.* a wide variety

- **gristmill** *n.* a building that houses machinery for grinding grain

- **tolerance** (TAH-luh-runts) *n.* acceptance of others

WDS CHART Complete a Word-Definition-Sentence (WDS) Chart for each Key Vocabulary word.

W conformity

D

S

W

D

S

W

D

S

W

D

S

Roots of American Democracy

VOCABULARY PRACTICE

KEY VOCABULARY

- **burgeon** (BUR-jehn) *v.* to grow quickly

- **Enlightenment** *n.* an intellectual movement that emphasized the use of reason to examine previously accepted beliefs

- **Great Awakening** *n.* a series of Protestant religious revivals that swept across the American colonies

- **libel** (LY-buhl) *n.* the publishing of lies

- **midwife** *n.* a person who is trained to help deliver babies

WORDS IN CONTEXT Follow the directions for using the Key Vocabulary words in context.

1. Describe what it means for something to *burgeon*.

_____

_____

2. Write the definition of *Enlightenment* in your own words.

_____

_____

_____

3. Write the sentence in which the term *Great Awakening* appears in the section.

_____

_____

4. Describe what *libel* means using your own words.

_____

_____

5. Who were *midwives* and what did they do?

_____

_____

UNIT 2

CHAPTER 4 SECTION 4
Roots of American Democracy

VOCABULARY PRACTICE

KEY VOCABULARY

- **natural rights** *n.* rights such as life or liberty that a person is born with

- **Parliament** (PAHR-luh-muhnt) *n.* the legislative body of England, and, later, Great Britain

- **salutary neglect** (SAL-yuh-tair-ee) *n.* the policy of the British government to not strictly enforce its colonial policies

- **salvation** (sal-VAY-shuhn) *n.* the act of being forgiven by one's deity (god) for one's wrongdoings, or sins

DEFINITION CHART   Complete a Three-Column Chart for the Key Vocabulary Words. Choose one of the words and draw a picture to illustrate in the space below.

WORD	DEFINITION	IN MY OWN WORDS

Vocabulary Illustration

UNIT 2

CHAPTER 4 SECTION 5
The French and Indian War

VOCABULARY PRACTICE

KEY VOCABULARY

- **trading post** *n.* a small settlement established for the purpose of exchanging goods

WORD WHEEL   Follow the instructions below to analyze the vocabulary word *trading post*.

1. Write the word in the center of the wheel.

2. Look in your textbook for examples of descriptions related to the word, or think of any related words you already know.

3. Write your descriptions and related words on the spokes of the wheel. Add more spokes if needed.

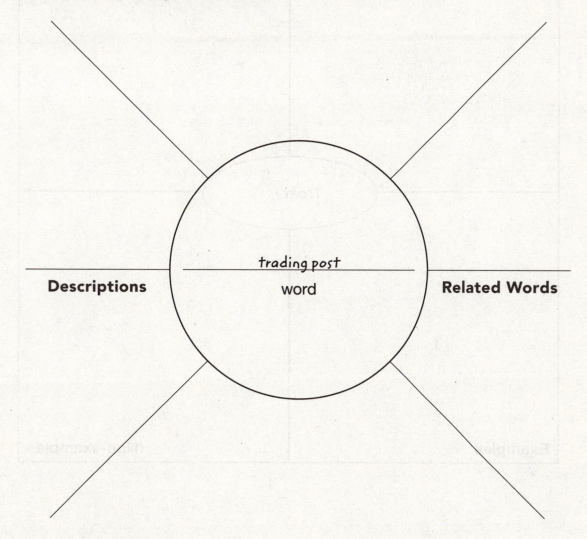

trading post

Descriptions   word   **Related Words**

UNIT **2** CHAPTER 4 SECTION 5
The French and Indian War

VOCABULARY PRACTICE

KEY VOCABULARY
- **treaty** *n.* a peace agreement

WORD SQUARE   Complete a Word Square for the Key Vocabulary word.

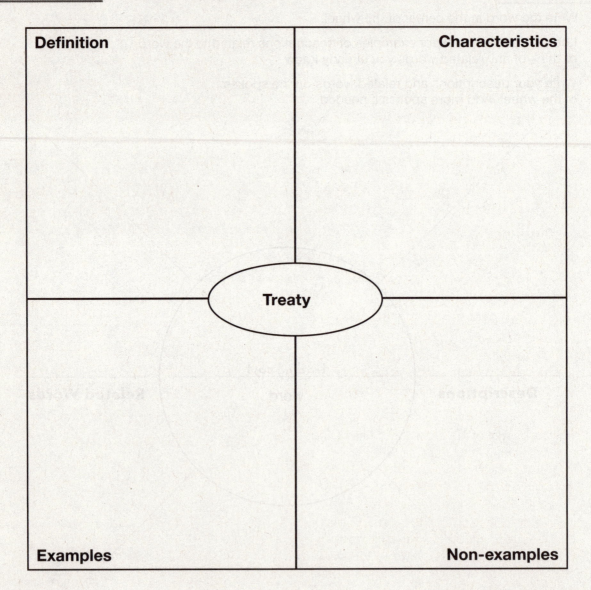

Definition	Characteristics

Treaty

Examples	Non-examples

AMERICAN VOICES
Sieur de la Salle
1643–1687

"I, René-Robert Cavelier de La Salle, by virtue of His Majesty's commission . . . have taken . . . all the nations, peoples, provinces, cities, towns, villages, mines, minerals, fisheries, streams and rivers, within the extent of the said Louisiana." — Sieur de la Salle

Engraving of Sieur de la Salle, c. 1685

©Pictorial Press Ltd/Alamy Stock Photo

René-Robert Cavelier, Sieur de la Salle, or La Salle, had become a Jesuit brother in France, but he was an explorer at heart. He led expeditions on ships and canoes along rivers and the Great Lakes from Montreal to the Gulf of Mexico.

La Salle was born in France in 1643. At age 22, he went to join his brother, a priest, in Canada, where he was given land near the St. Lawrence River. La Salle farmed the land, traded furs, and learned the languages of the Native Americans who lived near him. From them he heard tales of great rivers and vast territories beyond the settlements of New France. Intrigued, La Salle sold his land and set out exploring.

One of these tales was of the tremendous Mississippi River, by which one could travel from the Great Lakes to the sea. He and the governor of New France planned to set up trading posts and forts along the Great Lakes and the Mississippi River to expand and protect France's land claims. In 1680, La Salle sailed and canoed around the Great Lakes to the St. Joseph River, at the south end of Lake Michigan. From there, he found his way to the Kankakee River, to the Illinois, and finally to the Mississippi. In 1682, La Salle and his team canoed the length of that great river south to the Gulf of Mexico. He built forts along the route and claimed the entire Mississippi Basin for France and its king, Louis XIV, for whom he named the land "Louisiana."

La Salle sailed back to France. He returned with 200 men and four ships to secure the mouth of the Mississippi River at the Gulf of Mexico. But a navigation error sent the expedition to the Gulf coast of Texas, 500 miles off course. After many attempts, the explorers still did not find the Mississippi River. Following a shipwreck and sickness, an angry group of La Salle's men assassinated him in Texas in 1687.

HISTORICAL THINKING

IDENTIFY MAIN IDEAS AND DETAILS Why did La Salle explore the Mississippi River?

_____

_____

DETERMINE CHRONOLOGY What events led to La Salle's murder?

_____

_____

_____

UNIT 2
CHAPTER 4 LESSON 2.4
Slave Narratives

DOCUMENT-BASED QUESTION

Use the questions here to help you analyze the sources and write your paragraph.

DOCUMENT ONE: from *The Interesting Narrative of the Life of Olaudah Equiano*, 1789

1A What personal traits would have been necessary for those on the slave ship to survive?

_____

1B Constructed Response What details help you understand the horror the slaves endured in the Middle Passage?

_____

DOCUMENT TWO: from *A Narrative of the Most Remarkable Particulars in the Life of James Albert Ukawsaw Gronniosaw, An African Prince, as Related by Himself*, 1772

2A How did Gronniosaw's curiosity contribute to his decision to leave Africa?

_____

_____

2B Constructed Response How does the merchant make the idea of going with him sound like a fascinating adventure rather than the entry into a nightmare?

_____

DOCUMENT THREE: from *A Narrative of the Life and Adventures of Venture, a Native of Africa: But Resident Above Sixty Years in the United States of America*, 1798

3A What does Venture Smith have to do to achieve his own freedom and that of his family?

_____

3B Constructed Response What can you infer about the personal qualities that enabled Venture Smith to accomplish all that he describes?

_____

SYNTHESIZE & WRITE

How did formerly enslaved persons endure and overcome slavery?

Topic Sentence: _____

_____

Your Paragraph: _____

_____

_____

UNIT 3

CHAPTER 5 SECTION 1
British Control

NATIONAL GEOGRAPHIC LEARNING

READING AND NOTE-TAKING

SYNTHESIZE INFORMATION Use the text and the map in Section 1.1 to answer the questions below about the end of the French and Indian War.

1. What did King George think the role of the colony should be? _____

_____

2. Why might the colonists have been optimistic about their future after the French and Indian War?

_____

3. Describe the Proclamation of 1763. _____

_____

4. Did the colonists agree with the proclamation? Describe their reaction to it. _____

_____

5. Describe the Quartering Act. _____

_____

6. Explain the relationship between the colonists and the British as the King continued passing laws like the Proclamation of 1763 and the Quartering Act. _____

_____

SUMMARIZE

_____

_____

_____

_____

_____

_____

_____

_____

UNIT 3

CHAPTER 5 SECTION 1
British Control

NATIONAL GEOGRAPHIC LEARNING

READING AND NOTE-TAKING

IDENTIFY CAUSES AND EFFECTS   Use the chart below to record causes and effects that relate to the colonists' reactions to the taxes and control of the British government.

Causes	Effects
The French and Indian War had been expensive for the British government and they needed revenue to pay off their debt.	

UNIT 3

CHAPTER 5 SECTION 2
Rebellion in the Colonies

NATIONAL GEOGRAPHIC LEARNING

READING AND NOTE-TAKING

<u>**MAKE GENERALIZATIONS**</u>   After you finish reading about the growing tensions between the colonists and the British government in Section 2, read these excerpts from the text. Then, using your own words, write one or two generalizations about each excerpt.

1.	**EXCERPT:** "Colonists celebrated the Stamp Act's repeal. However, the British government insisted that it had not lost any authority over the colonies. But with the Stamp Act repealed, Britain had to figure out other ways of gaining revenue."
2.	**GENERALIZATION:** The colonists are going to continue to feel the control of the British government.

1.	**EXCERPT:** "By the 1770s, the ideas of the Great Awakening had helped create a revolutionary fervor among the colonists, which led them to challenge Britain's authority."
2.	**GENERALIZATION:**

UNIT 3

CHAPTER 5 SECTION 2

Rebellion in the Colonies *continued*

1.	**EXCERPT:** "Suddenly Preston's men were firing at the crowd. Five townspeople were killed and six were injured. This event soon became known as the Boston Massacre."
2.	**GENERALIZATION:**

1.	**EXCERPT:** "On the night of December 16, 1773, members of the Sons of Liberty disguised themselves as Native Americans and boarded three ships loaded with tea in Boston Harbor. Without harming the ships' other cargo, they dumped the tea into the icy water while thousands of people on shore watched the events of the Boston Tea Party unfold."
2.	**GENERALIZATION:**

UNIT 3

CHAPTER 5 SECTION 3
Lexington and Concord

NATIONAL GEOGRAPHIC LEARNING

READING AND NOTE-TAKING

SEQUENCE EVENTS   Fill in the Sequence Chart below as you read Section 3 to record information about the events that led up to the start of the American Revolution.

Parliament continued to punish the colonists. A series of laws were passed called the Coercive Acts. The colonists referred to these laws as the Intolerable Acts.

↓

↓

CHAPTER 5 SECTION 3
Lexington and Concord

**NATIONAL
GEOGRAPHIC
LEARNING**

READING AND NOTE-TAKING

SUMMARIZE   After you read Section 3, complete the T Chart below
with notes on the Patriots and Loyalists.

Patriots	Loyalists
Supported the right of the colonists to rule themselves.	

UNIT 3

CHAPTER 5 SECTION 4
Declaring Independence

NATIONAL GEOGRAPHIC LEARNING

READING AND NOTE-TAKING

ANNOTATE A TIME LINE   After you read Section 4, consider the dates listed below. Review the text and identify one event for each year listed. Write a description of the event in the box provided.

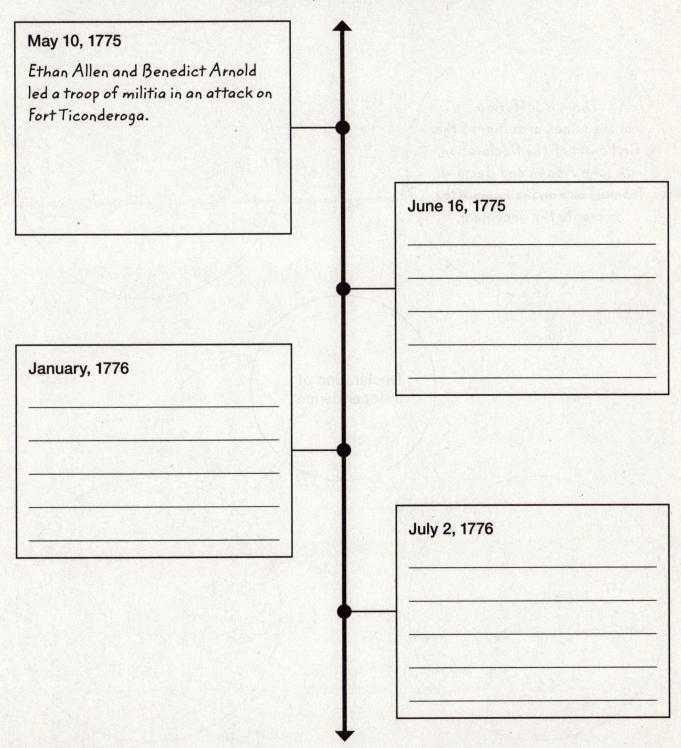

May 10, 1775

Ethan Allen and Benedict Arnold led a troop of militia in an attack on Fort Ticonderoga.

June 16, 1775

_____

_____

_____

_____

_____

January, 1776

_____

_____

_____

_____

July 2, 1776

_____

_____

_____

_____

_____

UNIT 3

CHAPTER 5 SECTION 4
Declaring Independence

READING AND NOTE-TAKING

IDENTIFY MAIN IDEA AND DETAILS   Use a Main Idea and Details Web to organize your notes on the Declaration of Independence.

Thomas Jefferson was the principal author of the first draft of the Declaration, with John Adams and Benjamin Franklin also on the committee to create the document.

Declaration of Independence

UNIT 3

CHAPTER 5 SECTION 1
British Control

VOCABULARY PRACTICE

KEY VOCABULARY

- **boycott** *n.* a form of protest that involves refusing to purchase goods or services
- **Currency Act** *n.* the British law that regulated paper money in the American colonies
- **duty** *n.* a tax on imports
- **grievance** (GREE-vuhnts) *n.* an objection or reason to complain
- **militia** (muh-LIH-shuh) *n.* military force made up of local citizens to help protect their town, land, or nation
- **Proclamation of 1763** *n.* a law requiring colonists to stay east of a line drawn on a map along the crest of the Appalachian Mountains
- **Quartering Act** *n.* one of several British laws that required American colonists to provide housing and food for British soldiers stationed in North America

THREE COLUMN CHART Complete the chart for each of the seven Key Vocabulary words. Write each word's definition, and then provide a definition in your own words.

WORD	DEFINITION	IN MY OWN WORDS
boycott	a form of protest that involves refusing to purchase goods or services	not buying things from people because you don't agree with them

UNIT **3**	CHAPTER 5 SECTION 1 **British Control**

VOCABULARY PRACTICE

KEY VOCABULARY

- **repeal** (rih-PEEL) *v.* to cancel or nullify, especially a law

- **revenue** *n.* income, money that is received

- **Sons of Liberty** *n.* the groups of merchants, shopkeepers, and craftsmen who successfully opposed the Stamp Act by establishing networks to boycott British goods

- **Stamp Act** *n.* the British law requiring colonists to purchase a stamp for official documents and published papers

- **Sugar Act** *n.* the British law that lowered the duty on molasses to cut out smuggling, so that the British would get the revenue

- **tyranny** (TEER-uh-nee) *n.* unjust rule by an absolute ruler

DEFINITION CHART   Complete a Definition Chart for the Key Vocabulary words.

WORD	DEFINITION	IN MY OWN WORDS
repeal		

UNIT 3

CHAPTER 5 SECTION 2
Rebellion in the Colonies

NATIONAL GEOGRAPHIC LEARNING

VOCABULARY PRACTICE

KEY VOCABULARY

- **Boston Massacre** *n.* the 1770 incident in which British soldiers fired on locals who had been taunting them

- **Boston Tea Party** *n.* the 1773 incident in which the Sons of Liberty boarded British ships and dumped their cargo in protest of British taxes on the colonists

- **committee of correspondence** *n.* in the Revolutionary era, a group of colonists whose duty it was to spread news about protests against the British

SUMMARY PARAGRAPH   Write a paragraph that describes the rebellion in the colonies. Use all of the Key Vocabulary words. Start with a strong topic sentence, and then write three to five sentences. Be sure to include a summary sentence at the end.

_____

_____

_____

_____

_____

_____

_____

_____

_____

_____

_____

_____

_____

UNIT 3

CHAPTER 5 SECTION 2
Rebellion in the Colonies

VOCABULARY PRACTICE

KEY VOCABULARY

- **Tea Act** *n.* the British law stating that only the East India Company was allowed to sell tea to the American colonists

- **Townshend Acts** *n.* a set of British laws that placed duties on tea, glass, paper, lead, and paint; required colonists to purchase from Britain

- **writs of assistance** *n.* a legal document giving authorities the right to enter and search a home or business

TOPIC TRIANGLE Use a Topic Triangle to help you understand the relationship between the Key Vocabulary words. Write three sentences about rebellion in the colonies, with the most general description on the top of the diagram and the most specific detail on the bottom level. Be sure that your diagram correctly uses all three Key Vocabulary words.

Topic Triangle

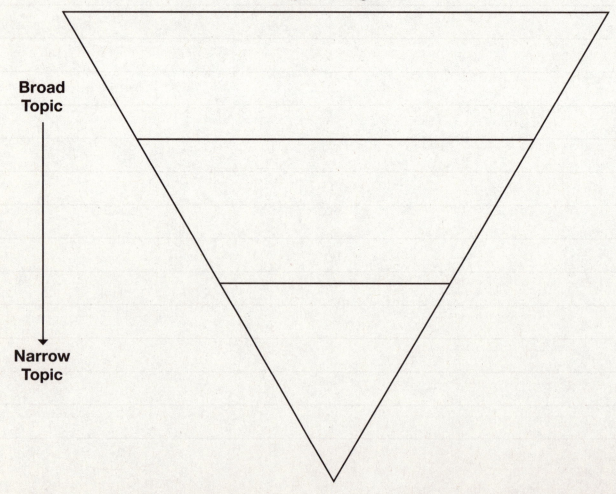

Broad Topic

Narrow Topic

UNIT 3

CHAPTER 5 SECTION 3
Lexington and Concord

NATIONAL GEOGRAPHIC LEARNING

VOCABULARY PRACTICE

KEY VOCABULARY

- **First Continental Congress** *n.* the 1774 meeting of representatives from American colonies to decide on a response to the Intolerable Acts

- **Intolerable Acts** *n.* the British laws passed to punish the people of Boston after the Boston Tea Party; also called the Coercive Acts

- **Loyalist** *n.* an American colonist who supported Britain during the American Revolution

RELATED IDEA WEB   Write one of the Key Vocabulary words inside each circle, along with its definition in your own words. Then draw lines or arrows connecting the circles to show how the words are related, based on what you read in Section 3. Write your explanation of the connection next to the line or arrow.

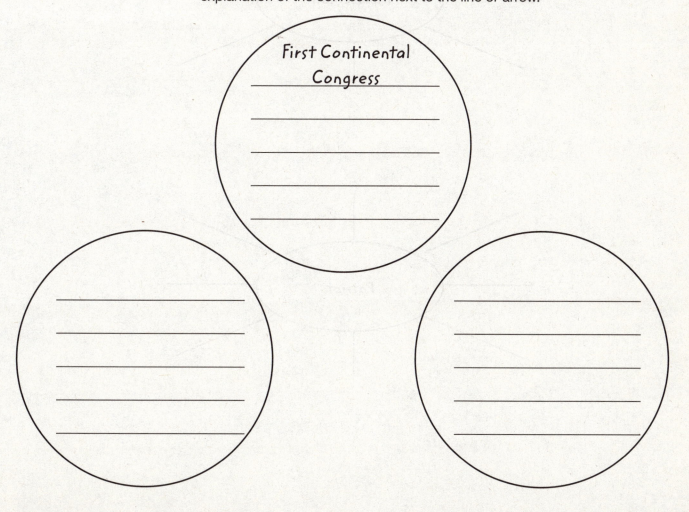

First Continental Congress

UNIT 3

CHAPTER 5 SECTION 3
Lexington and Concord

NATIONAL GEOGRAPHIC LEARNING

VOCABULARY PRACTICE

KEY VOCABULARY

- **minuteman** *n.* an American colonial militia member who was ready to join in combat at a moment's notice

- **Patriot** *n.* an American colonist who supported the right of the American colonies to govern themselves

WORD WHEEL   Complete a Word Wheel for each Key Vocabulary word.

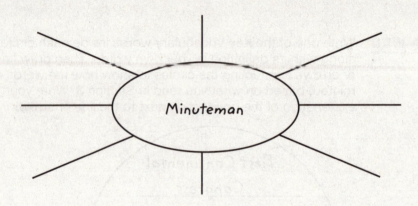

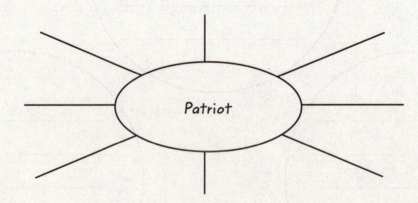

UNIT 3   CHAPTER 5 SECTION 4
Declaring Independence

VOCABULARY PRACTICE

KEY VOCABULARY

- **artillery** (ahr-TIH-luh-ree) *n.* large guns that can fire over a long distance

- **Continental Army** *n.* the American army formed in 1775 by the Second Continental Congress and led by General George Washington

- **Declaration of Independence** *n.* the document declaring American independence from Great Britain, adopted July 4, 1776

- **drumlin** (DRUHM-luhn) *n.* a smooth-sloped hill made of glacial sediments

- **earthworks** *n.* human-made land modifications

DEFINITION CLUES   Follow the instructions below for the Key Vocabulary word indicated.

1. Write the sentence in which the word *artillery* appears in the lesson.

   _____

   _____

2. Write the definition of the term *Continental Army* using your own words.

   _____

   _____

3. Use the term *Declaration of Independence* in a sentence of your own.

   _____

   _____

4. Now that you know what the word *drumlin* means, write a sentence describing two of the drumlins that were famous battlegrounds.

   _____

   _____

5. Write a sentence using the word *earthworks*.

   _____

   _____

UNIT 3 — CHAPTER 5 SECTION 4
Declaring Independence

NATIONAL GEOGRAPHIC LEARNING

VOCABULARY PRACTICE

KEY VOCABULARY

- **geology** *n.* the study of the processes that shape Earth's rocks and landforms

- **Hessians** (HEH-shuhnz) *n.* German soldiers hired by the British to fight during the American Revolution

- **Second Continental Congress** *n.* a group of leaders of the American colonies who met to address the problem of British tyranny, declared independence in 1776, and led the United States through the American Revolution

- **terrain** (tuh-RAYN) *n.* the physical features of the land

- **unalienable** (uhn-AY-lee-uhn-ah-buhl) **right** *n.* a right that cannot be taken away

KWL CHART   Fill in the KWL Chart for the Key Vocabulary words.

KWL Chart

K WHAT DO I KNOW	W WHAT DO I WANT TO LEARN?	L WHAT DID I LEARN?
Geology		

AMERICAN VOICES
John Adams
1735–1826

Abigail Adams
1744–1818

"I cannot say that I think you are very generous to the ladies; for, whilst you are proclaiming peace and good-will to men, emancipating all nations, you insist upon retaining an absolute power over wives." — from Abigail Adams's letter to her husband, John, May 7, 1776

"I pray… May none but honest and wise Men ever rule under this roof." — from John Adams's letter to his wife, Abigail, regarding the White House, November 1800

John Adams (1821) and his wife, Abigail (c. 1800-1815), wrote letters about the new country.

American Founding Father John Adams and his wife, Abigail Adams, shared trust, affection, and similar views on politics. Their letters offer personal looks at events surrounding the foundation of the new nation.

John Adams was born October 30, 1735, in Braintree, Massachusetts. Abigail Smith was born November 11, 1744, in Weymouth, Massachusetts. John attended Harvard and began practicing law in 1758. Abigail was schooled at home. Abigail and John met, fell in love, married in 1764, and raised five children together. Avid letter-writers, the Adamses shared their personal affections, as well as ideas and opinions about the colonies and, later, the United States.

John served as a Massachusetts delegate to the Continental Congress in Philadelphia from 1774–1776, where he helped write the Declaration of Independence. They kept in touch with letters. Both John and Abigail believed the colonies should gain independence from Great Britain. Additionally, Abigail wanted women to be treated fairly in the laws of the new nation. John's letters informed Abigail about the war and of his hopes for the new nation. Abigail's letters told John about their family and farm.

Following the American victory in the Revolutionary War, John Adams became the first vice president under President George Washington. Frustrated, John wrote to Abigail that the vice presidency was "the most insignificant office" ever created and he was able to do neither "good nor evil." In 1796, John was elected second president of the United States. The Adams's lived in the president's house in New York City during most of his term, but moved into the White House for the last few months. Their son, John Quincy Adams, became the nation's sixth president.

Abigail died in 1818 and John died in 1826. They are buried beside each other at their Quincy, Massachusetts, home.

HISTORICAL THINKING

MAKE GENERALIZATIONS How do you think letters written in the past, like those of John and Abigail Adams's, help people today better understand historical events and times?

_____

_____

UNIT 3 **CHAPTER 5 LESSON 4.5**
Declarations Of Freedom

DOCUMENT-BASED QUESTION

Use the questions here to help you analyze the sources and write your paragraph.

DOCUMENT ONE: from the Declaration of Independence, 1776

1A How would you explain in your own words what "unalienable Rights" are?

_____

1B Constructed Response In what ways is this vision of governing different from how the British monarchy governed?

_____

DOCUMENT TWO: from the Declaration of Independence, 1776

2A Why did the king dissolve (close down or bring to an end) certain Representative Houses?

_____

2B Constructed Response Why do you think the writers included such a complete list of grievances against the king?

_____

DOCUMENT THREE: from *Two Treatises on Government*, by John Locke, 1689

3A How did Locke describe the value of a community?

_____

_____

3B Constructed Response In what ways did Locke's ideas directly influence the actions of the colonies and the writing of the Declaration of Independence?

_____

SYNTHESIZE & WRITE

How did beliefs about the nature of government and human freedom lead to the colonies' break with Britain?

Topic Sentence: _____

_____

Your Paragraph: _____

_____

_____

READING AND NOTE-TAKING

IDENTIFY MAIN IDEA AND DETAILS

Use a Main Idea and Details Web to organize your notes on the Continental Army.

ill-prepared and disorganized

Continental Army

UNIT 3

CHAPTER 6 SECTION 1
Early War Years

NATIONAL GEOGRAPHIC LEARNING

READING AND NOTE-TAKING

SEQUENCE EVENTS   In the Sequence Chain below, list the major events addressed in Section 1. Start your Sequence Chain with the British troops' plan to capture the Hudson River Valley, and end with the Americans' success at Saratoga.

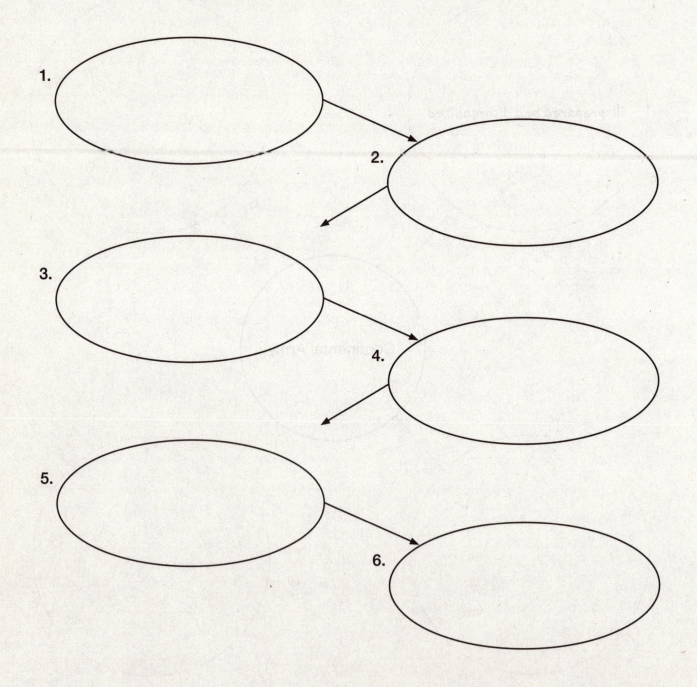

UNIT 3

CHAPTER 6 SECTION 2
The War Expands

NATIONAL GEOGRAPHIC LEARNING

READING AND NOTE-TAKING

OUTLINE AND TAKE NOTES As you read Section 2, use the headings and subheadings of each lesson to create an outline. Summarize each lesson as you finish taking notes.

2.1 Seeking Help from Europe

A. Powerful Friends

- _____
- _____
- _____

B. Heroes from Home and Abroad

- _____
- _____
- _____

Summarize

_____

_____

2.2

A.

- _____
- _____
- _____

B.

- _____
- _____
- _____

Summarize

_____

_____

2.3

A.

- _____
- _____
- _____

B.

- _____
- _____
- _____

Summarize

_____

_____

_____

2.4

A.

- _____
- _____
- _____

B.

- _____
- _____
- _____

Summarize

_____

_____

_____

UNIT **3**

CHAPTER 6 SECTION 3
The Path to Victory

NATIONAL
GEOGRAPHIC
LEARNING

READING AND NOTE-TAKING

MAKE PREDICTIONS Use the chart below to map out the events of the war in the Southern Colonies. Then make a prediction about the Americans' potential for victory.

Problem and Solution

Initial Event:

The British employed a new strategy in the Southern Colonies in 1778.

↓

Following Event:
Event 2:
Event 3:
Event 4:

↓

Prediction

UNIT 3

CHAPTER 6 SECTION 3
The Path to Victory

NATIONAL GEOGRAPHIC LEARNING

READING AND NOTE-TAKING

IDENTIFY CAUSES AND EFFECTS   Use the chart below to record causes and effects that relate to the end of the war as you read Section 3.

Cause-and-Effect Chart

Causes	Effects

UNIT 3

CHAPTER 6 SECTION 1
Early War Years

NATIONAL GEOGRAPHIC LEARNING

VOCABULARY PRACTICE

KEY VOCABULARY

- **Articles of Confederation** *n.* a set of laws adopted by the United States in 1777 that established each state in the union as a republic, replaced by the Constitution in 1789

- **counterattack** *n.* an attack made in response to a previous attack

- **defensive war** *n.* a war to protect one's own land, on familiar ground, from outside attackers

- **fortification** (fawr-tuh-fuh-KAY-shuhn) *n.* a structure built to protect a place from attack

WDS CHART   Complete a Word-Definition-Sentence (WDS) Chart for each Vocabulary word.

a set of laws adopted by the United States in 1777 that established each state in the union as a republic

Articles of Confederation

W

D   S

The Articles of Confederation allowed the states to govern themselves as small republics.

counterattack

W

D   S

defensive war

W

D   S

fortification

W

D   S

UNIT 3   CHAPTER 6 SECTION 1
Early War Years

VOCABULARY PRACTICE

KEY VOCABULARY

- **mercenary** (MUR-suh-nehr-ee) *n.* a soldier who is paid to fight for a country other than his or her own

- **reinforcements** *n.* more soldiers and supplies sent to help military troops engaged in warfare

- **republic** *n.* a form of government in which the people elect representatives to speak for them and enact laws based on their needs

WORD SQUARE   Complete a Word Square for the Key Vocabulary words *mercenary, reinforcements,* and *republic.*

Definition	Characteristics
mercenary	
Examples	Non-Examples

Definition	Characteristics
Examples	Non-Examples

Definition	Characteristics
Examples	Non-Examples

UNIT 3

CHAPTER 6 SECTION 2
The War Expands

VOCABULARY PRACTICE

KEY VOCABULARY

- **bayonet** (BAY-uh-nuht) *n.* a sharp blade attached to the end of a rifle
- **blockade** (blah-KAYD) *v.* to block ships from entering or leaving a harbor
- **financier** (fih-nuhn-SIHR) *n.* a person who lends or manage money for a business or undertaking

WORDS IN CONTEXT   Follow the directions for using the Key Vocabulary words in context.

1. Describe what a *bayonet* looks like.

_____

_____

_____

_____

_____

2. Describe how a *blockade* worked for the British ships.

_____

_____

_____

_____

_____

3. How did Americans deal with financial problems during the war?

_____

_____

_____

_____

_____

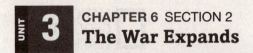

UNIT 3 CHAPTER 6 SECTION 2
The War Expands

NATIONAL GEOGRAPHIC LEARNING

VOCABULARY PRACTICE

KEY VOCABULARY

- **desert** (dih-ZURT) *v.* to run away from the army or another branch of the military to avoid military service

- **espionage** (EHS-pee-uh-nahzh) *n.* the practice of spying to obtain information

- **skirmish** *n.* a small, short-lasting battle

SUMMARY PARAGRAPH   Write a paragraph summarizing how the three Key Vocabulary words are related. Be sure to write a clear topic sentence as your first sentence. Then write several sentences with supporting details. Conclude your paragraph with a summarizing sentence.

_____

_____

_____

_____

_____

_____

_____

_____

_____

_____

_____

_____

_____

_____

_____

_____

U.S. HISTORY   Chapter 6 SECTION 2 **Activity B**   © National Geographic Learning, a part of Cengage Learning

UNIT 3
CHAPTER 6 SECTION 3
The Path to Victory

NATIONAL GEOGRAPHIC LEARNING

VOCABULARY PRACTICE

KEY VOCABULARY

- **expertise** (ehk-spur-TEEZ) *n.* an expert knowledge or skill

- **guerrilla** (guh-RIH-luh) *adj.* relating to an independent military group that uses methods such as sneak attacks and sabotage

- **pacifist** *n.* a person who stands against war and violence

- **provision** *n.* legal conditions that anticipate future needs

THREE-COLUMN CHART   Complete the chart for each of the four vocabulary words. Write the word's definition, and then provide a definition in your own words.

WORD	DEFINITION	IN MY OWN WORDS
expertise	expert knowledge or skill, often based on experience	

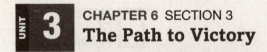

UNIT 3

CHAPTER 6 SECTION 3
The Path to Victory

NATIONAL GEOGRAPHIC LEARNING

VOCABULARY PRACTICE

KEY VOCABULARY

- **republicanism** *n.* a government in which people choose representatives to make their laws

- **Treaty of Paris of 1783** *n.* the binding agreement between Britain and the United States in which Britain acknowledged American independence, and the initial borders of the United States were determined

JOURNAL ENTRY   Imagine you are negotiating the details of the Treaty of Paris of 1783 at the end of the American Revolution. Write a journal entry describing what it was like to establish a new plan for government. Be sure to provide a headline and date. Use the Key Vocabulary words in your journal entry.

_____

_____

_____

_____

_____

_____

_____

_____

_____

_____

_____

_____

_____

_____

_____

_____

AMERICAN VOICES

Women of the Continental Army
1775–1783

"Amidst all the . . . sufferings of the Army . . . our Virtuous Country Women . . . have never been accused of withholding their most zealous efforts to support the cause we are engaged in."
— George Washington, regarding women nurses

Sybil Ludington spreads the news of a British attack on April 26, 1777.

Often overlooked by historical accounts, women contributed their time, skills, and courage to the Continental Army in many ways in order to assure an American victory over the British.

In colonial America in the late 18th century, women weren't allowed to enlist in the army. However, when the American Revolution broke out in 1775, many women played integral roles.

Some women who felt unsafe at home or needed paid work became what we now call "camp followers." They literally followed the troops as they traveled. Although not all officers were happy to have women along, the women performed beneficial chores, such as washing and mending uniforms. Soldiers usually did their own cooking, but some women, such as Sarah Osborne, cooked and baked for the troops.

Nursing became an important and profitable role during the war. Nurses could earn two dollars a month—and that pay rose later in the war. Plus, when women took on this responsibility, the male nurses were freed to fight. Nurses Rachel Clement and Mary DeCamp, among others, served at the Albany hospital in New York during the war. Nursing was dirty and dangerous, exposing the women to diseases such as fevers and smallpox.

Couriers—such as the famous Paul Revere who warned colonists of approaching Redcoats—carried messages of military importance. In spite of great peril, sixteen-year-old Sybil Ludington, of Putnam County, New York, became a military courier. On the night of April 26, 1777, a messenger arrived at the Ludington home, exhausted, and bearing news to Sybil's father of a British attack on nearby Danbury, Connecticut. Sybil agreed to spread the word. She climbed onto her horse and galloped nearly 40 miles through the darkness, mustering the militia.

A few women even dressed as men to fight in the war while others served as spies. All of these women, many of whose names are unknown, helped win the American Revolution.

HISTORICAL THINKING

IDENTIFY SUPPORTING DETAILS In what ways were women helpful to the Continental Army?

_____

_____

NATIONAL GEOGRAPHIC LEARNING

READING AND NOTE-TAKING

SEQUENCE EVENTS AND TAKE NOTES

As you read Section 1, take notes. First write the titles of the lessons and the headers. Then include details from those sections of text. Include at least four to six details in each box.

1.1

1.2

UNIT 3

CHAPTER 7 SECTION 1

The Confederation Era *continued*

1.3

Summarize Write a paragraph summarizing Section 1.

_____

_____

_____

_____

_____

_____

_____

_____

_____

_____

_____

_____

_____

_____

_____

_____

UNIT 3

CHAPTER 7 SECTION 2
Drafting the Constitution

READING AND NOTE-TAKING

IDENTIFY PROBLEMS AND SOLUTIONS Complete a Problem and Solution Chart to explain what the United States did about the Articles of Confederation.

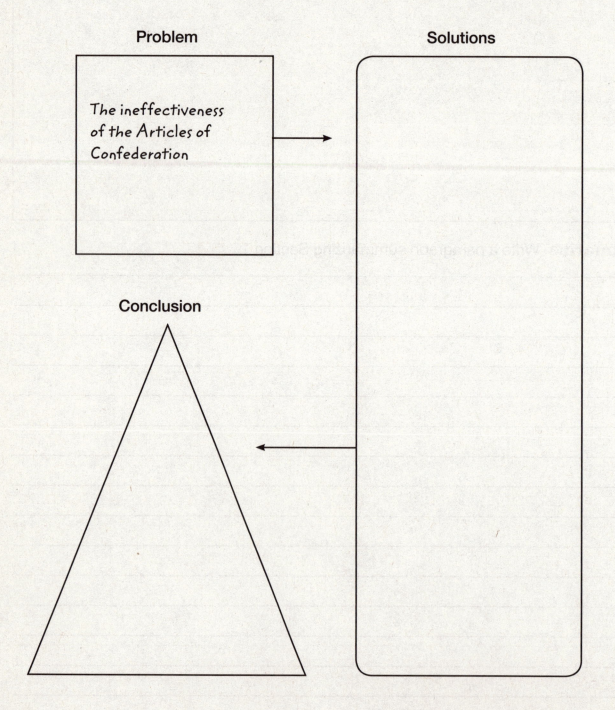

Problem

The ineffectiveness of the Articles of Confederation

Solutions

Conclusion

UNIT 3

CHAPTER 7 SECTION 2
Drafting the Constitution

READING AND NOTE-TAKING

OUTLINE AND TAKE NOTES As you read Section 3.3 use the outline below to organize and keep track of important information you read.

What is the title of the lesson? _____	
What is the Main Idea? _____ _____ _____	
Describe the Great Compromise. _____ _____ _____	What is the slave importation clause? _____ _____ _____
What is the fugitive slave clause? _____ _____ _____	Explain the commerce clause and the common market. _____ _____ _____

Summarize Write a paragraph summarizing this lesson.

_____
_____
_____
_____
_____
_____
_____
_____
_____
_____

UNIT 3

CHAPTER 7 SECTION 3
Ratification and the Bill of Rights

NATIONAL
GEOGRAPHIC
LEARNING

READING AND NOTE-TAKING

CATEGORIZE INFORMATION   As you read Section 3, use the T Chart below to categorize information about Federalists and Antifederalists.

Federalists	Antifederalists

UNIT 3

CHAPTER 7 SECTION 3
Ratification and the Bill of Rights

NATIONAL GEOGRAPHIC LEARNING

READING AND NOTE-TAKING

SYNTHESIZE VISUAL AND TEXTUAL INFORMATION Use visual and textual information from Section 3.3 to answer the questions below.

1. How has the U.S. Constitution survived for more than 200 years? _____
_____
_____

2. What must happen in order to change the Constitution? _____
_____
_____

3. What is the Bill of Rights? _____
_____
_____

4. Explain the First Amendment. _____
_____
_____

5. What is a *statute*? _____
_____
_____

6. What is the Sixth Amendment? _____
_____
_____

7. What do the first eight Amendments focus on? _____
_____
_____

8. Describe what the Ninth and Tenth Amendments say. _____
_____
_____

NATIONAL GEOGRAPHIC LEARNING

VOCABULARY PRACTICE

KEY VOCABULARY

- **constitution** *n.* a document that organizes a government and states its powers

- **constitutionalism** *n.* the concept of governing based on a constitution

- **credit** *n.* the privilege of purchasing something or borrowing money and paying the amount back over time

- **federal** *adj.* relating to a government where power is shared between the central, national government and that of states or provinces

- **Northwest Ordinance of 1787** *n.* legislation adopted by Congress to establish stricter control over the government of the Northwest Territory

DEFINITION CLUES   Follow the instructions below for the Key Vocabulary word indicated.

1. Write the sentence in which the word *constitution* appears in Section 1.

_____

_____

2. Write a definition of *constitutionalism* using your own words.

_____

_____

3. Use the word *credit* in a sentence of your own.

_____

_____

4. Write the sentence in which the word *federal* appears in Section 1.

_____

_____

5. Write a sentence using *Northwest Ordinance of 1787.*

_____

_____

UNIT 3 **CHAPTER 7 SECTION 1**

VOCABULARY PRACTICE

KEY VOCABULARY

- **ordinance** (OWRD-nuhnts) *n.* an official law, decree, or directive

- **Ordinance of 1785** *n.* a federal law that set up a system to allow settlers to purchase land in the undeveloped west

- **ratify** *v.* to approve formally, by vote

- **Shays's Rebellion** *n.* the 1786–1787 uprising of Massachusetts farmers in protest of high taxes

- **sovereign** (SAH-vruhn) *adj.* having the right to self-rule or independent government

DEFINITION CHART Complete a Definition Chart for the Key Vocabulary words.

WORDS	DEFINITION	IN MY OWN WORDS	ILLUSTRATION
ordinance			

UNIT 3   **CHAPTER 7 SECTION 2**

NATIONAL GEOGRAPHIC LEARNING

VOCABULARY PRACTICE

KEY VOCABULARY

- **checks and balances** *n.* the system established by the U.S. Constitution that gives each of the branches of government the power to limit the power of the other two

- **commerce clause** *n.* a provision in Article 1 of the U.S. Constitution granting Congress the power to make laws concerning foreign trade as well as trade among the states and with Native American nations

- **common market** *n.* a group of countries or states that allows the members to trade freely among them

- **delegate** (DEH-lih-guht) *n.* a person chosen or elected to represent a group of people

- **dual sovereignty** *n.* the concept that state governments have certain powers the federal government cannot overrule

- **electoral college** *n.* the group that elects the U.S. president; each state receives as many electors as it has congressional representatives and senators combined

- **executive branch** *n.* the section of the U.S. government headed by the president; responsible for enforcing the law

- **federalism** *n.* the support of a government where power is shared between the central, national government and that of states or provinces

- **Framers** *n.* delegates to the 1787 Constitutional Convention who helped shape the content and structure of the U.S. Constitution

- **fugitive slave cause** *n.* a provision in Article 4 of the U.S. Constitution that prevented free states from emancipating enslaved workers who had escaped from their masters in other states

- **judicial branch** *n.* the section of the U.S. government that includes the courts and legal system, led by the Supreme Court; responsible for interpreting the law

- **legislative branch** *n.* the section of the U.S. government led by Congress; responsible for making the law

- **Supreme Court** *n.* the highest court in the United States

- **separation of powers** *n.* the division of governmental power among the three branches of U.S. government: the executive branch, the judicial branch, and the legislative branch

- **slave importation clause** *n.* a provision in Article 1 of the U.S. Constitution that established the United States would not consider prohibiting the international slave trade in the United States until 1808

- **Three-Fifths Compromise** *n.* the agreement that determined that only three-fifths of the total population of enslaved persons in a state would be counted for purposes of taxation and representation

UNIT 3

CHAPTER 7 SECTION 2

NATIONAL GEOGRAPHIC LEARNING

VOCABULARY PRACTICE

SUMMARY PARAGRAPH   Write a paragraph summarizing Section 2. Use all of the Key Vocabulary words in your paragraph.

_____

_____

_____

_____

_____

_____

_____

_____

_____

_____

_____

_____

_____

_____

_____

_____

_____

_____

_____

_____

UNIT 3

CHAPTER 7 SECTION 3

Ratification and the Bill of Rights

NATIONAL GEOGRAPHIC LEARNING

VOCABULARY PRACTICE

KEY VOCABULARY

- **amendment** *n.* a formal change to a law, usually referring to a formal change to the U.S. Constitution

- **antifederalist** *n.* a person who opposed the U.S. Constitution of 1787 because of its emphasis on a strong national government

- **Bill of Rights** *n.* the first 10 amendments to the U.S. Constitution; a list of guarantees to which every person in a country is entitled

- **federalist** *n.* a person who supported the U.S. Constitution of 1787 as it was written during the process of ratification

- **statute** (STA-choot) *n.* a formal, written law

WDS TRIANGLES   Complete Word-Definition-Sentence Triangles for the Key Vocabulary words. Write the definition next to "D". Write a sentence using the word next to "S."

UNIT 3

CHAPTER 7 SECTION 3
Ratification and the Bill of Rights

_____

_____

_____

_____

_____

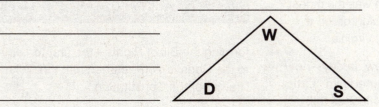

_____

_____

_____

_____

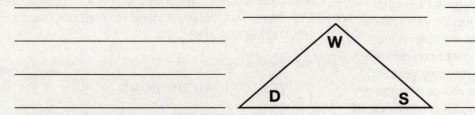

_____

_____

_____

_____

AMERICAN VOICES
James Madison
1751–1836

"Knowledge will forever govern ignorance: And a people who mean to be their own Governors, must arm themselves with the power which knowledge gives." — James Madison

Father of the Constitution, President James Madison, c. 1821

James Madison, called the "Father of the Constitution," wrote the first ten constitutional amendments—commonly known as the Bill of Rights—and served as the fourth president of the United States.

Born March 16, 1751, James Madison was the oldest of twelve children. His family lived at Montpelier, a tobacco plantation in Orange County, Virginia.

Madison attended the College of New Jersey—now Princeton—where his friends nicknamed him "Little Jemmy." Madison stood just 5 feet 4 inches tall, but he was not shy of debating and expressing his views. He completed a four-year course in two years, but remained another six months to study Hebrew and philosophy. He then returned to Montpelier, where he studied law.

As war broke out between the colonies and Great Britain, Madison was elected to the Virginia Convention in 1776 and to the Virginia Council of State one year later. In 1780, at just 29 years of age, Madison served as the youngest member of the Continental Congress. The Congress coordinated resistance to British rule during the early years of the American Revolution and served as a temporary national government. In 1786, Madison reintroduced the Virginia Statute for Establishing Religious Freedom, written by Thomas Jefferson in 1777. This statute served as a model for the U.S. Constitution's First Amendment.

Following America's victory in the Revolution, Madison helped create a constitution for the new nation. Madison's efforts, including his leadership in forming the Bill of Rights—the first ten amendments to the Constitution—earned him the nickname, "Father of the Constitution."

Madison became the fourth president of the United States in 1809. Three years later, the United States declared war on Great Britain, due to seizures of American seamen and cargoes. British forces attacked and burned Washington, D.C. However, under Madison's steady leadership, the United States won what became known as the War of 1812.

At his retirement in 1817, Madison returned home to Montpelier with his wife, Dolley. He died on June 28, 1836, at the age of 85.

HISTORICAL THINKING

MAKE INFERENCES How might Madison's work with the Continental Congress and in developing the Constitution have helped him as president?

_____

_____

©UniversalImagesGroup/Contributor

DOCUMENT-BASED QUESTION

Use the questions here to help you analyze the sources and write your paragraph.

DOCUMENT ONE: from "Federalist No. 1," by Alexander Hamilton, 1788

1A What does Hamilton seem to think about individual ambition?

_____

_____

1B Constructed Response What was the author's opinion about a strong government versus the opinions of those who advocated for more rights for the people?

_____

_____

DOCUMENT TWO: from "Objections to the Constitution of Government Formed by the Convention," by George Mason, 1787

2A How would you explain what Mason means by a "corrupt, tyrannical aristocracy"?

_____

_____

2B Constructed Response How does Mason's essay about government differ from ideas expressed in *The Federalist*?

_____

_____

DOCUMENT THREE: from "Observations on the New Constitution," by Mercy Otis Warren, 1788

3A What do you think Warren meant by the "rights of conscience"?

_____

_____

3B Constructed Response What concerns about the Constitution did Warren express?

_____

_____

SYNTHESIZE & WRITE

What were the main philosophies that supported the arguments for and against the ratification of the Constitution?

Topic Sentence: _____

_____

Your Paragraph: _____

_____

_____

UNIT 4

CHAPTER 8 SECTION 1
Washington's Presidency

READING AND NOTE-TAKING

IDENTIFY MAIN IDEA AND DETAILS Use a Main Idea and Details Web to organize your notes on George Washington as the nation's first president.

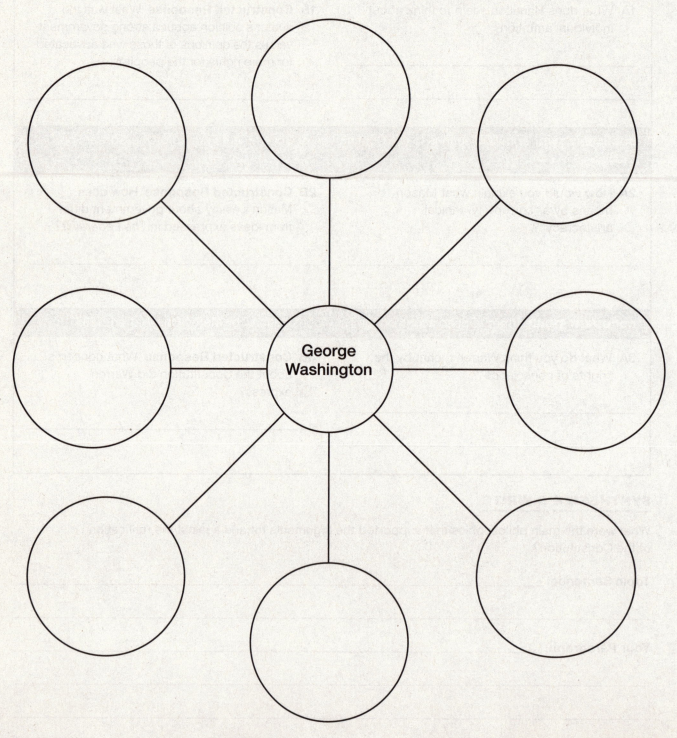

George Washington

UNIT 4

CHAPTER 8 SECTION 1
Washington's Presidency

NATIONAL GEOGRAPHIC LEARNING

READING AND NOTE-TAKING

CATEGORIZE INFORMATION   Use the boxes below to categorize information about Washington's cabinet, the Supreme Court, and Hamilton's economic plan.

Washington's Cabinet

Supreme Court

Hamilton's Economic Plan

UNIT 4
CHAPTER 8 SECTION 2
Politics in the 1790s

NATIONAL GEOGRAPHIC LEARNING

READING AND NOTE-TAKING

OUTLINE AND TAKE NOTES As you read Section 2, use the headings and subheadings of each lesson to create an outline. Summarize each lesson as you finish taking notes.

2.1 Political Parties Form

A. Taking Sides

- _____
- _____
- _____

B. Facing Off

- _____
- _____
- _____

Summarize

_____

_____

2.2 Competition for Territory and the French Revolution

A.

- _____
- _____
- _____

B.

- _____
- _____
- _____

Summarize

_____

_____

UNIT 4 CHAPTER 8 SECTION 2
Politics in the 1790s *continued*

NATIONAL GEOGRAPHIC LEARNING

2.4 *The Parties in Conflict*

A.

- _____
- _____
- _____

B.

- _____
- _____
- _____

Summarize

_____
_____
_____

Write a paragraph to summarize Section 2.

_____
_____
_____
_____
_____
_____
_____
_____
_____
_____
_____

UNIT **4**

CHAPTER 8 SECTION 1
Washington's Presidency

NATIONAL GEOGRAPHIC LEARNING

VOCABULARY PRACTICE

KEY VOCABULARY

- **attorney general** *n.* a member of the president's Cabinet, whose primary role is to represent the United States before the Supreme Court

- **cabinet** *n.* the heads of the departments that assist the president

- **Chief Justice** *n.* the head of the judicial branch of the government; presides over the Supreme Court

- **inauguration** (uh-NAW-gyuh-ray-shun) *n.* the ceremony that marks the beginning of a presidency

FOUR COLUMN CHART   Complete a Four-Column Chart for the Key Vocabulary words. In the last column, use the word in a sentence.

WORD	DEFINITION	ILLUSTRATION	SENTENCE

UNIT 4

CHAPTER 8 SECTION 1
Washington's Presidency

NATIONAL GEOGRAPHIC LEARNING

VOCABULARY PRACTICE

KEY VOCABULARY

- **national debt** *n.* the amount of money a government owes to all its creditors, incuding to other nations and to companies from which it purchases goods and services

- **precedent** (PREH-suh-duhnt) *n.* a prior event or decision that serves as an example for events or decisions that follow

- **tariff** (TAIR-uhf) *n.* taxes on imports and exports

<u>**THREE-COLUMN CHART**</u> Complete the chart for each of the Key Vocabulary words. Write the word and its definition. Then provide a definition using your own words.

WORD	DEFINITION	IN MY OWN WORDS

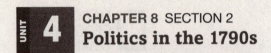

UNIT 4

CHAPTER 8 SECTION 2
Politics in the 1790s

NATIONAL GEOGRAPHIC LEARNING

VOCABULARY PRACTICE

KEY VOCABULARY

- **cede** (SEED) *v.* to give up

- **envoy** (AHN-voy) *n.* an ambassador

- **French Revolution** *n.* the 1789 rebellion against the French monarchy that sought to put an end to upper-class privilege and demanded equality for the lower classes

- **loose interpretation** *n.* an understanding of the Constitution as one that gives Congress and the president broad powers

- **power base** *n.* an area or group of people providing the biggest influence over a political candidate

KWL CHART   Fill in the KWL Chart for the Key Vocabulary words.

KWL Chart

WORD	WHAT I KNOW	WHAT I WANT TO KNOW	WHAT I LEARNED
cede			

UNIT 4

CHAPTER 8 SECTION 2
Politics in the 1790s

NATIONAL GEOGRAPHIC LEARNING

VOCABULARY PRACTICE

KEY VOCABULARY

- **Alien and Sedition Acts** *n.* a series of four laws passed to keep certain groups from immigrating to the United States; the laws gave the government power to expel aliens living in the United States and targeted U.S. citizens who criticized the U.S. government

- **radical** *n.* a person who supports complete social or political change

- **sedition** *n.* the act of provoking rebellion

- **states' rights** *n.* the concept that individual states have rights that the federal government cannot violate

- **strict interpretation** *n.* an understanding of the Constitution as one in which the Constituiton is strictly followed as it was written

- **Treaty of Greenville** *n.* a treaty between the United States and a number of Native American nations in which the Native American nations gave up their lands in present-day Ohio and Indiana to the United Sates

- **Whiskey Rebellion** *n.* a series of violent protests among farmers in western Pennsylvania against a tax on whiskey

- **XYZ Affair** *n.* the meeting with French agents after France began seizing American ships in an effort to prevent U.S. trade with Britain

SUMMARIZE   Use the Key Vocabulary words to write a summary paragraph.

_____

_____

_____

_____

_____

_____

_____

_____

_____

_____

AMERICAN VOICES
George Washington
1732–1799

President George Washington in 1821

"The Citizens of America . . . are now, by the late satisfactory pacification, acknowledged to be possessed of absolute Freedom and Independency." — George Washington to John Hancock, 1783

An ambitious, dedicated man, George Washington led the Continental Army to victory during the American Revolution and became the United States' first president.

George Washington was born in Westmoreland County, Virginia, on February 22, 1732. His father died when he was 11, leaving him in the care of his half-brother, Lawrence Washington. George grew up on Lawrence's plantation, later known as Mount Vernon, surrounded by people of status and culture. Ambitious and determined to make a name for himself, teenaged George became a surveyor, measuring and mapping portions of the Virginia frontier.

Washington joined the British Army in late 1753 and fought during the French and Indian War from 1754 to 1758. During this time, he gained a reputation for bravery and dedication. He eventually left military service and married the wealthy Martha Custis in 1759. For 15 years, Washington worked as a gentleman farmer at Mount Vernon, which he had inherited, experimenting with crops and expanding his house.

Meanwhile, tensions roiled the relationship between Great Britain and the colonies. To pay for the French and Indian War, the British government imposed taxes upon the colonies—taxes the colonists resented. As the burdens Great Britain placed on the colonies grew, so did hostilities. War broke out and the Continental Congress declared American independence from Great Britain. Washington accepted the challenging position of commander-in-chief of the Continental Army, a perilous and exhausting job. The Continental Army faced losses in battle and often had few supplies. Fatigued and discouraged, many soldiers deserted the army. Yet the determination and skills Washington had acquired in his younger years helped him lead the colonies to victory over the British in 1783.

Wasington was hailed as a national hero. He presided over the Constitutional Convention, a group of men who wrote the new nation's constitution. Elected the first U.S. president, Washington served from 1789 to 1797. After that, he returned to Mount Vernon, where he died in 1799.

HISTORICAL THINKING

DRAW CONCLUSIONS How did Washington's childhood prepare him for his role as the leader of a new nation?

_____

_____

UNIT 4

CHAPTER 8 LESSON 2.3
Washington's Farewell Address

NATIONAL GEOGRAPHIC LEARNING

DOCUMENT-BASED QUESTION

Use the questions here to help you analyze the sources and write your paragraph.

DOCUMENT ONE: from Washington's Farewell Address, 1796

1A What benefits of unity of government does Washington describe?

_____

_____

1B Constructed Response Why does Washington urge people to be proud to be called Americans?

_____

_____

DOCUMENT TWO: from Washington's Farewell Address, 1796

2A What problems did Washington think geographic differences might cause?

_____

_____

2B Constructed Response According to Washington, how might rival political parties affect a community?

_____

_____

DOCUMENT THREE: from Washington's Farewell Address, 1796

3A Why did Washington caution against "inveterate antipathies" and "passionate attachments" in regards to other countries?

_____

_____

3B Constructed Response What did Washington's speech suggest about the policy the United States should follow with other nations?

_____

_____

SYNTHESIZE & WRITE

What factors did Washington fear could disrupt the unity and peace of the United States?

Topic Sentence: _____

_____

Your Paragraph: _____

_____

_____

_____

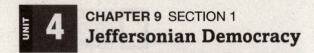

UNIT **4** CHAPTER 9 SECTION 1
Jeffersonian Democracy

READING AND NOTE-TAKING

SEQUENCE EVENTS As you read Section 1, take notes on the election of 1800.

Sequence Chart

First:

↓

Next:

↓

Last:

UNIT 4

CHAPTER 9 SECTION 1
Jeffersonian Democracy

NATIONAL GEOGRAPHIC LEARNING

READING AND NOTE-TAKING

IDENTIFY CAUSES AND EFFECTS Use the chart below to identify causes and effects that relate to John Adams and the Supreme Court as you read Section 1.

Cause-and-Effect Chart

Causes	Effects

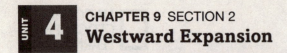

UNIT **4**   **CHAPTER 9** SECTION 2
Westward Expansion

READING AND NOTE-TAKING

SYNTHESIZE VISUAL AND TEXTUAL INFORMATION

As you read Section 2, take note of the map and photograph to synthesize
the information you read. Then answer the questions below.

1. What started happening as a result of population growth in the region between the
Appalachian Mountains and the Mississippi River?

_____

_____

_____

2. Why did Jefferson want to acquire New Orleans?

_____

_____

_____

3. Why was France a problem for Jefferson in acquiring New Orleans?

_____

_____

_____

4. Explain why the Spanish government returned Louisiana to France.

_____

_____

_____

5. Describe how France felt about Louisiana.

_____

_____

_____

6. Explain why negotiations between the United States and France over Louisiana began to stall.

_____

_____

_____

7. Describe what led up to the Louisiana Purchase and why France was willing to transfer that large amount of land to the United States.

_____

_____

_____

9. Why was Jefferson unsure of the Louisiana Purchase at first?

_____

_____

_____

10. Was Jefferson always upset about Louisiana? Explain.

_____

_____

_____

SUMMARIZE

_____

_____

_____

_____

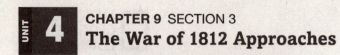

UNIT 4 CHAPTER 9 SECTION 3
The War of 1812 Approaches

NATIONAL
GEOGRAPHIC
LEARNING

READING AND NOTE-TAKING

ANNOTATE A TIMELINE   After you read Section 3.1, consider the dates listed below. Review the text and identify one event for each year listed. Write a description of the event in the box provided.

Timeline

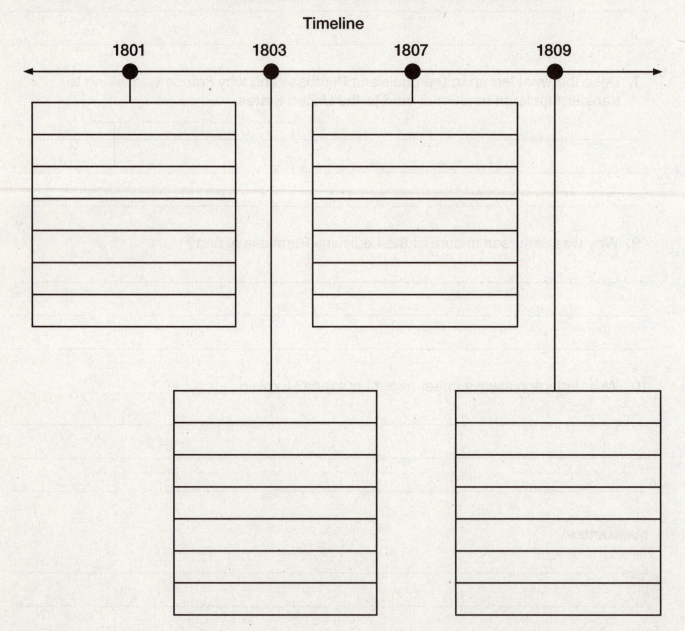

UNIT 4

CHAPTER 9 SECTION 3
The War of 1812 Approaches

NATIONAL GEOGRAPHIC LEARNING

READING AND NOTE-TAKING

IDENTIFY MAIN IDEAS AND DETAILS   Use a Main Idea Diagram to keep track of the details about America's relationship with Native American nations and the War of 1812.

Main-Idea Diagram

Main Idea:

Detail:

Detail:

Detail:

Main Idea:

Detail:

Detail:

Detail:

UNIT 4

CHAPTER 9 SECTION 1
Jeffersonian Democracy

NATIONAL GEOGRAPHIC LEARNING

VOCABULARY PRACTICE

KEY VOCABULARY

- **incumbent** *n.* the person currently in office; the incumbent president is the current president

- **judicial review** *n.* the power to invalidate any law the Supreme Court deems unconstitutional, even if it has been passed by Congress and signed into law by the president

- **Judiciary Act of 1801** *n.* the federal legislation that reduced the number of justices on the Supreme Court from 6 to 5

- **unconstitutional** *adj.* an idea or law that goes against the principles of the U.S. Constitution

- **writ** (WRIHT) *n.* a legal document

WORD SQUARE   Complete a Word Square for the Key Vocabulary words.

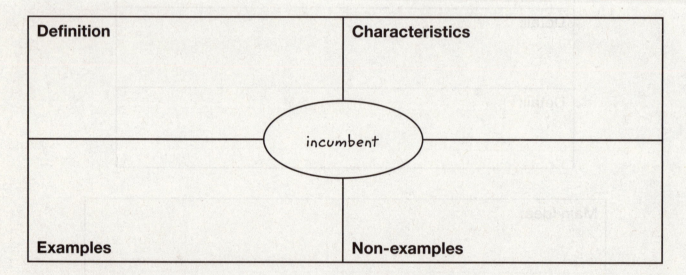

Definition | Characteristics

incumbent

Examples | Non-examples

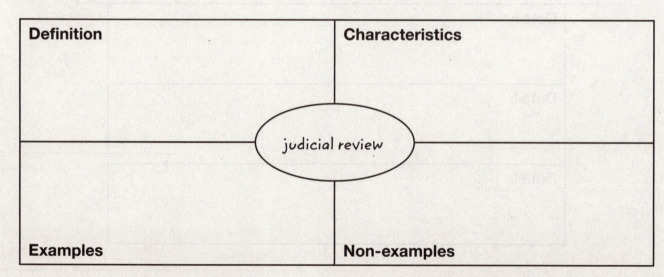

Definition | Characteristics

judicial review

Examples | Non-examples

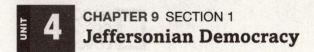

UNIT 4

CHAPTER 9 SECTION 1
Jeffersonian Democracy

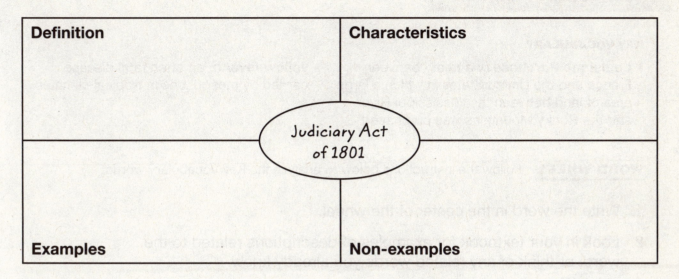

Definition	Characteristics

Judiciary Act of 1801

Examples	Non-examples

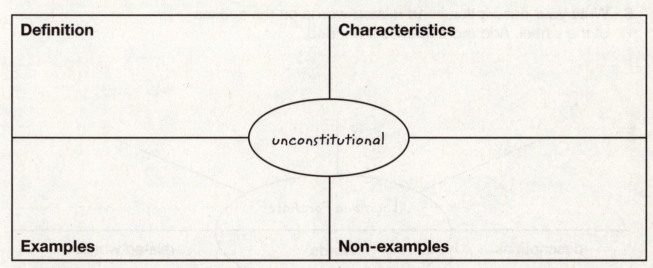

Definition	Characteristics

unconstitutional

Examples	Non-examples

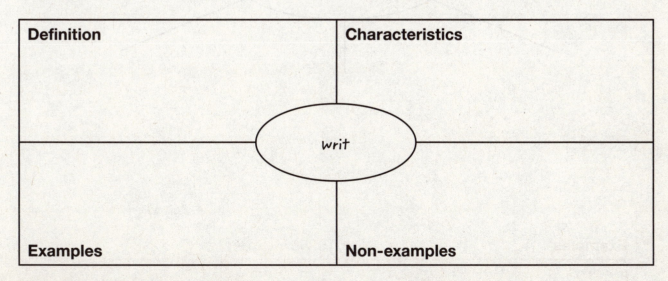

Definition	Characteristics

writ

Examples	Non-examples

UNIT 4

CHAPTER 9 SECTION 2
Westward Expansion

NATIONAL GEOGRAPHIC LEARNING

VOCABULARY PRACTICE

KEY VOCABULARY

- **Louisiana Purchase** *n.* a treaty between France and the United States in which a large area of land between the Mississippi River and the Rocky Mountains was purchased

- **yellow fever** *n.* an often fatal disease carried by mosquitoes in tropical climates

WORD WHEEL   Follow the instructions below to analyze the Key Vocabulary words.

1. Write the word in the center of the wheel.

2. Look in your textbook for examples of descriptions related to the word, or think of any related words you already know.

3. Write your descriptions and related words on the spokes of the wheel. Add more spokes if needed.

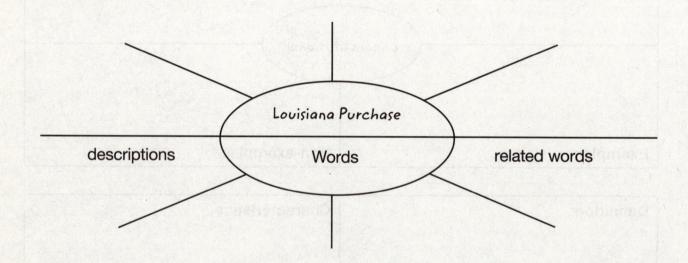

descriptions   Louisiana Purchase   Words   related words

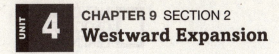

UNIT 4   **CHAPTER 9** SECTION 2
Westward Expansion

**NATIONAL
GEOGRAPHIC
LEARNING**

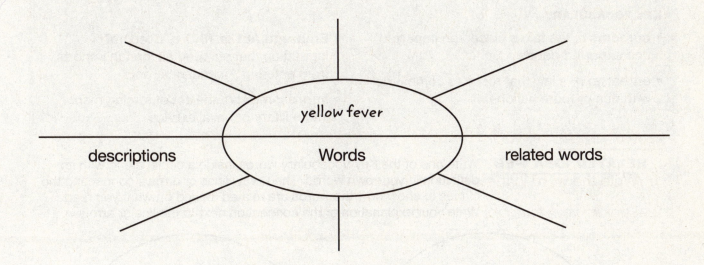

Write a paragraph summarizing what you learned about the Louisiana
Purchase in this section. Use the Key Vocabulary words.

_____

_____

_____

_____

_____

_____

_____

_____

_____

_____

UNIT 4

CHAPTER 9 SECTION 3

The War of 1812 Approaches

NATIONAL
GEOGRAPHIC
LEARNING

VOCABULARY PRACTICE

KEY VOCABULARY

- **customs** *n.* the taxes placed on imported and exported goods

- **embargo** *n.* a law that restricts commerce with one or more nations

- **Embargo Act of 1807** *n.* a federal legislation that stopped all foreign imports from entering American harbors

- **impressment** *n.* the act of forcing men into military or naval service

RELATED IDEA WEB   Write one of the Key Vocabulary words inside a circle, along with its definition in your own words. Then draw lines or arrows connecting the circles to show how the words are related, based on what you read. Write your explanation of the connection next to the line or arrow.

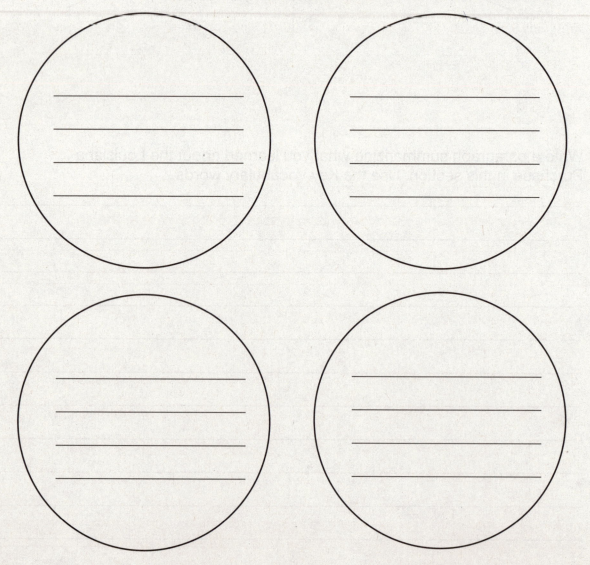

UNIT 4

The War of 1812 Approaches

NATIONAL GEOGRAPHIC LEARNING

VOCABULARY PRACTICE

KEY VOCABULARY

- **prophet** *n.* someone who is believed to deliver messages from God or some other divine source

- **War Hawks** *n.* a person who approves of and encourages war; Americans who favored war with Great Britain in 1812

- **War of 1812** *n.* the war against Great Britain that James Madison declared

WORDS IN CONTEXT   Follow the instructions below for the Key Vocabulary word indicated.

1. Explain what a *prophet* is.

_____

_____

2. Write the definition of *War Hawks* using your own words.

_____

_____

_____

3. Write the sentence in which the term *War of 1812* appears in the section.

_____

_____

4. Use the word *prophet* in a sentence of your own.

_____

_____

_____

5. Explain what happened as a result of the *War of 1812*.

_____

_____

_____

AMERICAN VOICES
Sacagawea
1790–1812

"The sight of This Indian woman, wife to one of our interprs. confirmed those people of our friendly intentions, as no woman ever accompanies a war party of Indians in this quarter." — journal of William Clark, referring to Sacagawea

Sacagawea, a Shoshone woman, helped Lewis and Clark's expedition succeed.

©MPI/Stringer/Getty Images

Sacagawea, a teenaged Shoshone, braved harsh conditions while serving as an interpreter for Meriwether Lewis and William Clark on their famed expedition across the Louisiana Purchase to the Pacific Ocean.

Sacagawea was born around 1790 in a region of what is now the state of Idaho. At about the age of 12, she was camping with her group near the headwaters of the Missouri River in Montana. Members of the Hidatsa tribe attacked the camp and kidnapped Sacagawea. They sold her to a French trapper named Toussaint Charbonneau, whom she married.

During the winter of 1804–1805, Meriwether Lewis, William Clark, and their party arrived at the Hidatsa village where Sacagawea and Charbonneau lived. These men were exploring the Louisiana Purchase, a huge territory acquired by the United States from France in 1803. This land stretched from the Mississippi River to the Rocky Mountains.

Lewis and Clark discovered that Sacagawea could speak the Shoshone language. They knew this would be a tremendous help when they met the Shoshone farther west. They asked Charbonneau and his wife to accompany them. The two agreed, even though Sacagawea was pregnant.

Sacagawea proved to be a crucial part of the team even while tending to her infant son, Jean Baptiste, who was born in February 1805. When one of the boats nearly capsized on the Missouri River,

Sacagawea quickly rescued papers, books, and medicines—things that would have been lost otherwise. She collected edible plants and made moccasins and clothing for the men. When suspicious Native Americans encountered the party, the sight of a woman and a baby suggested that the group was peaceful. Upon reaching Shoshone territory, Sacagawea was reunited with her brother, who gave them much-needed horses for the expedition. The group continued on, reaching the Pacific Ocean in November 1805.

Sacagawea, Charbonneau, and their son returned to the Hidatsa village with the expedition party in mid 1806. She died in 1812 when her daughter Lizette was an infant, but many stories suggest that Sacagawea lived until she was much older.

HISTORICAL THINKING

IDENTIFY MAIN IDEAS AND DETAILS What important roles did Sacagawea have in the Lewis and Clark expedition? Include supporting details from the biography in your answer.

_____

_____

CHAPTER 10 SECTION 1
America's First Industrial Revolution

READING AND NOTE-TAKING

SEQUENCE EVENTS As you read Section 1.1, take notes on the way the American economy and culture changed with the Industrial Revolution.

Beginning-Middle-End

```
┌─────────────────────────────────────────────────────────┐
│                                                           │
│                                                           │
│                                                           │
│                                                           │
│                                                           │
│                                                           │
└─────────────────────────────────────────────────────────┘
                            │
┌─────────────────────────────────────────────────────────┐
│                                                           │
│                                                           │
│                                                           │
│                                                           │
│                                                           │
│                                                           │
└─────────────────────────────────────────────────────────┘
                            │
┌─────────────────────────────────────────────────────────┐
│                                                           │
│                                                           │
│                                                           │
│                                                           │
│                                                           │
│                                                           │
└─────────────────────────────────────────────────────────┘
```

UNIT 4

CHAPTER 10 SECTION 1
America's First Industrial Revolution

NATIONAL GEOGRAPHIC LEARNING

READING AND NOTE-TAKING

SYNTHESIZE VISUAL AND TEXTUAL INFORMATION

Read about the textile industry in Section 1.1 and study the image to answer the questions below.

1. Describe how cloth was originally woven.

   _____

   _____

2. Explain the advantage of a single operator loom.

   _____

   _____

3. Who did mill owners hire as workers? Explain why they hired these workers.

   _____

   _____

4. Describe the *Lowell Offering*.

   _____

   _____

5. Why did the Lowell workers organize themselves in protest?

   _____

   _____

6. Use the image of a 19th-Century Textile Mill and write a paragraph describing how a mill worked.

   _____

   _____

   _____

   _____

   _____

   _____

   _____

UNIT 4

CHAPTER 10 SECTION 2
Plantations and Slavery Spread

NATIONAL
GEOGRAPHIC
LEARNING

READING AND NOTE-TAKING

IDENTIFY CAUSE AND EFFECT   As you read Section 2.2, use the chart below to record causes that relate to the expansion of slavery. Then summarize this lesson using your own words.

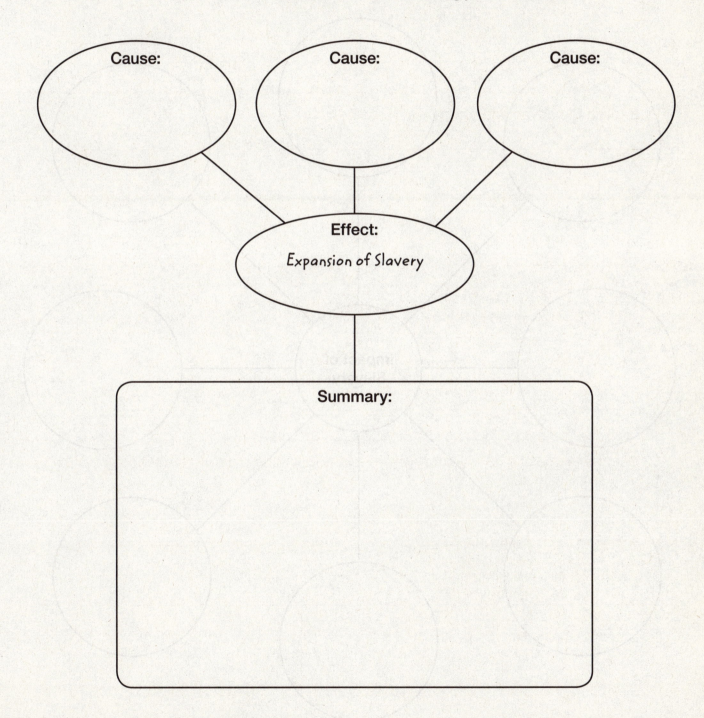

Cause:

Cause:

Cause:

Effect:

Expansion of Slavery

Summary:

UNIT 4

CHAPTER 10 SECTION 2
Plantations and Slavery Spread

NATIONAL GEOGRAPHIC LEARNING

READING AND NOTE-TAKING

IDENTIFY MAIN IDEA AND DETAILS Use a Main Idea and Details Web to organize your notes on the impact of the institution of slavery.

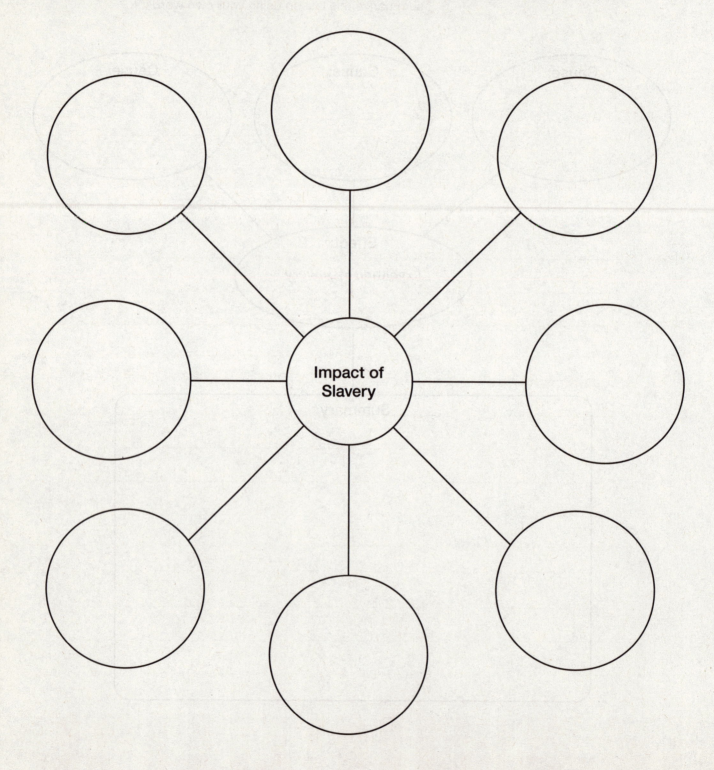

Impact of Slavery

UNIT **4**

CHAPTER 10 SECTION 3
Nationalism and Sectionalism

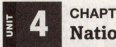
NATIONAL GEOGRAPHIC LEARNING

READING AND NOTE-TAKING

OUTLINE AND TAKE NOTES As you read Section 3, take notes using the headings and subheadings of Sections 3.1, 3.2, and 3.4 as a starting point. Then write a paragraph to summarize the content.

3.1 A Young Nation Expands

A. Transportation and Commerce

- _____
- _____
- _____
- _____

B. New Boundaries, New Decisions

- _____
- _____
- _____
- _____

3.2 Increasing Regional Tensions

A. _____

- _____
- _____
- _____
- _____

B. _____

- _____
- _____
- _____
- _____

UNIT 4

CHAPTER 10 SECTION 3

Nationalism and Sectionalism *continued*

NATIONAL GEOGRAPHIC LEARNING

3.4 Women in the Early Republic

A. _____

- _____

- _____

- _____

- _____

B. _____

- _____

- _____

- _____

- _____

SUMMARY

_____

_____

_____

_____

_____

_____

_____

_____

_____

_____

_____

_____

_____

UNIT 4

CHAPTER 10 SECTION 1
America's First Industrial Revolution

NATIONAL GEOGRAPHIC LEARNING

VOCABULARY PRACTICE

KEY VOCABULARY

- **factory system** *n.* a method of production in which large crews of people performed work in one location

- **Industrial Revolution** *n.* an era in which widespread production by machinery replaced goods made by hand

- **interchangeable parts** *n.* parts of a mechanism that can be substituted one for another

- **reaper** (REE-pur) *n.* a machine that cuts stalks of wheat or oats

WDS CHART Complete a Word-Definition-Sentence (WDS) Chart for each Key Vocabulary word.

W _____

D _____

S _____

W _____

D _____

S _____

W _____

D _____

S _____

W _____

D _____

S _____

UNIT 4

CHAPTER 10 SECTION 1
America's First Industrial Revolution

**NATIONAL
GEOGRAPHIC
LEARNING**

VOCABULARY PRACTICE

KEY VOCABULARY

- **steamboat** *n.* a boat outfitted with steam boiler engines to power the paddle wheels that propel it forward

- **strike** *n.* a work stoppage in order to force an employer to comply with demands

- **telegraph** *n.* a machine that sent messages long distances by sending electrical pulses in code over electrical wires

- **textile** (TEHK-styl) *n.* the cloth and clothing made from cotton and other raw materials

SUMMARY PARAGRAPH

Write a paragraph summarizing how the four Key Vocabulary words are related. Be sure to write a clear topic sentence as your first sentence. Then write several sentences with supporting details. Conclude your paragraph with a summarizing sentence.

_____

_____

_____

_____

_____

_____

_____

_____

_____

_____

_____

_____

_____

_____

_____

UNIT **4**

CHAPTER 10 SECTION 2
Plantations and Slavery Spread

NATIONAL GEOGRAPHIC LEARNING

VOCABULARY PRACTICE

KEY VOCABULARY

- **cotton gin** *n.* a machine that separates the cotton seeds and hulls from the cotton boll (tuft of cotton)

- **interstate slave trade** *n.* the buying and selling of slaves within the United States

VOCABULARY CLUSTER   Complete a Vocabulary Cluster for the Vocabulary words *cotton gin* and *interstate slave trade*. Write down the definition for each word. Then add information, ideas, examples and related words to help show what the word means.

Word: _____   Word: _____

Definition

Definition

Plantations and Slavery Spread

NATIONAL
GEOGRAPHIC
LEARNING

VOCABULARY PRACTICE

KEY VOCABULARY

- **antebellum** (an-tih-BEH-luhm) *adj.* before the American Civil War

- **passive resistance** *n.* a nonviolent refusal to obey authority and laws

- **spiritual** *n.* a religious song based on scripture and biblical figures in the Christian Bible, first sung by enslaved people in the South

THREE-COLUMN CHART Complete the chart for each of the three Key Vocabulary words. Write the word and its definition. Then provide a definition using your own words.

WORD	DEFINITION	IN MY OWN WORDS

UNIT 4

CHAPTER 10 SECTION 3
Nationalism and Sectionalism

VOCABULARY PRACTICE

KEY VOCABULARY

- **abolition** *n.* the act of putting an end to something, such as slavery

- **nationalism** *n.* the concept of loyalty and devotion to one's nation

- **sectionalism** *n.* a loyalty to whichever section or region of the country one was from, rather than to the nation as a whole

- **subsidy** (SUHB-suh-dee) *n.* government funds for improvements or support of commerce

- **unorganized territory** *n.* lands governed by the federal government but not belonging to any state

WORDS IN CONTEXT   Answer the questions below about the vocabulary words.

1. In what ways are *nationalism* and *sectionalism* similar and different?

_____

_____

_____

2. What is a *subsidy*?

_____

_____

_____

3. What is *abolition*? What did the women want to abolish?

_____

_____

_____

4. Find and write the sentence in Section 3 that defines *unorganized territory*.

_____

_____

_____

UNIT 4

CHAPTER 10 SECTION 3
Nationalism and Sectionalism

NATIONAL GEOGRAPHIC LEARNING

VOCABULARY PRACTICE

KEY VOCABULARY

- **American System** *n.* a policy of promoting the U.S. industrial system through the use of tariffs, federal subsidies to build roads and other public works, and a national bank to control currency

- **implied power** *n.* a power not explicitly stated in the Constitution

- **Missouri Compromise** *n.* an agreement that stated the people of Missouri could own slaves and be admitted to the Union along with Maine, a free state

- **monopoly** (muh-NAH-puh-lee) *n.* the complete and exclusive control of an industry by one company

- **Monroe Doctrine** *n.* an approach to foreign policy that stated the American continents were no longer under European influence

- **republican motherhood** *n.* the idea that women should raise their children to be good citizens who participated in the government

SUMMARIZE   Use the Key Vocabulary words to write a summary paragraph.

_____

_____

_____

_____

_____

_____

_____

_____

_____

_____

_____

_____

AMERICAN VOICES
Francis Cabot Lowell
1775–1817

Lucy Larcom
1824–1893

"From the first starting of the first power loom there was no hesitation or doubt about the success of this manufacture." — an investor in Francis Cabot Lowell's fully integrated mill

"Sometimes the confinement of the mill became very wearisome." — Lucy Larcom

Lucy Larcom (right) worked as a mill girl in a textile factory inspired by Francis Cabot Lowell. There are no known photos of Lowell.

American industrialist Francis Cabot Lowell helped launch the American Industrial Revolution with a new kind of textile mill. Writer Lucy Larcom shared her experiences working as a "mill girl" in a textile factory of that era.

Francis Cabot Lowell, born April 7, 1775, in Newburyport, Massachusetts, revolutionized American cotton fabric production. In 1810, he traveled to Scotland to study British textile industries and returned to Massachusetts with exciting new ideas. He founded the Boston Manufacturing Company and, with the inventor Paul Moody, created an efficient power loom and spinning machine. Lowell's company built the world's first integrated textile mill, which transformed raw cotton into finished fabric all in one building.

Lowell died August 10, 1817, but his legacy continued. Between 1814 and 1850, many textile mills were built throughout New England. The mills Lowell built in East Chelmsford, Massachusetts, brought the community such prosperity that the citizens renamed their town Lowell in his honor. By the mid-19th century, the New England textile industry employed 85,000 people. Many girls and young women had left farms and families to work in these mills for a chance at a better life.

One of these "mill girls" was Lucy Larcom, born March 5, 1824, in Beverly, Massachusetts. Her father died when she was eight, and the family struggled financially. They moved to Lowell, where the older daughters took jobs in the mills. Lucy quit school at 11 and joined her sisters as a millworker, where wages for female workers were typically $3.00 to $3.50 per week. An avid writer, Larcom penned poems and stories during her free time. They were published in *The Operatives' Magazine*, a magazine published by female machine operators.

After 10 years, Larcom left the mills and began teaching English literature. She continued writing and publishing poetry, and in 1889, published the book for which she is best known, *A New England Girlhood*, describing her life as a millworker. The book remains in print today. She died April 17, 1893.

HISTORICAL THINKING

MAKE INFERENCES Why might it make good sense to build a factory in which every step—from processing raw cotton to weaving finished textiles—could be performed?

_____

_____

AMERICAN VOICES

Samuel Morse
1791–1872

Mary Dixon Kies
1752–1837

"What hath God wrought." — First message sent by Samuel Morse by way of his invention, the electric telegraph, May 24, 1844

". . . a new and useful improvement in weaving straw with silk or thread." — patent description of Mary Dixon Kies's invention

Samuel Morse and Mary Dixon Kies were both inventors in their own right.

In the early 19th century, American inventor Samuel Morse created the electric telegraph and code that transformed long-distance communication. Inventor Mary Dixon Kies, the first American woman to receive a patent, came up with a better way to make fashionable hats of her day.

Samuel Morse, the inventor of the electric telegraph, was born April 27, 1791, in Charlestown, Massachusetts. He attended Yale College (now Yale University), where he enjoyed painting and became intrigued with the study of electricity. After graduating, Morse traveled to England and other parts of Europe to study art.

While sailing back home in 1832, he overheard a conversation about electromagnets. Fascinated, he spent the next few years designing a working model of an electric telegraph while also painting and teaching art. He and Alfred Vail created a system of dots and dashes that, when tapped in various patterns, represented different letters. This system became known as the Morse Code. For more than 100 years, the electric telegraph system served as the primary method for sending information by radio wave or wire. Wealthy at the end of his life, Morse donated money to colleges, churches, and mission societies. He died April 2, 1872.

Mary Dixon Kies' story follows a very different arc. Born March 21, 1752, in South Killingly, Connecticut, Kies was a weaver and a hat maker. An innovative woman, she created a new method for weaving straw with silk to make fashionable ladies' hats.

By 1790, men and women could apply for patents in the United States. But since women could not own property, most didn't try to patent their inventions. Kies pursued a patent anyway. On May 5, 1809, she secured a patent for her straw and silk weaving design, the first patent ever issued to a woman in the United States. At the time, the United States had stopped importing European goods, making Kies's invention a solid contribution to domestic manufacturing. First Lady Dolley Madison was so impressed that she sent Kies a complimentary letter. But fashions changed over time, and, unlike Samuel Morse, Kies died penniless in 1837.

HISTORICAL THINKING

EVALUATE Why is each of these inventions historically important?

_____

_____

_____

AMERICAN VOICES
James Monroe
1758–1831

"I trust that we shall not only continue, to be free and happy, but to present an example, which will be useful to other nations."

— James Monroe

1816 portrait of the fifth president of the United States, James Monroe

James Monroe, fifth president of the United States, established the Monroe Doctrine, warning European nations to stop colonizing the American continents.

James Monroe was born in Westmoreland County, Virginia, on April 28, 1758. After attending the College of William and Mary for two years, Monroe left in 1776 to fight in the American Revolution. During the Battle of Trenton, he suffered a near-fatal shoulder wound. He returned to the army after he recovered to fight in the Brandywine, Germantown, and Monmouth battles.

Following the war, Monroe studied law while working for Thomas Jefferson's law practice. He married Elizabeth Kortright. They had a son, who died in infancy, and two daughters. Monroe embarked on a career in politics, serving in the Virginia legislature, as a U.S. senator, and as governor of Virginia. He served as minister to France from 1794 to 1796 under President Washington. In 1803 under President Jefferson, he negotiated with France for the Louisiana Purchase, which doubled the size of the nation.

In 1816, Monroe was elected the fifth president of the United States. A time of relative prosperity and calm enveloped the nation after years of war. However, an issue continued to vex the government—whether new states should be admitted to the Union as slave or free states. In 1820, Monroe signed the Missouri Compromise into law. The compromise accepted Missouri as a slave state, admitted Maine as a free state, and declared that the unorganized territories north of the 36° 30' N latitude line would be admitted as free states.

One of Monroe's lasting achievements is the Monroe Doctrine. This 1823 doctrine warned European nations that attempting to colonize lands in the Western Hemisphere would be considered an act of aggression. Having served two terms as president, Monroe died in New York City on July 4, 1831.

HISTORICAL THINKING

MAIN IDEAS AND DETAILS What were James Monroe's major political accomplishments and what effects did they have on the country?

_____

_____

DRAW CONCLUSIONS Why might President Monroe have wanted other countries to stop attempting to colonize land in North America?

_____

_____

UNIT 4

CHAPTER 10 LESSON 3.3

The Monroe Doctrine

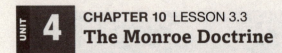
NATIONAL GEOGRAPHIC LEARNING

DOCUMENT-BASED QUESTION

Use the questions here to help you analyze the sources and write your paragraph.

DOCUMENT ONE: from War Message to Congress, by James Madison, June 1, 1812

1A How has Britain responded to American complaints of interference on the seas?

_____

_____

1B Constructed Response How does Madison's summary of British actions make a case for retaliation?

_____

_____

DOCUMENT TWO: from Seventh Annual Message to Congress, by James Monroe, December 2, 1823

2A Under what circumstances, according to Monroe, would the United States take part in a European situation?

_____

_____

2B Constructed Response How does Monroe's speech communicate a strategy for both peacetime and military action, if provoked?

_____

_____

DOCUMENT THREE: from "The Monroe Doctrine and Spanish America," by Juan Bautista Alberdi, c. 1850

3A What economic impact does Alberdi foresee?

_____

_____

3B Constructed Response How does Alberdi's opinion of the Monroe Doctrine differ from Monroe's description of his new policy?

_____

_____

SYNTHESIZE & WRITE

Support or oppose: In the early 1800s, the United States established itself as a world power through a policy of protection and European nonintervention in the Americas.

Topic Sentence: _____

_____

Your Paragraph: _____

_____

_____

UNIT 5 · CHAPTER 11 SECTION 1
Jacksonian Democracy and States' Rights

NATIONAL GEOGRAPHIC LEARNING

READING AND NOTE-TAKING

OUTLINE AND TAKE NOTES As you read Section 1, take notes using the headings and subheadings of Lessons 1.1–1.3 as a starting point. Then write a paragraph to summarize the content.

1.1 Expanding Democracy

A. The Tight Election of 1824

- The presidential election of 1824 was between John Quincy Adams and Andrew Jackson.

- _____

- _____

- _____

B. Ready for a Rematch

- _____

- _____

- _____

1.2 President of the People?

A. _____

- _____

- _____

- _____

- _____

B _____

- _____

- _____

- _____

UNIT 5

CHAPTER 11 SECTION 1
Jacksonian Democracy and States' Rights *continued*

**NATIONAL
GEOGRAPHIC
LEARNING**

1.3 *Debating States' Rights*

A. _____

- _____
- _____
- _____
- _____

B. _____

- _____
- _____
- _____

SUMMARY

_____
_____
_____
_____
_____
_____
_____
_____
_____
_____
_____
_____
_____
_____

UNIT 5 — CHAPTER 11 SECTION 2
Jackson's Policy Toward Native Americans

NATIONAL GEOGRAPHIC LEARNING

READING AND NOTE-TAKING

IDENTIFY MAIN IDEA AND DETAILS Use a Main Idea and Details Web to organize your notes on the Indian Removal Act and the Native American Resistance.

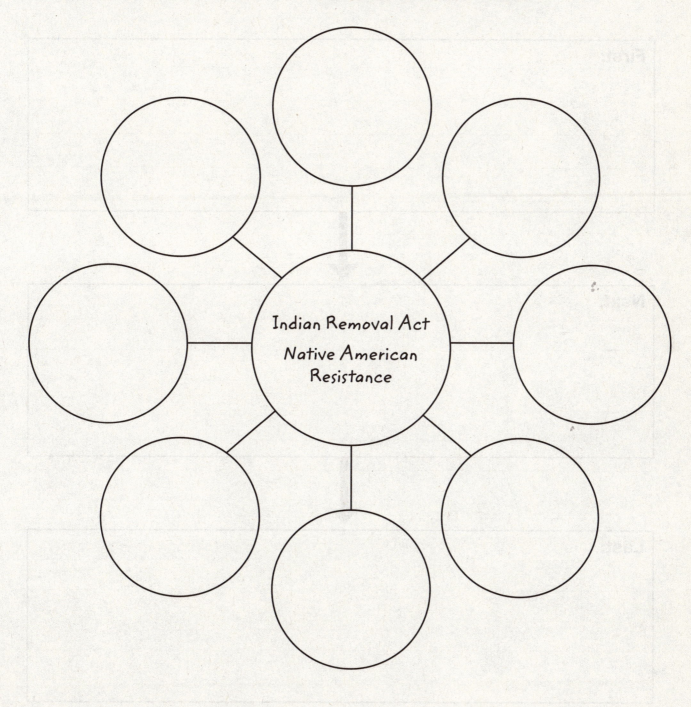

Indian Removal Act
Native American Resistance

UNIT 5

CHAPTER 11 SECTION 2
Jackson's Policy Toward Native Americans

NATIONAL GEOGRAPHIC LEARNING

READING AND NOTE-TAKING

ANALYZE CAUSE AND EFFECT   As you read Section 2, complete a flow chart to show what happened to the Cherokee in what came to be known as the Trail of Tears.

First:

Next:

Last:

UNIT 5

CHAPTER 11 SECTION 3
Prosperity and Panic

READING AND NOTE-TAKING

POSE AND ANSWER QUESTIONS   Use a Pose and Answer Questions Chart to ask any questions that arise before or while you read Section 3.1. Answer the questions after you have finished reading.

QUESTIONS	ANSWERS

UNIT 5

CHAPTER 11 SECTION 3
Prosperity and Panic

READING AND NOTE-TAKING

SEQUENCE EVENTS   In the Sequence Chain below, list the major events addressed in Section 3.2.

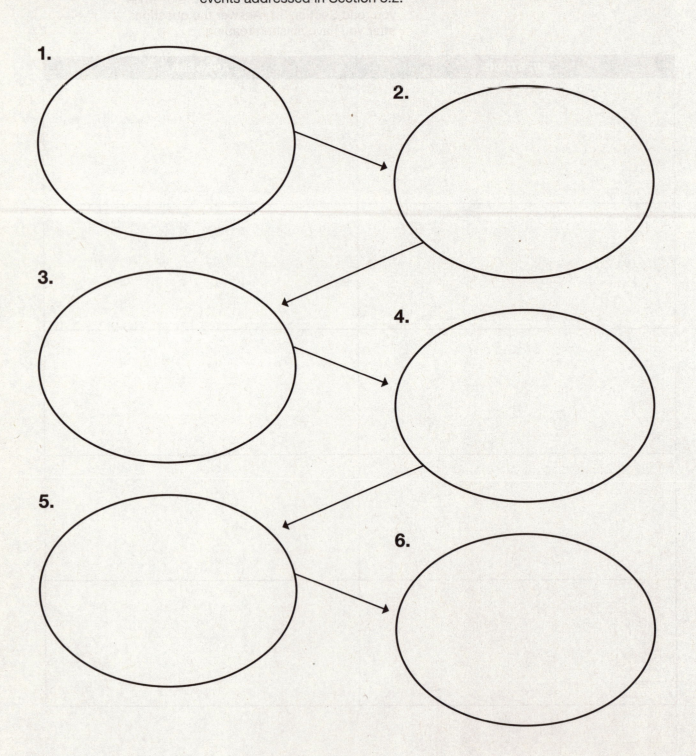

1.

2.

3.

4.

5.

6.

UNIT **5**

CHAPTER 11 SECTION 1
Jacksonian Democracy and States' Rights

NATIONAL GEOGRAPHIC LEARNING

VOCABULARY PRACTICE

KEY VOCABULARY

- **agrarian** (ah-GRAR-ee-ehn) *adj.* related to agriculture or farming

- **doctrine of nullification** *n.* a doctrine that said a state could nullify, or reject, a federal law they feel is unconstitutional, held by some southern politicians before the Civil War

- **Jacksonian democracy** *n.* a political movement that celebrated the common man and defended the will of the people, named for President Andrew Jackson

- **secession** (seh-SEHSH-ehn) *n.* the act of formally withdrawing from an organization, a nation, or any other group in order to be independent

KWL CHART   Fill in the KWL Chart for the Key Vocabulary words.

K What Do I Know	W What Do I Want to Learn?	L What Did I Learn?
agrarian		

UNIT 5

CHAPTER 11 SECTION 1

Jacksonian Democracy and States' Rights

NATIONAL GEOGRAPHIC LEARNING

VOCABULARY PRACTICE

KEY VOCABULARY

- **slogan** *n.* a catchy phrase meant to attract and keep attention

- **spoils system** *n.* the practice of rewarding political backers with government jobs

- **Tariff of Abominations** *n.* the term used by southerners to refer to the Tariff of 1828 because it stirred feelings of disgust and hatred

- **treason** (TREE-sehn) *n.* the crime of aiding the enemy of one's nation or plotting to overthrow one's nation; being disloyal to one's nation

- **voting rights** *n.* the laws that tell who can vote and when; the civil right to vote

DEFINITION CHART Complete a Definition Chart for the Key Vocabulary words. In the last column, use the word in a sentence.

Word	Definition	In My Own Words	Sentence

UNIT 5

CHAPTER 11 SECTION 2

Jackson's Policy Toward Native Americans

NATIONAL
GEOGRAPHIC
LEARNING

VOCABULARY PRACTICE

KEY VOCABULARY

- **assimilate** (ah-SIM-ih-late) *v.* to adopt the culture or way of life of the nation in which one currently lives

- **Indian Removal Act** *n.* a law that ended the U.S. government's earlier policy of respecting the rights of Native Americans to remain on their land

- **Indian Territory** *n.* the area of land in present-day Oklahoma and parts of Kansas and Nebraska to which Native Americans were forced to migrate

- **Trail of Tears** *n.* the route the Cherokees and other Native Americans took during their forced migration from the southeast United States to Oklahoma

- **truce** (TROOS) *n.* an agreement to stop fighting

I READ, I KNOW, AND SO   Complete the graphic organizers below. Write down the sentence in which the Key Vocabulary word appears in Section 1. Then write down what else you read about the word. Finally, draw a conclusion about the word based on what you have learned.

I read	
I know	And so

I read	
I know	And so

UNIT 5

CHAPTER 11 SECTION 2
Jackson's Policy Toward Native Americans *continued*

NATIONAL GEOGRAPHIC LEARNING

I read

I know   And so

I read

I know   And so

I read

I know   And so

UNIT **5** **CHAPTER 11 SECTION 3**
Prosperity and Panic

VOCABULARY PRACTICE

KEY VOCABULARY

- **depression** *n.* a period of slow economic activity when many people are without work

- **inflation** *n.* a decrease in the value of money that causes an increase in the price of goods and services

WORD WHEEL   Complete a Word Wheel for each Key Vocabulary word.

UNIT 5

CHAPTER 11 SECTION 3
Prosperity and Panic

VOCABULARY PRACTICE

KEY VOCABULARY

- **Panic of 1837** *n.* the widespread fear of a failing economy that caused the beginning of a U.S. economic recession that lasted until 1840

- **veto** (VEE-toh) *v.* to formally reject a decision or proposal made by a legislature

- **Whig Party** *n.* a political party formed to oppose the policies of Andrew Jackson, who the party believed had exceeded his power as president

SUMMARY PARAGRAPH   Write a paragraph summarizing Section 3. Use the Key Vocabulary words in your paragraph.

_____

_____

_____

_____

_____

_____

_____

_____

_____

_____

_____

_____

_____

_____

_____

_____

AMERICAN VOICES
Sequoyah
c. 1776–1843

"Your invention of the alphabet is worth more to your people than two bags full of gold in the hands of every Cherokee." — Sam Houston, of Sequoyah's writing system.

Sequoyah, a Cherokee, created a writing system in order to help the Cherokee people maintain their independence.

Sequoyah was born around 1776 in what is now Tennessee. His father was a white fur trader, and his mother was the daughter of a Cherokee chief. Sequoyah's mother raised him in a traditional Cherokee home in which she and Sequoyah spoke only their native language. He didn't learn to write, read, or speak English.

After some training, Sequoyah became a skilled silversmith, creating tools and jewelry. Through his dealings with customers, Sequoyah saw the importance of a written language. With writing, people had more independence. They could communicate on paper instead of speaking directly to one another. However, the Cherokee people had only a spoken language—they did not have a writing system.

Around the year 1809, Sequoyah began working on a Cherokee system of writing, which he called "talking leaves." Some friends were doubtful of its usefulness, while others saw it as witchcraft. These attitudes did not deter Sequoyah, and he turned his focus from silversmithing to developing the writing system. He initially tried to create a picture for each word, and then one for every idea, but both systems were too complicated.

When Sequoyah became a United States soldier during the War of 1812, he became even more resolved to develop his writing system. He saw the powerful advantages the white soldiers had in being able to read written orders and to send and receive letters.

Circa 1828 portrait of Sequoyah holding his writing system

By 1821, Sequoyah had created a written language featuring 86 symbols that represented all the syllables in the spoken Cherokee language. He taught the language to young Cherokee and used it to send written messages between Cherokee in the West and those in the East. Soon people throughout the Cherokee Nation were communicating with each other in writing and through books and newspapers published in their own language. After Sequoyah died in 1843, giant redwood trees were named "sequoia" in his honor.

HISTORICAL THINKING

ANALYZE CAUSE AND EFFECT Why did Sequoyah decide to create a written language for the Cherokee people?

_____

_____

AMERICAN VOICES
John Ross
1790–1866

"Spare our people! . . . Let not our deserted homes become the monuments of our desolation!" —John Ross

An 1843 print of Cherokee chief John Ross

Cherokee chief John Ross spent his life trying to protect native lands in Georgia and surrounding areas, but the U.S. government eventually forced him to move his people to Oklahoma.

Born October 3, 1790, in present-day Alabama, John Ross (also called Tsan-Usdi) had an unusual heritage for a future Cherokee chief. His father was a Scotsman and his mother was part Cherokee. His mother raised him in a traditional Cherokee home, teaching him tribal traditions. When he was older, she sent him to Kingston Academy, a private school in Tennessee.

In the early 1800s, white settlers pushed to acquire native lands in Georgia and surrounding regions. Ross became a leader resisting the loss of those lands. From 1819 until 1826, he was president of the Cherokee National Council, a group that spoke and wrote on behalf of the Cherokee people. He also exposed an attempt by government officials to bribe him to approve the sale of Cherokee lands.

In 1828, newly elected President Andrew Jackson resolved to claim the Cherokee lands for white settlers. By May 1830, Congress had passed the Indian Removal Act. It forced southeastern tribes to give up their lands and move to territory west of the Mississippi River. The government gave the Cherokee two years to leave voluntarily. Some did. Ross and other chiefs refused because they saw the command as unjust. Ross sent petitions to President Jackson, but Jackson was not swayed.

When the two years were up, Ross knew he would not be able to save his native lands. He reluctantly led his people westward to Indian Territory in what is now the state of Oklahoma. This journey was part of the "Trail of Tears." Thousands died along the way. When the survivors arrived in the new settlement, Ross was named chief. He remained in power until his death on August 1, 1866.

HISTORICAL THINKING

SUMMARIZE Why was the Indian Removal Act passed?

_____

_____

DRAW CONCLUSIONS Why do you think John Ross was named chief of the new Oklahoma settlement even after the "Trail of Tears" journey?

_____

_____

UNIT 5

CHAPTER 12 SECTION 1
Trails West

NATIONAL
GEOGRAPHIC
LEARNING

READING AND NOTE-TAKING

SEQUENCE EVENTS As you read Section 1, complete the Sequence Chain with details about Manifest Destiny and the trails west.

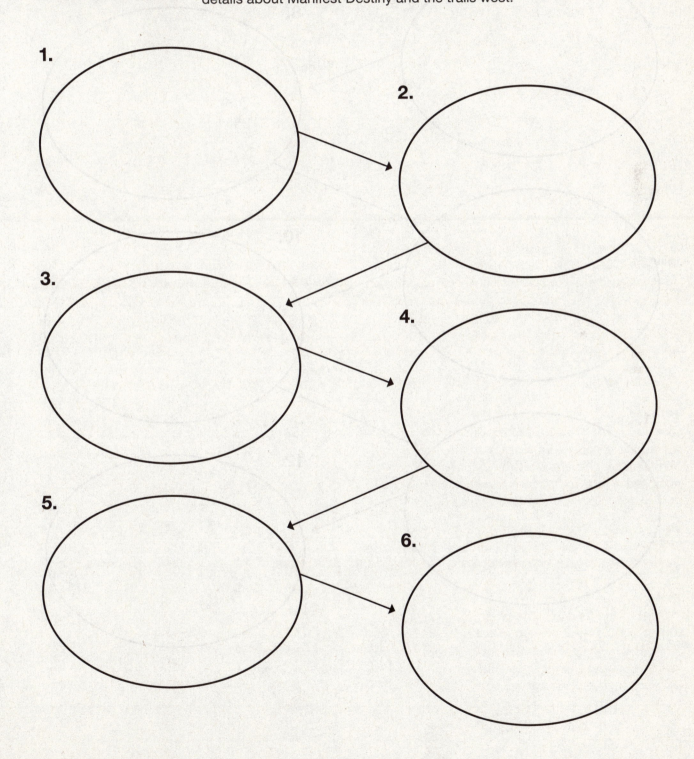

1.

2.

3.

4.

5.

6.

UNIT 5

CHAPTER 12 SECTION 1
Trails West continued

NATIONAL
GEOGRAPHIC
LEARNING

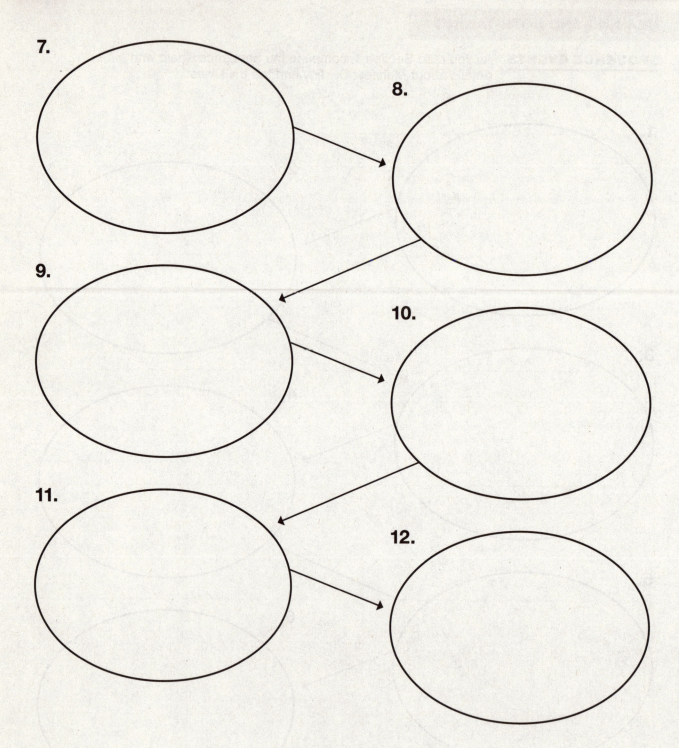

7.

8.

9.

10.

11.

12.

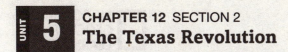

UNIT 5

CHAPTER 12 SECTION 2

The Texas Revolution

NATIONAL GEOGRAPHIC LEARNING

READING AND NOTE-TAKING

IDENTIFY CAUSES AND EFFECTS

Use the chart below to record causes and effects that relate to Texas and the fight for independence.

Causes	Effects
Tejanos, forbidden by Spain to trade with other countries, attacked Spanish settlements so they could trade with Americans.	

UNIT 5

CHAPTER 12 SECTION 2
The Texas Revolution

NATIONAL GEOGRAPHIC LEARNING

READING AND NOTE-TAKING

SUMMARIZE After you read Section 2.3, complete the boxes below with notes on the events that happened as Texas went from becoming independent to being annexed. Once you have noted each event, write a summary.

Initial Event

↓

Event 1:

Event 2:

Event 3:

↓

Summary

UNIT 5

CHAPTER 12 SECTION 3
The War With Mexico

NATIONAL GEOGRAPHIC LEARNING

READING AND NOTE-TAKING

SYNTHESIZE VISUAL AND TEXTUAL INFORMATION

As you read Section 3, take note of the maps, photographs, and other visuals that will help you to synthesize the information you read. Then answer the questions below.

1. Why was Polk interested in the annexation of Texas?

_____

_____

_____

2. How did Southerners and Northerners each feel about Polk and his plans to annex Texas? Explain.

_____

_____

_____

3. Why did the annexation of Texas worsen relations between the United States and Mexico?

_____

_____

_____

4. Explain why Polk felt he had an excuse to start a war with Mexico.

_____

_____

_____

5. How did the American people feel about the war with Mexico? Explain.

_____

_____

_____

UNIT 5

CHAPTER 12 SECTION 3

The War With Mexico *continued*

NATIONAL GEOGRAPHIC LEARNING

6. What happened when General Stephen Kearny and his troops marched into Santa Fe?

_____

_____

_____

7. How did the Bear Flag Revolt get its name?

_____

_____

_____

8. How did Taylor gain control of northern Mexico?

_____

_____

_____

9. After Mexico surrendered and the war was over, how were politicians divided about what to do with the land?

_____

_____

_____

10. Write a paragraph describing what happened to the borders of the United States as a consequence of the war. Use the map in Section 3.3 to gather information for your paragraph.

_____

_____

_____

_____

_____

_____

UNIT 5 — CHAPTER 12 SECTION 4
The California Gold Rush

NATIONAL GEOGRAPHIC LEARNING

READING AND NOTE-TAKING

MAKE GENERALIZATIONS In the boxes below, write general statements that summarize the most important events in Section 4. Then write a summary of the section.

4.1 THE SPANISH AND MEXICANS IN CALIFORNIA

The Spanish established missions in California.

4.2 THE GOLD RUSH

UNIT 5

CHAPTER 12 SECTION 4
The California Gold Rush *continued*

4.3 THE MINING FRONTIER

Write a paragraph summarizing Section 4.

_____

_____

_____

_____

_____

_____

_____

_____

_____

_____

_____

_____

_____

_____

UNIT 5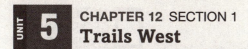

CHAPTER 12 SECTION 1
Trails West

VOCABULARY PRACTICE

KEY VOCABULARY

- **annex** (a-NEX) *v.* to add

- **Continental Divide** *n.* the high point in the Rocky Mountains that divides the watersheds of the Atlantic and Pacific oceans

- **exodus** (EHK-suh-duhs) *n.* a mass departure

- **individualism** *n.* self-reliant independence

- **manifest destiny** *n.* the idea that the United States had the right and the obligation to expand its territory across North America to the Pacific Ocean

WORDS IN CONTEXT   Follow the directions for using the Key Vocabulary words in context.

1. Write the sentence in which the word *annex* appears in the lesson.

_____

_____

2. Write the definition of *Continental Divide* using your own words.

_____

_____

3. Write the definition of *exodus*.

_____

_____

4. Describe what *individualism* means.

_____

_____

5. Write the sentence in which the word *manifest destiny* appears in the lesson.

_____

_____

UNIT 5

CHAPTER 12 SECTION 1
Trails West

VOCABULARY PRACTICE

KEY VOCABULARY

- **mountain men** *n.* the American fur trappers and explorers who began to explore and move west

- **pioneer** *n.* a settler moving to a new and unfamiliar land

- **rendezvous** (RAHN-day-voo) *n.* a temporary market where trappers met to trade and socialize

- **wagon train** *n.* a large group of covered wagons that traveled together across the North American continent as American pioneers moved westward

WDS CHART   Complete a Word-Definition-Sentence (WDS) Chart for each Key Vocabulary word.

W _____

D _____

S _____

W _____

D _____

S _____

W _____

D _____

S _____

W _____

D _____

S _____

UNIT 5
CHAPTER 12 SECTION 2
The Texas Revolution

NATIONAL GEOGRAPHIC LEARNING

VOCABULARY PRACTICE

KEY VOCABULARY
- **presidio** (preh-SIHD-eoh) *n.* a military post or settlement

WORD MAP Complete a Word Map for *presidio*.

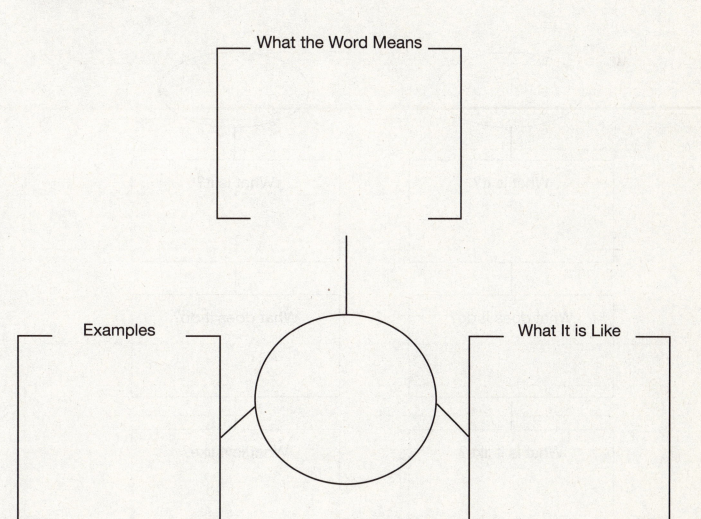

What the Word Means

Examples

What It is Like

The Texas Revolution

NATIONAL GEOGRAPHIC LEARNING

VOCABULARY PRACTICE

KEY VOCABULARY

- **siege** (SEEJ) *n.* a military tactic in which troops surround a city with soldiers in an attempt to take control of it

- **margin** *n.* the amount by which something is won or lost

WORD MAP   Complete a Word Map for each of the Key Vocabulary words.

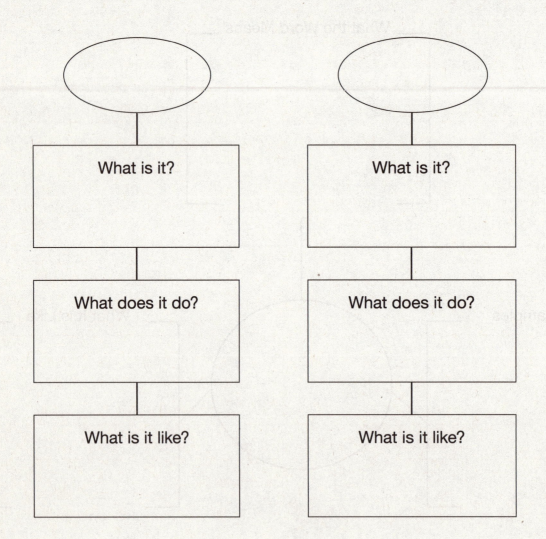

UNIT 5

CHAPTER 12 SECTION 3

The War with Mexico

NATIONAL GEOGRAPHIC LEARNING

VOCABULARY PRACTICE

KEY VOCABULARY

- **contiguous** (kuhn-TIH-gyuh-wuhs) *adj.* connected
- **diplomat** *n.* a person sent to another nation to represent his or her country's interests
- **Gadsden Purchase** *n.* a sale of land in 1853 from Mexico to the United States that established the current U.S. southwestern border

WORD SQUARE   Complete a Word Square for each Key Vocabulary word.

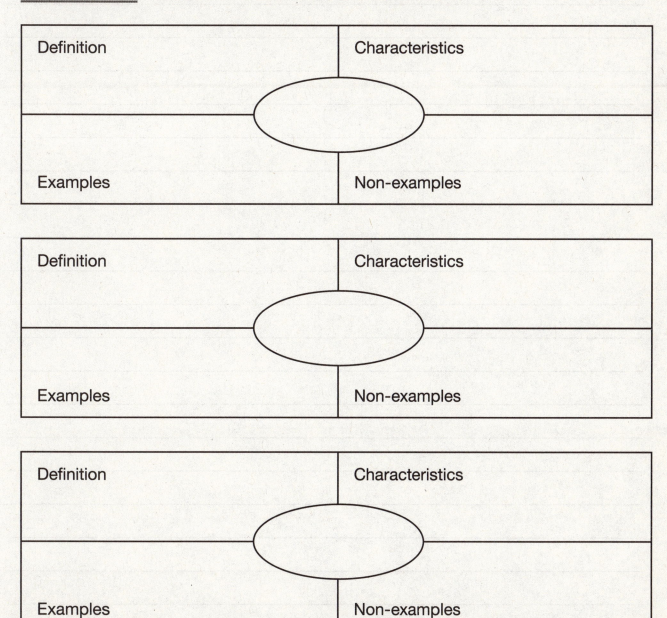

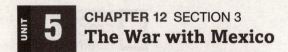

UNIT 5

CHAPTER 12 SECTION 3

The War with Mexico

NATIONAL GEOGRAPHIC LEARNING

VOCABULARY PRACTICE

KEY VOCABULARY

- **insurrection** *n.* a rebellion
- **parallel** *n.* a line of latitude
- **proviso** (pruh-VEY-zoh) *n.* a condition attached to a legal document or legislation

WRITE A SUMMARY Write a summary of the war with Mexico using the Key Vocabulary words above. Use the words in a way that defines and explains them.

_____

_____

_____

_____

_____

_____

_____

_____

_____

_____

_____

_____

_____

_____

_____

_____

_____

_____

_____

_____

UNIT 5 — CHAPTER 12 SECTION 4
The California Gold Rush

VOCABULARY PRACTICE

KEY VOCABULARY

- **boomtown** *n.* a town that experiences a great population increase in only a short time period

- **Californio** (kal-uh-fowr-nee-oh) *n.* a resident of California who was of Spanish or Mexican descent and lived there before the gold rush

VOCABULARY CLUSTER Complete a Vocabulary Cluster for the Key Vocabulary words. Add information, ideas, examples, and related words to help show what the words mean.

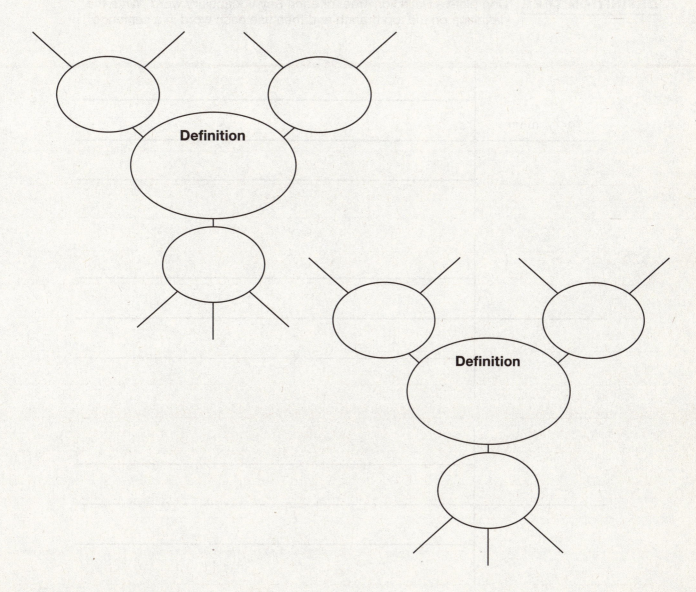

UNIT 5

CHAPTER 12 SECTION 4
The California Gold Rush

NATIONAL GEOGRAPHIC LEARNING

VOCABULARY PRACTICE

KEY VOCABULARY

- **forty-niner** *n.* one of the thousands of prospective miners who traveled to California seeking gold in 1849

- **prospector** *n.* a person who searches in the earth for valuable resources, such as gems or precious metals

- **rancho** (RAN-choh) *n.* land granted by Mexico to settlers in the form of large estates in what is now California

DEFINITION TREE   Complete a Definition Tree for each Key Vocabulary word. Write the definition on the top branch and then use each word in a sentence.

forty-niner

AMERICAN VOICES
David Crockett
1786–1836

James Bowie
c. 1796–1836

"I am determined to do my duty to my country, let the consequences be as they may."
— David Crockett

"We will rather die in these ditches than give it up to the enemy." — James Bowie

Outdoorsmen David Crockett (1816) and James Bowie (c. 1830) fought for Texas independence.

Frontiersman and politician David Crockett and military leader James Bowie joined the struggle for Texas independence from Mexico, a struggle that ended with the ill-fated battle of the Alamo.

David Crockett was born in the Tennessee wilderness in 1786. When David was twelve, his father hired him to help drive cattle to Virginia. On his return, David started school but often played hooky, preferring to be outdoors. As a young man, Crockett hunted and explored, earning a reputation as a brave frontiersman.

In 1813, Crockett joined the Tennessee militia as a scout and hunter during its battles against Native Americans. In 1821, he was elected to the Tennessee legislature and then served two terms in the U.S. Congress. Frustrated with politics, he left Congress in 1835 and traveled to Texas. At the time, Texas was part of Mexico. However, the Mexican government imposed restrictive laws on non-Mexicans, so many Texans wanted independence from Mexico. Crockett, who had grown to love Texas, sided with those who sought independence.

James Bowie was born in Kentucky around 1796. At 18, the adventurous Bowie left home to serve in the War of 1812. He later made money trading slaves and investing in land. Bowie was a bold and skilled

fighter, one who—as his family claimed—could ride both wild horses and alligators.

In his desire for more land, Bowie moved into Texas where he befriended members of the Mexican government. He became a Mexican citizen, but was sympathetic to the cause for Texas independence. He joined the Texas army and fought in several battles to free Texas from Mexican control.

In December 1835, a band of about 200 Texan volunteers, including David Crockett and James Bowie, drove Mexican soldiers from the settlement of San Antonio. The men then took over the Alamo, a local abandoned Spanish mission. When the Mexican army besieged and attacked the Alamo, nearly everyone in it was killed. Crockett and Bowie died fighting for a cause they believed in.

HISTORICAL THINKING

FORM AND SUPPORT OPINIONS How might Crockett's and Bowie's early lives as free, adventurous men have influenced their feelings about Texas independence?

_____

_____

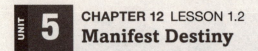

UNIT 5

CHAPTER 12 LESSON 1.2
Manifest Destiny

NATIONAL GEOGRAPHIC LEARNING

DOCUMENT-BASED QUESTION

Use the questions here to help you analyze the sources and write your paragraph.

DOCUMENT ONE: from "The Great Nation of Futurity," by John L. O'Sullivan, 1839

1A How does O'Sullivan describe the future of the United States?

_____

_____

1B Constructed Response On what authorities does O'Sullivan rest his ideas about the "onward march" of the United States?

_____

_____

DOCUMENT TWO: Wheel from a covered wagon, wood and iron, c. 1830

2A Why would Americans today preserve artifacts like this wheel?

_____

_____

2B Constructed Response What characteristics of the wheel can you see that make it suited to carrying a one-ton load more than 1,000 miles?

_____

_____

DOCUMENT THREE: from "The Letters and Journals of Narcissa Whitman," by Narcissa Whitman, 1836

3A What kind of attitude toward her situation does Whitman display?

_____

_____

3B Constructed Response How does Whitman describe the hardships of travel to the West?

_____

_____

SYNTHESIZE & WRITE

In what ways did Americans incorporate the idea of manifest destiny into their decisions about moving west?

Topic Sentence: _____

_____

Your Paragraph: _____

_____

_____

UNIT 5

CHAPTER 13 SECTION 1
The Immigrant Experience

NATIONAL GEOGRAPHIC LEARNING

READING AND NOTE-TAKING

IDENTIFY MAIN IDEA AND DETAILS   Use a Main Idea and Details Web to organize your notes on the United States' story of immigration.

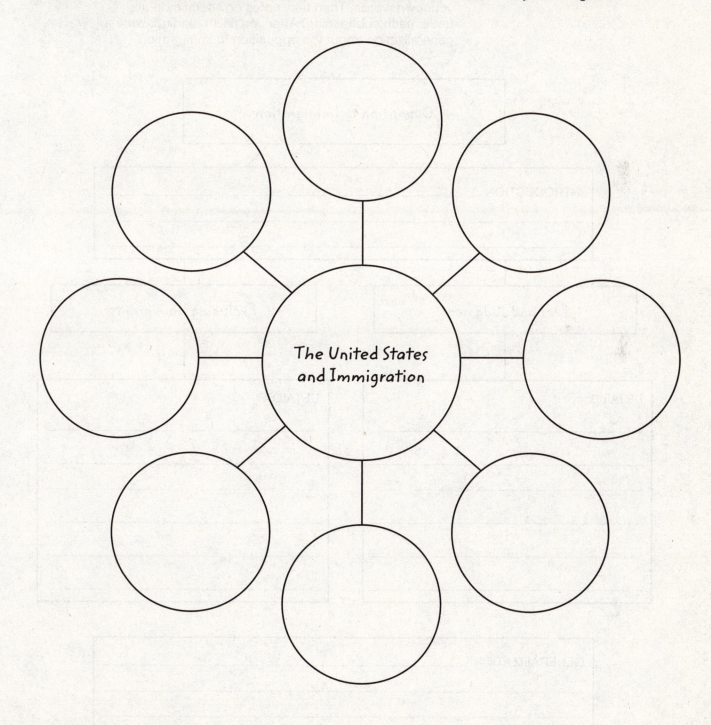

The United States and Immigration

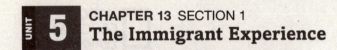

UNIT 5

CHAPTER 13 SECTION 1
The Immigrant Experience

READING AND NOTE-TAKING

MAKE GENERALIZATIONS   Complete an Idea Diagram about the information in Section 1.4. Rewrite the introduction to the section in your own words. Then take notes on specific details under each subheading. After you finish reading, write a generalization about the opposition to immigration.

Opposition to Immigration

INTRODUCTION _____
_____
_____

Fear and Judgment

Excluding Immigrants

DETAILS:
_____
_____
_____
_____
_____

DETAILS:
_____
_____
_____
_____
_____

GENERALIZATION: _____
_____
_____

UNIT 5

CHAPTER 13 SECTION 2
Reforming American Society

NATIONAL GEOGRAPHIC LEARNING

READING AND NOTE-TAKING

OUTLINE AND TAKE NOTES As you read Section 2, take notes using the headings and subheadings as a starting point.

2.1 The Second Great Awakening

A. A Return to the Church

- _____
- _____
- _____
- _____

B. Reforming Social Problems

- _____
- _____
- _____
- _____

2.2 Educating and Advocating

A. _____

- _____
- _____
- _____
- _____

B. _____

- _____
- _____
- _____
- _____

UNIT 5

CHAPTER 13 SECTION 2
Reforming American Society *continued*

2.3 Fighting for Better Pay

A. _____

- _____
- _____
- _____
- _____

B. _____

- _____
- _____
- _____
- _____

2.4 Creative Expression

A. _____

- _____
- _____
- _____
- _____

B. _____

- _____
- _____
- _____
- _____

UNIT 5

CHAPTER 13 SECTION 3
Abolition and Women's Rights

NATIONAL GEOGRAPHIC LEARNING

READING AND NOTE-TAKING

IDENTIFY ABOLITIONISTS Use a chart to take notes on details about the people who fought against slavery.

ABOLITIONIST	DETAILS

UNIT 5 — CHAPTER 13 SECTION 3
Abolition and Women's Rights

NATIONAL GEOGRAPHIC LEARNING

READING AND NOTE-TAKING

IDENTIFY ACTIVISTS Use a chart to take notes on details about the women who were activists in the women's rights movement.

ACTIVIST	DETAILS

UNIT 5

CHAPTER 13 SECTION 1
The Immigrant Experience

NATIONAL GEOGRAPHIC LEARNING

VOCABULARY PRACTICE

KEY VOCABULARY

- **assimilate** *v.* to become absorbed in a culture or country

- **blight** (BLYT) *n.* a fungus or an insect that causes plants to dry up and die

- **domestic service** *n.* housework in another person's home, performed as a job

- **emigrate** *v.* to a move away from a country in order to live in another

- **famine** (FA-muhn) *n.* an extreme lack of crops or food causing widespread hunger

- **immigrate** *v.* to permanently move to another country

THREE-COLUMN CHART   Complete the chart for each of the six Key Vocabulary words. Write each word's definition, and then provide a definition in your own words.

WORD	DEFINITION	IN MY OWN WORDS

UNIT 5

CHAPTER 13 SECTION 1
The Immigrant Experience

VOCABULARY PRACTICE

KEY VOCABULARY

- **Know-Nothing party** *n.* a political party formed in the 1850s to oppose immigration, also called the American Party

- **nativist** (NA-tiv-ihst) *n.* a person who believes native-born people should be favored more than immigrants

- **prejudice** (PREH-juh-duhs) *n.* a broad judgment about a group of people not based on reason or fact

- **push-pull factor** *n.* a reason why people immigrate, such as lack of economic opportunity or freedom in one country and the promise of a better life in another

- **steerage** (STEER-ehg) *n.* the inferior section of a ship housing passengers who pay the lowest fare for the journey

DEFINITION CHART Complete a Definition Chart for the Key Vocabulary words. In the last column, use the word in a sentence.

WORD	DEFINITION	IN MY OWN WORDS	SENTENCE

UNIT 5

CHAPTER 13 SECTION 2
Reforming American Society

VOCABULARY PRACTICE

KEY VOCABULARY

- **asylum** (uh-SY-luhm) *n.* a hospital dedicated to treating the mentally ill

- **common school movement** *n.* an educational reform movement in the 1830s that promoted free public schools funded by property taxes and managed by local governments

- **craft union** *n.* a labor union that advocates for workers' rights and protections, whose members are specialized skilled workers, or craftsmen

- **evangelize** (ih-VAN-juh-lyz) *v.* to spread one's religious beliefs through public speaking and personal witness

WDS CHART Complete a Word-Definition-Sentence (WDS) Chart for each Key Vocabulary word.

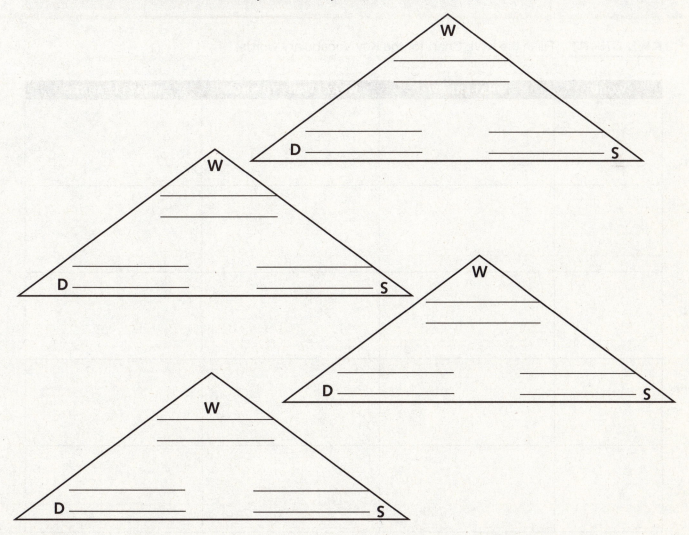

UNIT 5

CHAPTER 13 SECTION 2
Reforming American Society

NATIONAL GEOGRAPHIC LEARNING

VOCABULARY PRACTICE

KEY VOCABULARY

- **labor union** *n.* a voluntary association of workers that uses its power to negotiate better working conditions

- **revival meeting** *n.* an informal religious gathering meant to inspire people to join the faith, often held outdoors or in tents

- **Second Great Awakening** *n.* an American Protestant movement based on revival meetings and a direct and emotional relationship with God

- **temperance movement** *n.* 19th century reform movement that encouraged the reduction or elimination of alcoholic beverage consumption

- **transcendentalism** *n.* an intellectual and social movement of the 1830s and 1840s that called for rising above society's expectations

KWL CHART   Fill in the KWL Chart for the Key Vocabulary words.

WORD	WHAT I KNOW	WHAT I WANT TO KNOW	WHAT I LEARNED

UNIT 5 CHAPTER 13 SECTION 3
Abolition and Women's Rights

VOCABULARY PRACTICE

KEY VOCABULARY

- **abolitionist** *n.* a person who wants to end slavery

- **emancipation** *n.* the ending of slavery

- **Seneca Falls Convention** *n.* an 1848 women's rights convention organized by Elizabeth Cady Stanton and Lucretia Mott in Seneca Falls, New York

- **suffrage** (SUH-frihj) *n.* the right to vote

- **Underground Railroad** *n.* a network of people who worked together to help African Americans escape from slavery from the southern United States to the northern states or to Canada before the Civil War

DEFINITION AND DETAILS Complete a Definition and Details Chart for the Key Vocabulary words. For each word, write its definition and examples or other details related to the word from the section.

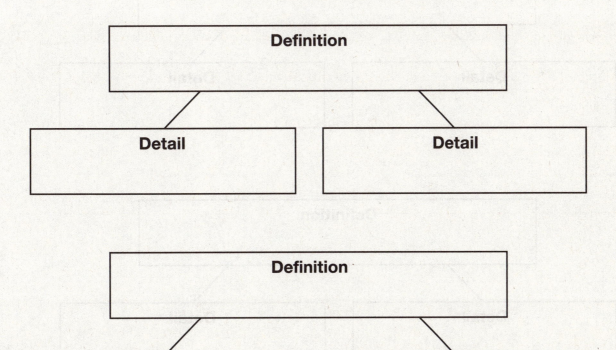

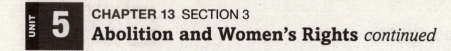

UNIT 5

CHAPTER 13 SECTION 3
Abolition and Women's Rights *continued*

NATIONAL GEOGRAPHIC LEARNING

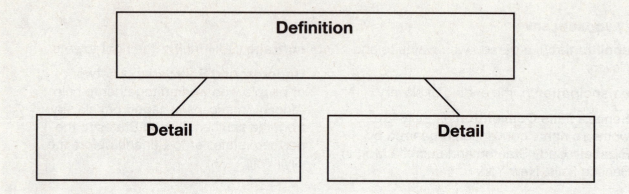

Definition

Detail	Detail

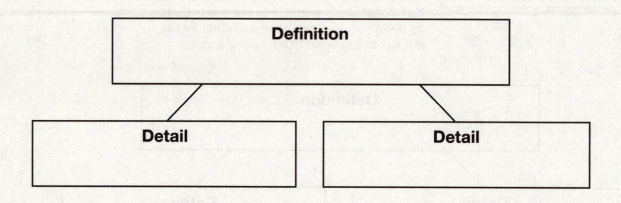

Definition

Detail	Detail

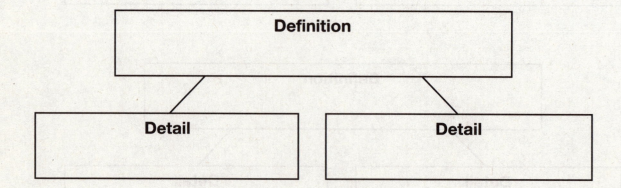

Definition

Detail	Detail

AMERICAN VOICES
The Know-Nothing Party
1849–1859

A print labeled "Uncle Sam's youngest son, Citizen Know-Nothing" (c. 1854) was a common, and most likely idealized, nativist image.

"When the Know-Nothings get control, it will read 'all men are created equal, except negroes, and foreigners, and Catholics.'"

— Abraham Lincoln, about the Know-Nothing party

The American political party known as the Know-Nothing party formed in the 1850s, arising from anti-immigrant sentiments.

In the 1840s, the United States became home to a large number of new immigrants. Many were Germans, who settled mainly in the Midwest, and Irish Catholics, who settled mainly in the East. This worried some of the native-born Protestant population, who viewed the new immigrants as threats to their political and economic security. They feared losing their jobs to immigrants who were often poor and more willing to work for lower wages. They also resented tax money being spent on schooling, police, and other services needed in cities where new immigrants settled.

In response, nativists in New York City formed a secret organization called The Order of the Star Spangled Banner in 1849. Before long, more of this organization's lodges opened in other American cities. If members were asked about its political views, they were to respond that they "knew nothing." This anti-immigration movement grew into a political party. Although named the American Party, most people called it the Know-Nothing party. Its policies included imposing a severe limit on immigration and refusing foreign-born people the right to vote or hold public office. The American Party also wanted to require people to live in the United States for 21 years before becoming citizens.

Even with their derisive nickname, the Know-Nothings had some political success. By 1855, they had managed to elect 43 members to Congress. In 1856, the American Party held its convention in

Philadelphia and nominated former U.S. president Millard Fillmore to run for office again. But the party began to crumble over its southern delegates' proslavery demands. Fillmore and many of their Congressmen lost in the 1856 election because of other conflicts in the nation. After 1859, the Know-Nothing party was all but gone.

HISTORICAL THINKING

ANALYZE CAUSE AND EFFECT Why was the Know-Nothing party created?

_____

_____

SUMMARIZE What policies did the Know-Nothing party promote?

_____

_____

AMERICAN VOICES
Sojourner Truth
1797–1883

©The Library of Congress

Sojourner Truth, photographed c. 1864

"And ain't I a woman? Look at me! Look at my arm! I have ploughed and planted, and gathered into barns, and no man could head me! And ain't I a woman?" — Sojourner Truth

Sojourner Truth, a former slave, raised a powerful voice for abolition and women's rights.

Sojourner Truth was born to enslaved parents around 1797 in Ulster County, New York. Her name at birth was Isabella Baumfree. She never learned to read or write, but could quote the Bible extensively. She was bought and sold many times and lived under abusive masters. She fell in love with an enslaved man named Robert and bore a child, but Robert's master beat him for associating with her, and he died from his injuries. She married another slave named Thomas and bore four more children.

In 1817, the state of New York declared that all slaves born before 1799 should be freed by 1827. Isabella's master had promised to set her free before then, but he went back on his promise. Isabella ran away with her baby in late 1826. Two years later, she gained custody of her son Peter, who had been illegally sold to a man in Alabama—where slavery was still legal. She became the first black woman to sue a white man in court and win.

Isabella moved to New York City and worked as a housekeeper until a powerful religious experience changed her life. She changed her name to Sojourner Truth in 1843 and became a traveling preacher, sharing her message of God's compassion. She spoke out against slavery and for women's rights—especially the right to vote. Truth became well known for her powerful presentations, including her most famous speech delivered in 1851 before the Women's Rights Convention in Ohio. The "Ain't I a Woman?" speech, quoted above, challenged the idea that men were stronger and should have more rights than women.

In 1857, Truth moved to Battle Creek, Michigan. As the Civil War broke out, Truth collected supplies for African-American volunteer regiments. Near the end of the war, she met with President Lincoln at the White House and thanked him for helping end slavery. She continued to lobby against segregation laws until her death in 1883.

HISTORICAL THINKING

FORM AND SUPPORT OPINIONS Do you think Sojourner Truth's life has had a lasting influence on American life today? Give reasons to support your opinion.

_____

_____

_____

AMERICAN VOICES

Elizabeth Cady Stanton
1815–1902

Susan B. Anthony
1820–1906

"Resolved, that it is the duty of the women of this country to secure to themselves their sacred right to the elective franchise."
— Elizabeth Cady Stanton

"I really believe I shall explode if some of you young women don't wake up." — Susan B. Anthony

Women's rights activists Elizabeth Cady Stanton (c. 1900) and Susan B. Anthony (1890) devoted their lives to the suffrage movement.

Elizabeth Cady Stanton and Susan B. Anthony agreed that full citizenship requires the right to vote. Together they fought for women's suffrage so that American women could gain more control over their lives.

Elizabeth Cady Stanton was born in Johnstown, New York, on November 12, 1815. As she studied law in her father's office, Stanton noticed how the law favored men over women regarding jobs, property, and other issues. In 1848 she and Lucretia Mott called for a convention on women's rights to take place in Seneca Falls, New York. At the convention, Stanton shared her "Declaration of Sentiments," a statement on the inferior social position that women endured. She also shared a resolution demanding women's suffrage.

Susan B. Anthony was born in Adams, Massachusetts, on February 15, 1820. Raised a Quaker, Anthony learned about fairness and independence from an early age. Living with her family near Rochester, New York, she met abolitionist Frederick Douglass and women's suffrage leader Elizabeth Cady Stanton. These leaders inspired Anthony to raise her voice against slavery and for women's right to vote.

In January 1869, Anthony organized the first Woman Suffrage Convention, held in Washington, D.C. In May of that year, Stanton and Anthony formed the National Woman Suffrage Association.

Anthony and Stanton worked together for 50 years. They spoke before legislative bodies, circulated petitions, and organized campaigns. Anthony focused on women's suffrage, while Stanton addressed the unfairness of rights granted to men but not to women. Stanton wrote powerful speeches that were persuasively delivered by Anthony. In 1872, Anthony dared to vote and was arrested.

Stanton died in 1902 and Anthony in 1906. Their work set in motion the movement that resulted in the passage of the 19th Amendment, ratified in 1920, which granted women the right to vote.

HISTORICAL THINKING

SUMMARIZE How did Elizabeth Cady Stanton and Susan B. Anthony work together toward women's suffrage?

_____

_____

UNIT 5

CHAPTER 13 LESSON 3.2
Voices Against Slavery

NATIONAL GEOGRAPHIC LEARNING

DOCUMENT-BASED QUESTION

Use the questions here to help you analyze the sources and write your paragraph.

DOCUMENT ONE: from "Address to the Slaves of the United States," by William Lloyd Garrison, 1843

1A What arguments does Garrison use to persuade enslaved people to take action?

_____

_____

1B Constructed Response How does Garrison describe enslaved people, and what specific actions does he encourage them to take?

_____

DOCUMENT TWO: from "On the Injustice of Slavery" by Sojourner Truth, 1856

2A What does Truth mean when she says, "I have had two husbands, but I never possessed one of my own."?

_____

2B Constructed Response How does Truth's account reflect the lack of basic freedom enslaved people endured?

_____

DOCUMENT THREE: from "What the Black Man Wants," by Frederick Douglass, 1865

3A What does Douglass identify as his only goal?

_____

_____

3B Constructed Response Why does Douglass reject the pity and sympathy of other abolitionists?

_____

SYNTHESIZE & WRITE

In what ways did abolitionists appeal to their fellow citizens' morality in order to gather support to abolish slavery?

Topic Sentence: _____

_____

Your Paragraph: _____

_____

_____

UNIT 6

CHAPTER 14 SECTION 1
Growing Tensions Between North and South

READING AND NOTE-TAKING

SEQUENCE EVENTS   In the Sequence Chain below, list the major events addressed in Section 1.

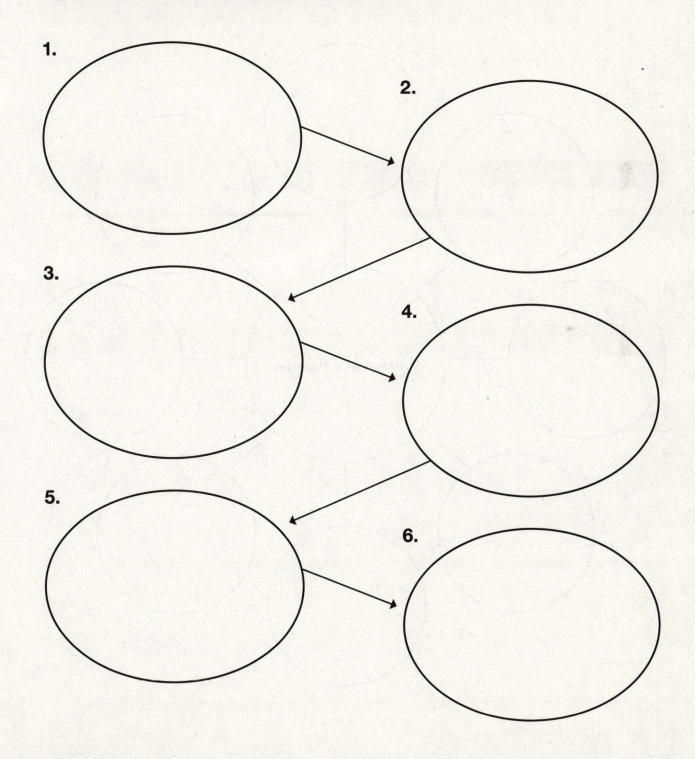

1.

2.

3.

4.

5.

6.

© National Geographic Learning, a part of Cengage Learning

READING AND NOTE-TAKING

IDENTIFY MAIN IDEA AND DETAILS Use a Main Idea and Details Web to organize your notes on slavery and racism.

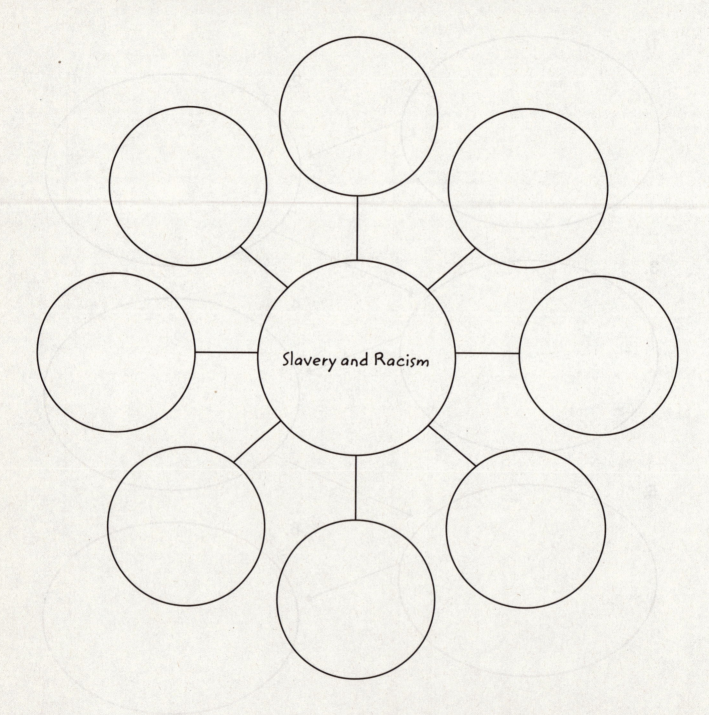

CHAPTER 14 SECTION 2
Slavery Dominates Politics

NATIONAL GEOGRAPHIC LEARNING

READING AND NOTE-TAKING

IDENTIFY CAUSES AND EFFECTS
Use the chart below to record causes and effects that relate to the Kansas-Nebraska Act.

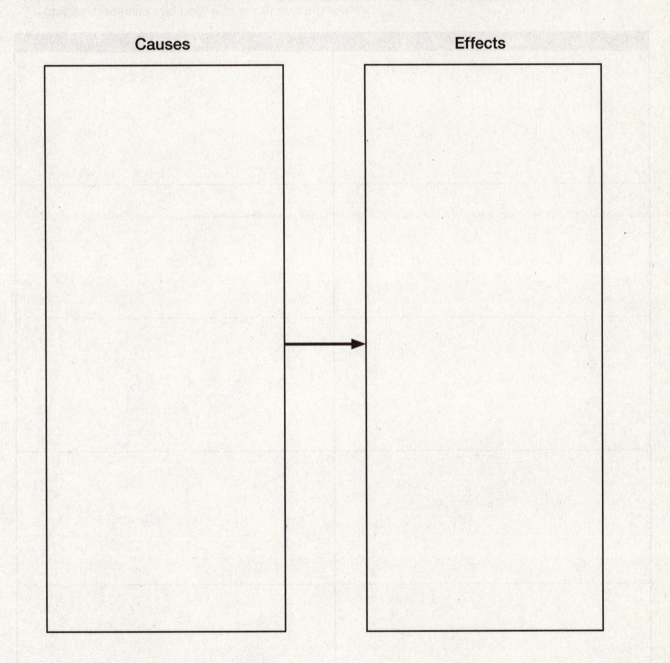

Causes   Effects

UNIT 6   CHAPTER 14 SECTION 2
Slavery Dominates Politics

NATIONAL GEOGRAPHIC LEARNING

READING AND NOTE-TAKING

POSE AND ANSWER QUESTIONS   Use a Pose and Answer Questions Chart to ask any questions that arise before or while you read Section 2. Answer the questions after you have finished reading.

QUESTIONS	ANSWERS

6
UNIT

CHAPTER 14 SECTION 3
Lincoln's Election and Southern Secession

READING AND NOTE-TAKING

OUTLINE AND TAKE NOTES As you read Section 3, take notes using the headings and subheadings. Then write a paragraph to summarize the content.

3.1 The Election of 1860

A. Political Parties Break Apart

- _____
- _____
- _____
- _____

B. The Nomination of Lincoln

- _____
- _____
- _____
- _____

3.2 Southern States Secede

A. _____

- _____
- _____
- _____
- _____

B. _____

- _____
- _____
- _____
- _____

UNIT 6

CHAPTER 14 SECTION 3
Lincoln's Election and Southern Secession *continued*

NATIONAL
GEOGRAPHIC
LEARNING

3.3 *Efforts at Compromise*

A. _____

- _____
- _____
- _____
- _____

B. _____

- _____
- _____
- _____
- _____

Summary

_____
_____
_____
_____
_____
_____
_____
_____
_____
_____
_____
_____
_____
_____
_____

UNIT 6 CHAPTER 14 SECTION 1
Growing Tensions Between North and South

NATIONAL
GEOGRAPHIC
LEARNING

VOCABULARY PRACTICE

KEY VOCABULARY

- **federal marshall** *n.* a law enforcement officer who works for the United States government

WORD WHEEL   Follow the instructions below to analyze the Key Vocabulary word *federal marshall.*

1. Write the word in the center of the wheel.

2. Look in this section for descriptions related to the word, or think of any related words you already know.

3. Write your descriptions and related words on the spokes of the wheel. Add more spokes if needed.

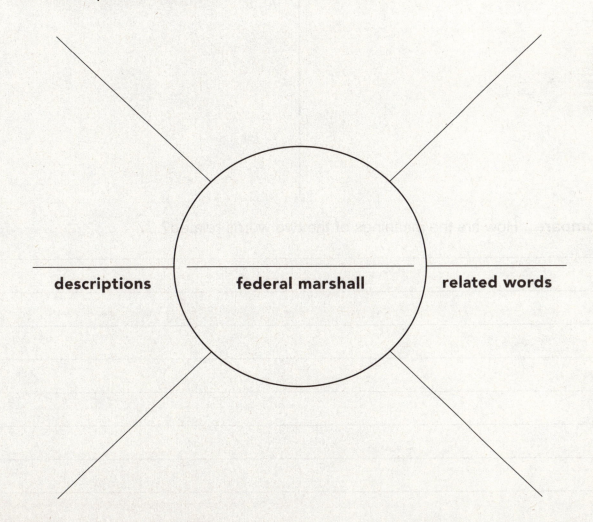

descriptions   federal marshall   related words

UNIT 6

CHAPTER 14 SECTION 1
Growing Tensions Between North and South

NATIONAL GEOGRAPHIC LEARNING

VOCABULARY PRACTICE

KEY VOCABULARY

- **racism** *n.* the belief that one race is better than others

- **segregation** (seh-grih-GAY-shuhn) *n.* separation of people based on race

VOCABULARY T CHART   Use the T Chart to compare the meanings of the Key Vocabulary words *racism* and *segregation*. Write the definition of each word and fill in details about each word from what you know and what you have read. Then answer the question.

Compare   How are the meanings of the two words related?

_____

_____

_____

_____

_____

_____

_____

UNIT 6

CHAPTER 14 SECTION 2
Slavery Dominates Politics

VOCABULARY PRACTICE

KEY VOCABULARY

- **Dred Scott decision** *n.* a Supreme Court decision that African Americans held no rights as citizens and that the Missouri Compromise of 1820 was unconstitutional; Dred Scott, the escaped slave at the center of the case, was returned to slavery

DESCRIPTIVE PARAGRAPH   Write a paragraph describing the Dred Scott decision. Write a clear topic sentence as your first sentence. Then write sentences with supporting details. Conclude your paragraph with a summarizing sentence.

_____

_____

_____

_____

_____

_____

_____

_____

_____

_____

_____

_____

_____

_____

_____

UNIT 6

CHAPTER 14 SECTION 2
Slavery Dominates Politics

NATIONAL
GEOGRAPHIC
LEARNING

VOCABULARY PRACTICE

KEY VOCABULARY

• **popular sovereignty** *n.* the idea that the residents of a region or nation decide an issue by voting

• **Republican Party** *n.* a political party founded in 1854 by antislavery leaders

DEFINITION CHART Complete a Definition Chart for the Key Vocabulary words.

WORD	POPULAR SOVEREIGNTY
Definition	
In My Own Words	
Symbol or Diagram	

WORD	REPUBLICAN PARTY
Definition	
In My Own Words	
Symbol or Diagram	

UNIT 6

CHAPTER 14 SECTION 3
Lincoln's Election and Southern Secession

NATIONAL
GEOGRAPHIC
LEARNING

VOCABULARY PRACTICE

KEY VOCABULARY

- **Confederacy** *n.* the 11 southern states that seceded from the Union to form their own nation, the Confederate States of America

- **Crittenden Plan** *n.* a proposal that stated the federal government would have no power to abolish slavery in the states where it already existed; it reestablished and extended the Missouri Compromise line to the Pacific Ocean

I READ, I KNOW, AND SO Use the graphic organizers below to explore your understanding of *Confederacy* and *Crittenden Plan*.

I Read		
I Know	**Confederacy**	And So

I Read		
I Know	**Crittenden Plan**	And So

UNIT 6

CHAPTER 14 SECTION 3
Lincoln's Election and Southern Secession

NATIONAL
GEOGRAPHIC
LEARNING

VOCABULARY PRACTICE

KEY VOCABULARY

- **garrison** *n.* a defense force of soldiers

- **secede** (seh-SEED) *v.* to formally withdraw from a nation or organization in order to become independent

- **Unionist** *n.* a member of the Constitutional Union Party

DEFINITION TREE For each Key Vocabulary word in the Definition Tree below, write the definition on the top branch and then use each word in a sentence.

garrison

_____

_____

_____

secede

_____

_____

_____

Unionist

_____

_____

_____

AMERICAN VOICES
Abraham Lincoln
1809–1865

". . . that we here highly resolve that these dead shall not have died in vain . . . and that government of the people, by the people, for the people shall not perish from the earth."
— Abraham Lincoln, the Gettysburg Address

Abraham Lincoln, the 16th U.S. President, led the nation during the devastating Civil War. He set into motion actions that would end slavery in the United States.

Abraham Lincoln was born February 12, 1809, in a one-room log cabin in Kentucky. He lived there with his older sister, Sarah, and his parents, who were both uneducated. Lincoln's younger brother, Thomas, died in infancy. Though rarely able to attend school, Lincoln loved books and became an avid reader.

Lincoln spent his first seven years on farms in Kentucky, and then his father moved the family to a forested region of Indiana. Young still, but strong and tall in stature, Lincoln was given an axe, which he used to chop down trees. He continued clearing trees, plowing, and harvesting the land.

In 1818, Lincoln's mother died, leaving Sarah in charge of her younger brother and the housework. One year later, their father remarried a loving woman with three children of her own. In 1826, Sarah died in childbirth.

Lincoln and his father built log cabins when the family moved to Illinois in 1830. Lincoln also worked in a store where he impressed people with his wit and intelligence. He became a lawyer and served in the Illinois legislature for eight years. In 1842, he married Mary Todd.

In 1858, Lincoln ran for the U.S. Senate. He lost the race, and others as well, but gained national recognition. Then, in 1860, Abraham Lincoln was elected the 16th president of the United States. Disagreements raged between the North and the

Portrait of Abraham Lincoln, painted in 1916, 51 years after his death

South, and soon the nation was at war.

Four years later, the bloody Civil War ended. During that time, Lincoln issued the Emancipation Proclamation, making slaves forever free. He also gave his famous speech, the *Gettysburg Address*. Lincoln was reelected for a second term, but was shot and killed by John Wilkes Booth on April 14, 1865.

Lincoln's coffin traveled by train from Washington, D.C., to Springfield, Illinois. Watching it pass through New York City, an African-American woman exclaimed, "He died for me! God bless him!"

HISTORICAL THINKING

ANALYZE CAUSE AND EFFECT How did an uneducated child like Abraham Lincoln become such a well-respected president?

_____

_____

U.S. HISTORY

©Bridgeman Images

AMERICAN VOICES
Jefferson Davis
1808–1889

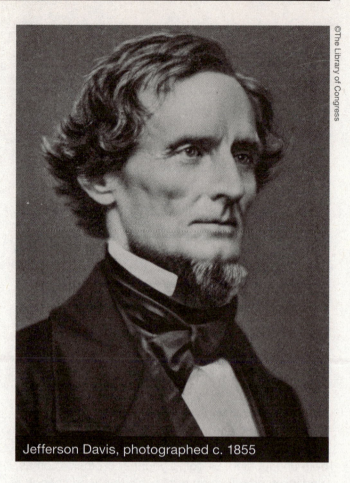

Jefferson Davis, photographed c. 1855

©The Library of Congress

"I have for many years advocated, as an essential attribute of State sovereignty, the right of a State to secede from the Union."
— Jefferson Davis

At first, Jefferson Davis promoted peace between the North and the South, but as the president of the Confederate States of America, he answered the call to war—the American Civil War.

Born June 3, 1808, in Kentucky, Jefferson Davis moved with his family to a plantation near Woodville, Mississippi, when he was three years old. He spent much of his childhood in boarding schools. At age 16, he enrolled in the United States Military Academy at West Point and graduated in 1828. He served in the U.S. Army until 1835, when he married Sarah Knox. Sarah died from malaria three months after their wedding, causing Davis to withdraw and spend much of his time alone, working and reading.

In 1845, Davis was elected to the U.S. House of Representatives. He married his second wife, Varina Howell, with whom he had six children. Davis resigned his position in Congress one year later to fight in the Mexican-American War. He was gravely wounded, but survived. After the war, Davis was elected to the Senate and served as Secretary of War under President Franklin Pierce.

Meanwhile, tensions between the North and the South escalated. In December 1860, South Carolina seceded from the Union. Mississippi soon followed. Davis reluctantly left the Senate and returned to Mississippi, where he was inaugurated provisional president of the Confederate States of America on February 18, 1861. Davis sent an unsuccessful peace commission to Washington, D.C., hoping to prevent armed conflict between the North and the South.

However, when Lincoln sent armed ships to resupply Union troops at Fort Sumter, South Carolina, Davis felt he had no choice. He ordered Confederate troops to fire on the fort, thus beginning the Civil War.

Davis struggled with many issues during his presidency, including an uncooperative Congress, a lack of resources, and an unpopular law that ordered military service. On May 10, 1865, a month after Lee's surrender to Grant, Union forces captured and imprisoned Davis. He was charged with treason, but the charges were eventually dropped. Davis died in New Orleans on December 6, 1889.

HISTORICAL THINKING

IDENTIFY How did Jefferson Davis try to prevent fighting between the North and the South?

_____

_____

UNIT 6 **CHAPTER 14 LESSON 2.3**
Lincoln And Douglas

NATIONAL GEOGRAPHIC LEARNING

DOCUMENT-BASED QUESTION

Use the questions here to help you analyze the sources and write your paragraph.

DOCUMENT ONE: from Abraham Lincoln's speech at the Republican Convention in Springfield, Illinois, on June 16, 1858

1A In your own words, explain the two factions that have formed in the country.

_____

_____

1B Constructed Response What does Lincoln think will happen to the Union if the division continues?

_____

_____

DOCUMENT TWO: from Stephen Douglas's speech at the Lincoln-Douglas debate in Freeport, Illinois, on August 27, 1858

2A What does Douglas say is essential for slavery to exist anywhere?

_____

_____

2B Constructed Response Describe how Douglas uses cause and effect to explain how people can keep slavery out of a territory.

_____

_____

DOCUMENT THREE: Political Cartoon from *Harper's Weekly*, 1860

3A How effective do you find this cartoon for expressing the state of the country at the time?

_____

_____

3B Constructed Response What details in the cartoon suggest that slavery is tearing the United States apart?

_____

_____

SYNTHESIZE & WRITE

What differing positions did Lincoln and Douglas take on the issue of slavery?

Topic Sentence: _____

_____

Your Paragraph: _____

_____

_____

NATIONAL GEOGRAPHIC LEARNING

READING AND NOTE-TAKING

SYNTHESIZE VISUAL AND TEXTUAL INFORMATION

After you read Section 1.1, use the visual and textual information as well as the map to answer the questions below.

1. Which states seceded after the fall of Fort Sumter? Which was the first to secede?

_____

_____

_____

2. Describe what the border states were.

_____

_____

_____

3. What color are the border states on the map? How do you know?

_____

_____

_____

4. What did Lincoln do to keep Maryland in the Union?

_____

_____

_____

5. What was the last state to secede?

_____

_____

_____

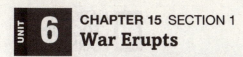

UNIT 6 CHAPTER 15 SECTION 1
War Erupts

NATIONAL GEOGRAPHIC LEARNING

READING AND NOTE-TAKING

COMPARE AND CONTRAST Use a Venn Diagram to compare and contrast the Union and the Confederacy as the Civil War began.

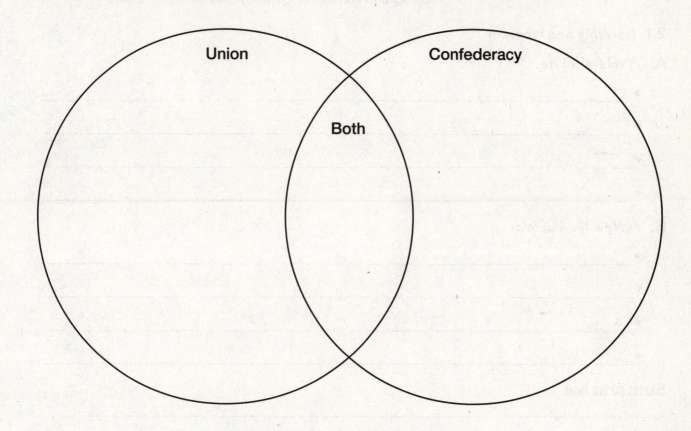

Union

Both

Confederacy

Summarize your notes on the Union and the Confederacy.

_____

_____

_____

_____

_____

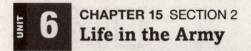

UNIT 6

CHAPTER 15 SECTION 2
Life in the Army

READING AND NOTE-TAKING

OUTLINE AND TAKE NOTES   As you read Section 2, take notes using the headings and subheadings as a starting point. Then write a paragraph summarizing the content of each lesson.

2.1 Hardship and Weapons

A. A soldier's Life

- _____
- _____
- _____
- _____

B. A New Kind of War

- _____
- _____
- _____
- _____

Summarize

_____
_____
_____
_____
_____
_____
_____
_____
_____

UNIT 6 **CHAPTER 15** SECTION 2
Life in the Army *continued*

2.2 Women and the War

A. Women on the Battlefield

- _____
- _____
- _____
- _____

B. Women at Home

- _____
- _____
- _____
- _____

Summarize

_____
_____
_____
_____
_____
_____
_____
_____
_____
_____
_____
_____

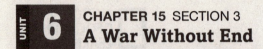

UNIT 6

CHAPTER 15 SECTION 3
A War Without End

READING AND NOTE-TAKING

SEQUENCE EVENTS   As you read Section 3, take note of major events as the war continued.

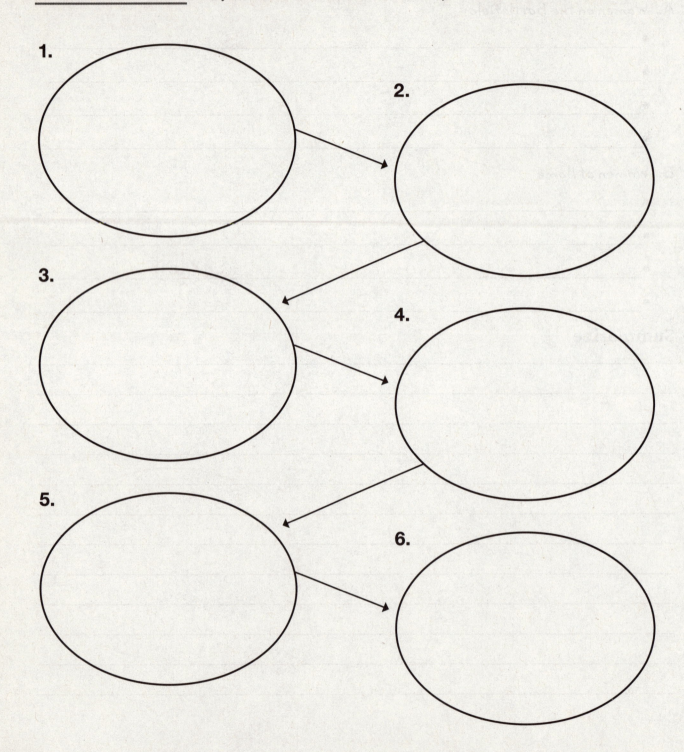

1.

2.

3.

4.

5.

6.

UNIT **6**

CHAPTER 15 SECTION 3
A War Without End continued

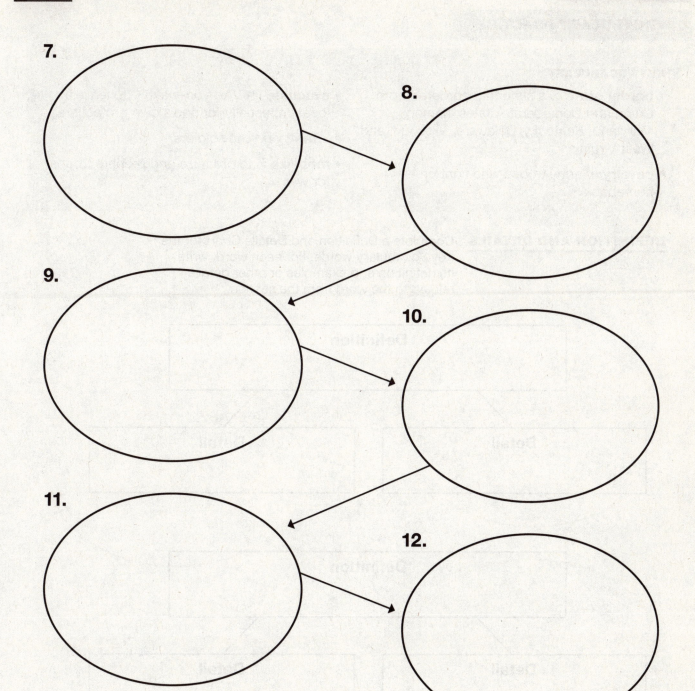

7.

8.

9.

10.

11.

12.

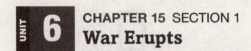

UNIT 6

CHAPTER 15 SECTION 1
War Erupts

NATIONAL GEOGRAPHIC LEARNING

VOCABULARY PRACTICE

KEY VOCABULARY

- **border state** *n.* a state that bordered both Union and Confederate states, namely Maryland, Kentucky, Delaware, Missouri, and West Virginia

- **cavalry** *n.* army troops who fight on horseback

- **evacuate** (ih-VA-kyoo-wayt) *v.* to leave a location, usually for one's own protection

- **infantry** *n.* foot soldiers

- **mobilize** *v.* to organize and prepare troops for war

DEFINITION AND DETAILS

Complete a Definition and Details Chart for the Key Vocabulary words. For each word, write its definition and examples or other details related to the word from the section.

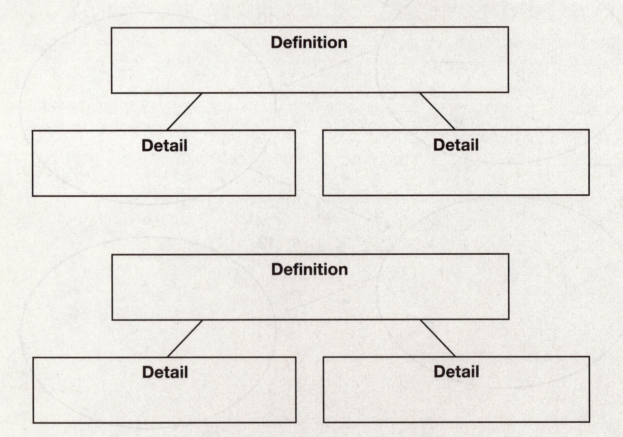

Definition

Detail   Detail

Definition

Detail   Detail

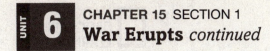

UNIT 6 **CHAPTER 15** SECTION 1
War Erupts *continued*

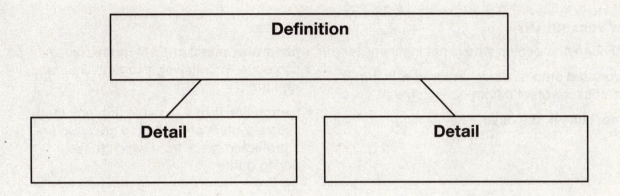

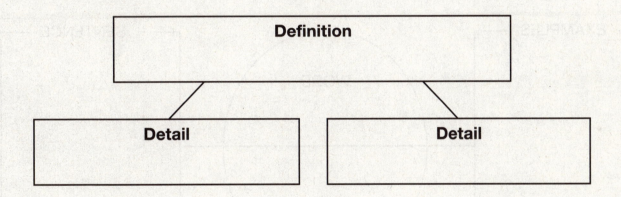

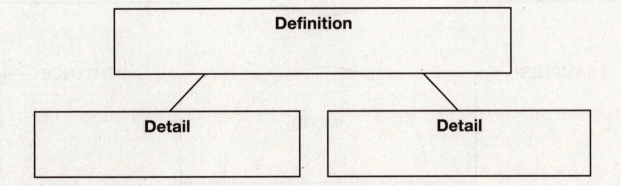

UNIT 6

CHAPTER 15 SECTION 2
Life in the Army

VOCABULARY PRACTICE

KEY VOCABULARY

- **civilian** *n.* a person who is not in the military

- **ironclad ship** *n.* a ship armored with iron plates to protect it from cannon fire

- **mortality** *n.* the death rate

- **philanthropist** (fuh-LAN-thruh-pihst) *n.* someone who actively promotes human welfare

- **trench warfare** *n.* a battle strategy that uses a system of ditches to give soldiers a protected place from which to fire during battle

DEFINITION MAP   Complete a Definition Map for each Key Vocabulary word.

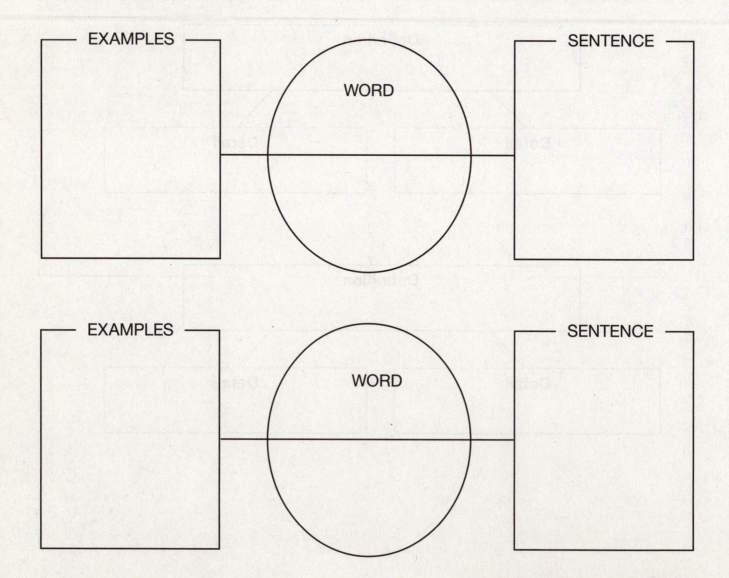

CHAPTER 15 SECTION 2
Life in the Army *continued*

WORD

WORD

SENTENCE

EXAMPLES

WORD

SENTENCE

EXAMPLES

WORD

SENTENCE

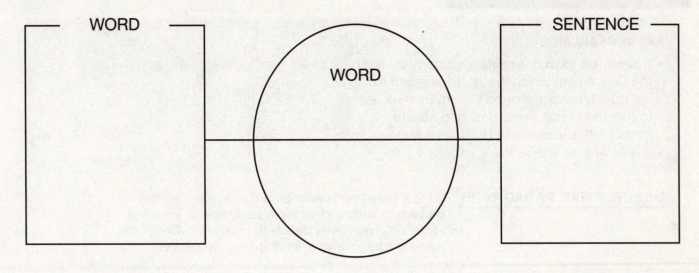
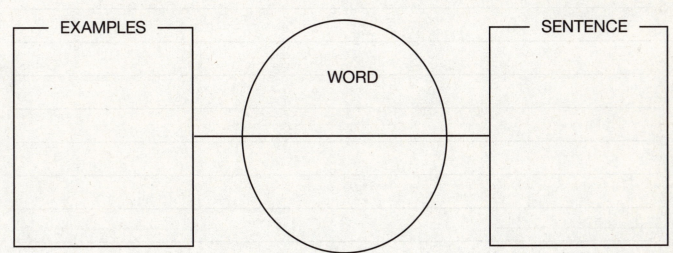
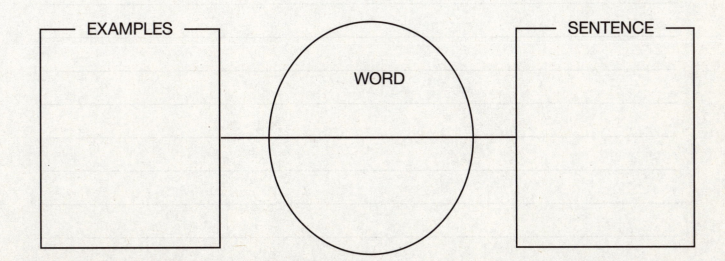

UNIT 6 — CHAPTER 15 SECTION 3
A War Without End

NATIONAL
GEOGRAPHIC
LEARNING

VOCABULARY PRACTICE

KEY VOCABULARY

- **Anaconda Plan** *n.* a military strategy during the Civil War in which the North planned to set up a blockade around the southern coast to ruin the South's economy and secure ports on the Mississippi River, as a huge snake, like an anaconda, crushes its prey

DESCRIPTIVE PARAGRAPH

Write a paragraph describing the Anaconda Plan. Be sure to write a clear topic sentence as your first sentence. Then write details to support it. Conclude your paragraph with a summarizing sentence.

_____

_____

_____

_____

_____

_____

_____

_____

_____

_____

_____

_____

_____

_____

_____

_____

CHAPTER 15 SECTION 3
A War Without End

NATIONAL
GEOGRAPHIC
LEARNING

VOCABULARY PRACTICE

KEY VOCABULARY

- **gunboat** *n.* a small, fast ship carrying mounted guns

- **pontoon** *n.* a portable, cylindrical float used to build a temporary bridge

DEFINITION CHART
Complete the Definition Chart for each of the Key Vocabulary words and draw a picture to illustrate each word in the space below.

WORD	DEFINITION	IN MY OWN WORDS

Illustration

UNIT 6 CHAPTER 16 SECTION 1
The Emancipation Proclamation

NATIONAL
GEOGRAPHIC
LEARNING

READING AND NOTE-TAKING

IDENTIFY MAIN IDEA AND DETAILS
Use a Main Idea and Details Web to organize your notes on the Emancipation Proclamation.

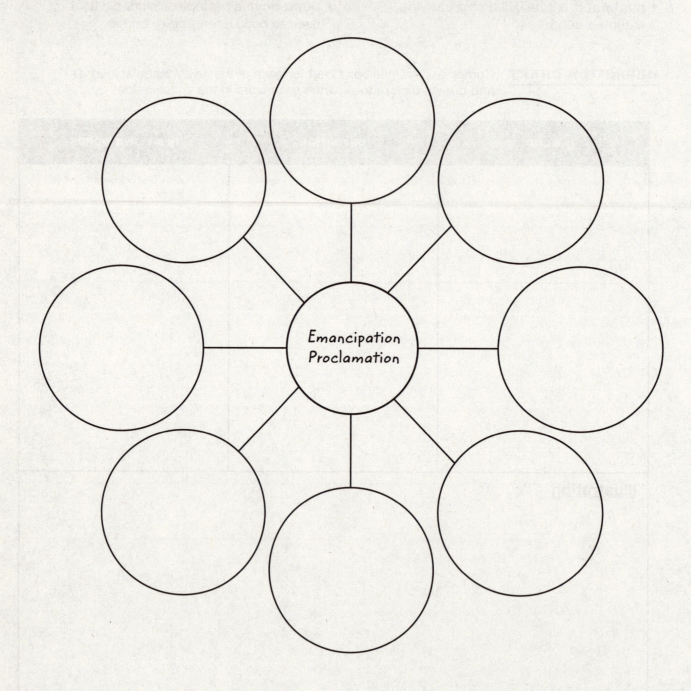

UNIT 6

CHAPTER 16 SECTION 1
The Emancipation Proclamation

NATIONAL GEOGRAPHIC LEARNING

READING AND NOTE-TAKING

ANALYZE CAUSE AND EFFECT

As you read Section 1.3, complete a flow chart to show which events led to such a large number of African American soldiers fighting in the war and then what effect that had on the outcome of the war.

First:

↓

Next:

↓

Last:

UNIT 6

CHAPTER 16 SECTION 2
Americans at War

READING AND NOTE-TAKING

POSE AND ANSWER QUESTIONS   Use a Pose and Answer Questions Chart to ask any questions that arise while reading about the draft or the cost of war in Section 2. Answer the questions after you have finished reading.

QUESTIONS	ANSWERS

UNIT 6

CHAPTER 16 SECTION 2
Americans at War

NATIONAL GEOGRAPHIC LEARNING

READING AND NOTE-TAKING

DRAW CONCLUSIONS   Use an Idea Diagram to help you draw a conclusion about the wartime prison camps. Be sure to include details under each main idea.

TOPIC: _Civil War prison camps_ _____

INTRODUCTION: _____

MAIN IDEAS: _____   _____

DETAILS: _____   _____

CONCLUSION: _____

UNIT 6

CHAPTER 16 SECTION 3
The Tide Turns

NATIONAL GEOGRAPHIC LEARNING

READING AND NOTE-TAKING

OUTLINE AND TAKE NOTES As you read Section 3, take notes using the headings and subheadings as a starting point.

3.1 Battles of Vicksburg and Gettysburg

A. Splitting the Confederacy

- _____
- _____
- _____
- _____

B. The Tide Turns at Gettysburg

- _____
- _____
- _____
- _____

3.2 Sherman's March and Grant's Victory

A. _____

- _____
- _____
- _____
- _____

B. _____

- _____
- _____
- _____
- _____

UNIT 6   **CHAPTER 16** SECTION 3
The Tide Turns *continued*

NATIONAL GEOGRAPHIC LEARNING

3.4 Appomattox

A. _____

  - _____

  - _____

  - _____

  - _____

B. _____

  - _____

  - _____

  - _____

  - _____

SUMMARIZE Write a paragraph summarizing the information from Section 3.

_____
_____
_____
_____
_____
_____
_____
_____
_____
_____
_____
_____
_____
_____
_____
_____

UNIT 6
CHAPTER 16 SECTION 4
The War's Aftermath

NATIONAL GEOGRAPHIC LEARNING

READING AND NOTE-TAKING

SEQUENCE EVENTS As you read Section 4, complete the Sequence Chain with details about the end of slavery and rebuilding the nation after the war.

Sequence Chain

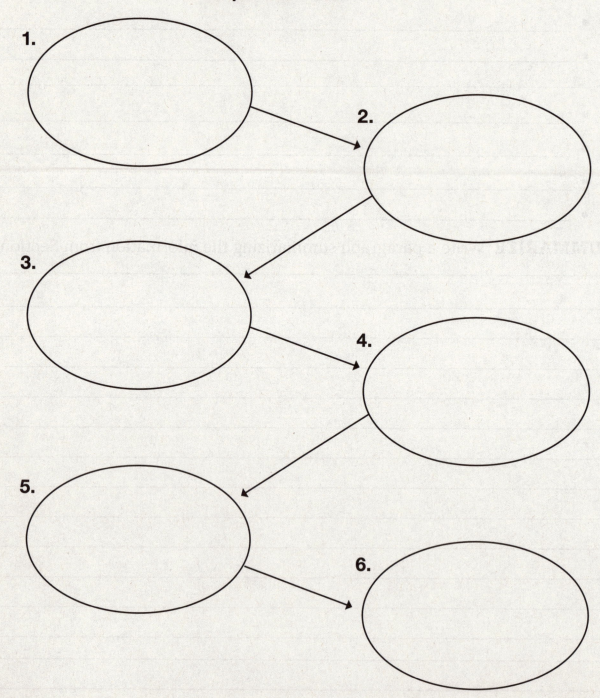

1.

2.

3.

4.

5.

6.

UNIT 6

CHAPTER 16 SECTION 4
The War's Aftermath *continued*

Sequence Chain

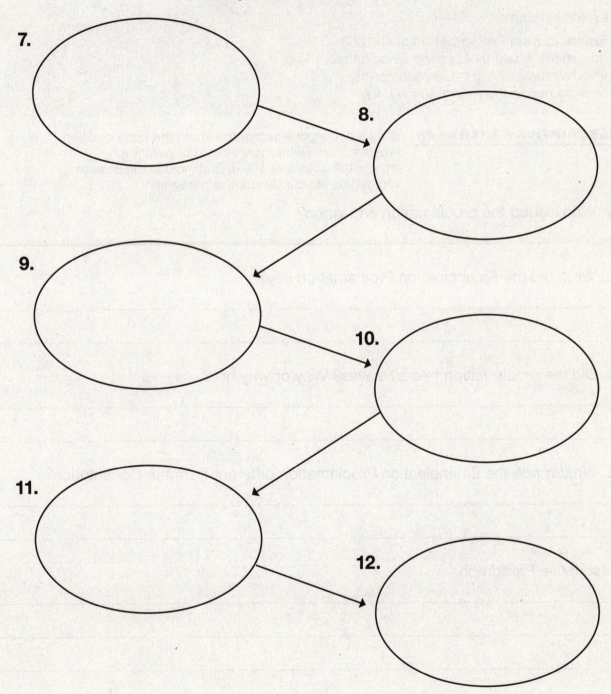

7.

8.

9.

10.

11.

12.

UNIT 6

CHAPTER 16 SECTION 1
The Emancipation Proclamation

NATIONAL GEOGRAPHIC LEARNING

VOCABULARY PRACTICE

KEY VOCABULARY

• **Emancipation Proclamation** *n.* an 1863 document issued by Abraham Lincoln that freed all slaves living in Confederate-held territory during the American Civil War

DESCRIPTIVE PARAGRAPH   Write a descriptive paragraph about the Emancipation Proclamation. Before you write your paragraph, answer the questions below and include the answer information in your descriptive paragraph.

1. Who issued the proclamation and when?

_____

2. What did the Emancipation Proclamation say?

_____

_____

3. Did the proclamation free all slaves? Why or why not?

_____

_____

4. What made the Emancipation Proclamation different from the Constitution?

_____

_____

Descriptive Paragraph

_____

_____

_____

_____

_____

UNIT 6

CHAPTER 16 SECTION 1
The Emancipation Proclamation

NATIONAL GEOGRAPHIC LEARNING

VOCABULARY PRACTICE

KEY VOCABULARY

- **enlist** (ehn-LIST) *v.* to join

- **stalemate** *n.* a situation in which neither side in a conflict is able to win

DEFINITION CLUES   Follow the instructions below for the Key Vocabulary word indicated.

ENLIST	STALEMATE
1. Write the sentence in which the word appears in the section.	1. Write the sentence in which the word appears in the section.
2. Write the definition using your own words.	2. Write the definition using your own words.
3. Use the word in a sentence of your own.	3. Use the word in a sentence of your own.
4. Describe an example of a person enlisting in something.	4. Describe an example of a stalemate.

235

UNIT 6 · CHAPTER 16 SECTION 2
Americans at War

VOCABULARY PRACTICE

KEY VOCABULARY

- **bond** *n.* a certificate offered for sale to the public with the promise that the government will pay the money back at a later date

- **Conscription Act** *n.* a law instituted by the Union in 1863 stating that men between the ages of 20 and 45 years of age were liable to be drafted into the military, but they could pay $300 to avoid service

- **draft** *n.* a mandatory term of military service

- **exemption** *n.* a release from obligations

- *habeas corpus* (HA-be-as COR-pus) *n.* the right of an arrested person to be brought before a judge before going to jail

KWL CHART   Fill in the KWL Chart for the Key Vocabulary words.

WHAT DO I KNOW	WHAT DO I WANT TO LEARN	WHAT DID I LEARN
bond a certificate offered for sale to the public with the promise that the government will pay the money back at a later date		

UNIT 6

CHAPTER 16 SECTION 2
Americans at War

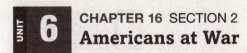

NATIONAL GEOGRAPHIC LEARNING

VOCABULARY PRACTICE

KEY VOCABULARY

- **Legal Tender Act** *n*. an act that replaced the notes of individual banks with a unified national currency

- **quarantine** (KWAWR-uhn-teen) *v*. to keep infected people away from those who had not yet contracted a disease

- **rations** (RA-shuhnz) *n*. supplied food

- **scapegoat** *n*. an individual or group blamed for the mistakes or faults of others

- **scurvy** (SCUR-vee) *n*. a disease linked to malnutrition and a diet lacking in fruits and vegetables

DEFINITION CHART   Complete a Definition Chart for the Key Vocabulary words. In the last column, use the word in a sentence.

WORD	DEFINITION	IN MY OWN WORDS	SENTENCE

UNIT 6

CHAPTER 16 SECTION 3
The Tide Turns

VOCABULARY PRACTICE

KEY VOCABULARY

- **bluff** *n.* a cliff
- **flotilla** (flo-TIHL-ah) *n.* a small fleet
- **morphine** (MAWR-feen) *n.* a powerful painkiller

DEFINITION TREE For each Key Vocabulary word in the Definition Tree below, write the definition on the top branch and then use each word in a sentence.

bluff

flotilla

morphine

UNIT 6

CHAPTER 16 SECTION 3
The Tide Turns

NATIONAL GEOGRAPHIC LEARNING

VOCABULARY PRACTICE

KEY VOCABULARY

- **total war** *n.* a war in which all rules and laws of war are ignored and all resources are used for defeating the enemy

- **veteran** *n.* a person who has served in the military

- **Gettysburg Address** *n.* an 1863 speech delivered by President Lincoln to commemorate the loss of life at the Battle of Gettysburg and to dedicate a military cemetery there

RELATED IDEA WEB
Write one of the Key Vocabulary words inside a circle, along with its definition in your own words. Then draw lines or arrows connecting the circles to show how the words are related, based on what you read in Section 3. Write your own explanation of the connection next to the line or arrow.

UNIT 6 — CHAPTER 16 SECTION 4
The War's Aftermath

VOCABULARY PRACTICE

KEY VOCABULARY

- **assassinate** *v.* to murder for political reasons
- **casualty** *n.* a dead or injured person
- **Homestead Act** *n.* an act which started a program of public land grants to small farmers

- **jurisdiction** *n.* the authority to enforce laws within a given area
- **reconstruction** *n.* the effort to rebuild and reunite the United States following the Civil War
- **servitude** *n.* state of being enslaved

I READ, I KNOW, AND SO Complete the charts below for the Key Vocabulary words in Section 4. Write the sentence in which the word appears. Then write what else you read about the word. Finally, draw a conclusion about the word based on what you have learned.

I Read		
	assassinate	
I Know		And So

I Read		
	casualty	
I Know		And So

NATIONAL GEOGRAPHIC LEARNING

I Read		
	Homestead Act	
I Know		And So

I Read		
	jurisdiction	
I Know		And So

I Read		
	reconstruction	
I Know		And So

I Read		
	servitude	
I Know		And So

AMERICAN VOICES
Dr. Martin Luther King, Jr.
1929–1968

"I have a dream that my four children will one day live in a nation where they will not be judged by the color of their skin but by the content of their character."
— Martin Luther King, Jr., "I Have A Dream" speech, August 28, 1963

Dr. Martin Luther King, Jr., speaking at an antiwar demonstration in New York City, 1967

Civil rights activist Dr. Martin Luther King, Jr., was a Baptist minister who believed in peaceful, nonviolent protests to bring an end to racial discrimination.

Martin Luther King, Jr., was born on January 15, 1929, in Atlanta, Georgia, to a family deeply rooted in their Baptist faith. He grew up during a time when racial discrimination and inequalities were ever-present in our nation. After many years of questioning his religion, King enrolled in a seminary. Here he met Benjamin E. Mays, a staunch advocate for racial equality, who encouraged him to use Christianity to enact change. King later earned a doctoral degree at Boston University, where he met Coretta Scott, a musician and singer. The couple married in 1953 and had four children.

King became a pastor of the Dexter Avenue Baptist Church in Montgomery, Alabama, and, in 1955, completed his Ph.D. In December of that year, Rosa Parks was told to give up her seat on a bus for a white man. When she refused, Rosa was arrested. Backed by other civil rights leaders, Martin Luther King, Jr., led a peaceful 381-day bus boycott in response. The group faced violence and discrimination, but the U.S. Supreme Court eventually ruled that public bus segregation was illegal.

After this victory, the Southern Christian Leadership Conference was formed. A key participant, King spoke out against racism and worked tirelessly to give African Americans a voice. In 1960, King and his family returned to Atlanta, Georgia. King continued to inspire people around the nation with his eloquent speeches and by using peaceful methods to achieve equality. On August 28, 1963, King gave his famous "I Have a Dream" speech during the March on Washington. One year later, he received the Nobel Peace Prize.

King worked throughout the 1960s to bring awareness to racial injustices. Some people said his approach was passive and ineffective, but hundreds of thousands believed in his message. On April 3, 1968, King gave his last speech. The next day, he was shot and killed by James Earl Ray in Memphis, Tennessee. In 1986, a federal holiday was named to honor the life and legacy of Dr. Martin Luther King, Jr.

HISTORICAL THINKING

MAKE CONNECTIONS In what ways can you support the work of Dr. Martin Luther King, Jr., on his national holiday?

_____

_____

AMERICAN VOICES
Robert E. Lee
1807–1870
Ulysses S. Grant
1822–1885

"But what a cruel thing is war . . . to fill our hearts with hatred instead of love for our neighbours." — Robert E. Lee

"Although a soldier by profession, I have never felt any sort of fondness for war." — Ulysses S. Grant

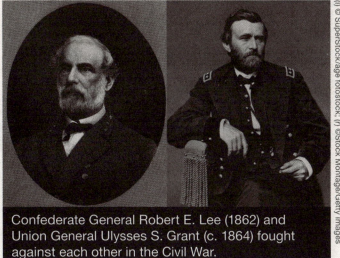

Confederate General Robert E. Lee (1862) and Union General Ulysses S. Grant (c. 1864) fought against each other in the Civil War.

Although enemies on the battlefield, Confederate General Robert E. Lee and Union General Ulysses S. Grant shared common experiences, including fighting for their ideals during the Civil War.

Robert E. Lee was born in Stratford, Virginia, on January 19, 1807. He enrolled in the United States Military Academy at West Point and graduated second in his class. During the Mexican-American War, Lee gained a reputation as an outstanding soldier and leader.

When the southern states seceded from the Union in 1860, President Lincoln offered Lee command of an army to force those states back into the Union. Lee didn't approve of secession but opposed Lincoln's plan, so he resigned his commission. He became commander of the Army of Northern Virginia and then commander of all Confederate armies. He secured major victories until the Confederate failures at Gettysburg in 1863. Not long after, he faced his most formidable opponent, Union General Ulysses S. Grant.

Grant was born April 27, 1822, in Point Pleasant, Ohio. He was not interested in a military career but his father enrolled him in the United States Military Academy at West Point. Grant graduated near the bottom of his class. Although courageous during the Mexican-American War, Grant opposed the war.

During the Civil War, Grant secured many Union victories. In March 1864, Lincoln named Grant "lieutenant general," a title first held by George Washington. Grant was given command of all Union armies. His success at stopping Confederate troops, along with two Union victories—the demolition of Virginia railroads and the ravaging of Georgia— forced Lee to surrender at Appomattox Courthouse in 1865, successfully ending the war.

The U.S. government claimed Lee's home and land near Arlington, Virginia, which has become Arlington National Cemetery. Lee moved to Lexington, Virginia, and became the president of a college now known as Washington and Lee University. He died October 12, 1870.

Grant was elected 18th president of the United States in 1869 and served two terms. He died July 23, 1885, in New York, after having just finished writing his memoir.

HISTORICAL THINKING

COMPARE AND CONTRAST In what ways were Ulysses S. Grant and Robert E. Lee similar?

_____

_____

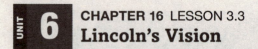

DOCUMENT-BASED QUESTION

Use the questions here to help you analyze the sources and write your paragraph.

DOCUMENT ONE: The Gettysburg Address, by Abraham Lincoln, November 19, 1863

1A What did Lincoln mean by "testing whether that nation or any nation so conceived and so dedicated can long endure"?

_____

_____

_____

1B Constructed Response What action did Lincoln propose as the best way to honor those who had died at Gettysburg?

_____

_____

_____

DOCUMENT TWO: from Second Inaugural Address, by Abraham Lincoln, March 4, 1865

2A What does Lincoln call for in the last lines of this passage?

_____

_____

_____

_____

2B Constructed Response What was Lincoln referring to when he called on Americans "to bind up the nation's wounds"?

_____

_____

_____

SYNTHESIZE & WRITE

What was President Lincoln's vision for the United States after the Civil War, and how did he try to persuade Americans to support that vision?

Topic Sentence: _____

_____

Your Paragraph: _____

_____

_____

_____

_____

_____

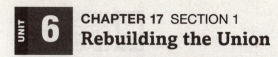

UNIT 6

CHAPTER 17 SECTION 1
Rebuilding the Union

READING AND NOTE-TAKING

ANALYZE CAUSE AND EFFECT As you read Section 1, complete a flow chart to show events from the end of the war and Lincoln's death to the creation of the Freedmen's Bureau.

First:

Next:

Last:

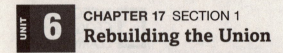

UNIT 6

CHAPTER 17 SECTION 1
Rebuilding the Union

READING AND NOTE-TAKING

SYNTHESIZE VISUAL AND TEXTUAL INFORMATION Use the chart below to record visual and textual information from Section 1.2.

What is the title of the lesson? _____	
What is the Main Idea? _____ _____ _____	
What were the black codes? _____ _____ _____ _____ _____	**What did Republicans do in response to the black codes?** _____ _____ _____ _____ _____
Which states made up Military District No. 3? _____ _____ _____ _____	**Which state was the first to be readmitted to the Union?** _____ _____ _____ _____
Why was President Johnson impeached? _____ _____ _____	

UNIT 6

CHAPTER 17 SECTION 2
Reconstruction Changes Daily Life

NATIONAL GEOGRAPHIC LEARNING

OUTLINE AND TAKE NOTES As you read Section 2, take notes using the headings and subheadings as a starting point.

2.1 Free African Americans Gain a Voice

A. *Taking Public Office*

- _____
- _____
- _____
- _____

B. *Church and Family*

- _____
- _____
- _____
- _____

2.2 Education and Land

A. _____

- _____
- _____
- _____
- _____

B. _____

- _____
- _____
- _____
- _____

UNIT 6

CHAPTER 17 SECTION 2
Reconstruction Changes Daily Life *continued*

NATIONAL GEOGRAPHIC LEARNING

2.3 Resistance in the South

A. _____

- _____
- _____
- _____
- _____

B. _____

- _____
- _____
- _____
- _____

SUMMARIZE Write a paragraph summarizing the information from Section 2.

_____
_____
_____
_____
_____
_____
_____
_____
_____
_____
_____
_____
_____
_____
_____

UNIT 6

CHAPTER 17 SECTION 3
The End of Reconstruction

READING AND NOTE-TAKING

<u>**SEQUENCE EVENTS**</u>   As you read Section 3, complete the Sequence Chain with details about Grant's presidency and the election of 1876.

Sequence Chain

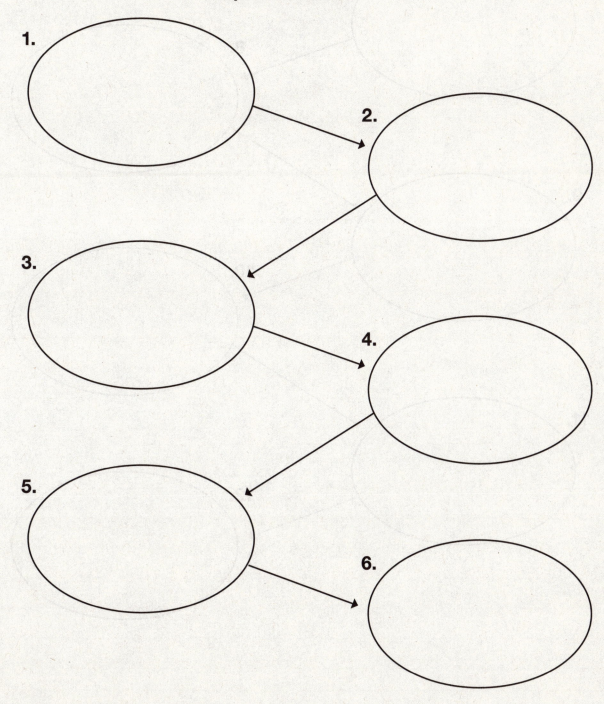

1.

2.

3.

4.

5.

6.

UNIT 6

CHAPTER 17 SECTION 3
The End of Reconstruction *continued*

Sequence Chain

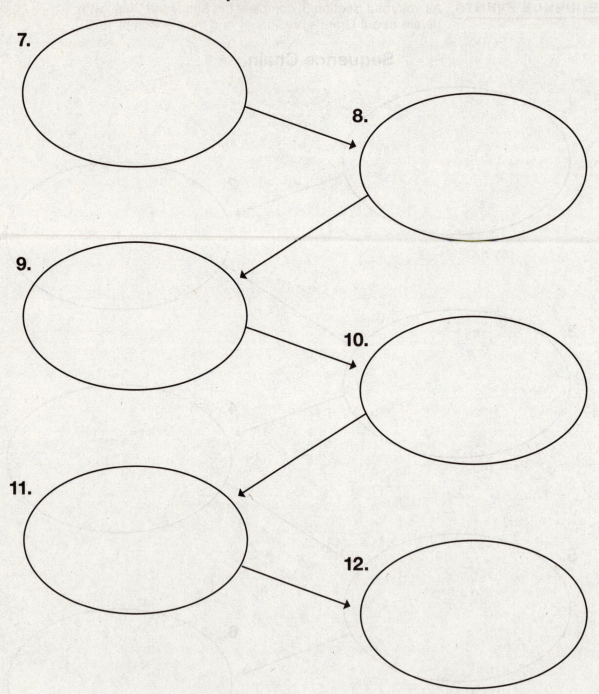

7.

8.

9.

10.

11.

12.

UNIT 6 — CHAPTER 17 SECTION 1
Rebuilding the Union

NATIONAL GEOGRAPHIC LEARNING

VOCABULARY PRACTICE

KEY VOCABULARY

- **black codes** *n.* laws passed by southern states immediately after the Civil War for controlling African Americans and limiting their rights, repealed by Reconstruction in 1866

- **Civil Rights Act of 1866** *n.* a bill granting full equality and citizenship to every race and color

COMPARISON CHART Complete the chart below. Write the definition and details for each word, and then explain how the two words are related.

black codes	Civil Rights Act of 1866

How are these two words related?

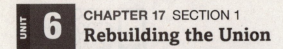

NATIONAL
GEOGRAPHIC
LEARNING

VOCABULARY PRACTICE

KEY VOCABULARY

- **Freedmen's Bureau** *n.* Bureau of Refugees, Freedmen, and Abandoned Lands created by Congress in 1865 to help former slaves as well as poor white southerners

- **impeachment** (ihm-PEECH-muhnt) *n.* the official charge of a president with misconduct while in office

- **Presidential Reconstruction** *n.* a policy which stated Confederate states must ratify the 13th Amendment and create new governments with new constitutions before they could rejoin the Union

- **Radical Reconstruction** *n.* the name given to the Republicans' plan in passing the Reconstruction Acts of 1867

- **Reconstruction Acts of 1867** *n.* acts that put the Republican Congress in charge of Reconstruction instead of the president

DEFINITION CHART Complete a Definition Chart for the Key Vocabulary words. In the last column, use the word in a sentence.

WORD	DEFINITION	IN MY OWN WORDS	SENTENCE
Freedmen's Bureau			

UNIT 6 CHAPTER 17 SECTION 2
Reconstruction Changes Daily Life

VOCABULARY PRACTICE

KEY VOCABULARY

- **arson** (AR-son) *n.* the purposeful burning of buildings illegally

- **black peonage** (PE-eh-nij) *n.* economic slavery that tied African Americans to sharecropping landlords' lands

- **Ku Klux Klan** *n.* the group whose purpose was to maintain the social and political power of white people

- **literacy** *n.* the ability to read and write

WDS CHART Complete a Word-Definition-Sentence (WDS) Chart for each Key Vocabulary word.

W
D   S

W
D   S

W
D   S

W
D   S

UNIT 6

CHAPTER 17 SECTION 2
Reconstruction Changes Daily Life

VOCABULARY PRACTICE

KEY VOCABULARY

- **lynch** *v.* to hang someone illegally by mob action

- **sharecropping** *n.* an agricultural system in which a farmer raises crops for a landowner in return for part of the money made from selling the crops

- **social justice** *n.* the fair distribution of opportunities and privileges, including racial equality

- **wage economy** *n.* an economy in which people are paid for their work

RELATED IDEA WEB Write one of the Key Vocabulary words inside a circle along with its definition in your own words. Then draw lines or arrows connecting the circles to show how the words are related, based on what you read in Section 2. Write your explanation of the connection next to the line or arrow.

UNIT 6

CHAPTER 17 SECTION 3
The End of Reconstruction

VOCABULARY PRACTICE

KEY VOCABULARY

- **15th Amendment** *n.* amendment to the Constitution that says that federal and state governments cannot restrict the right to vote because of race, color, or previous condition of servitude

- **bribery** *n.* offers of money or privileges to those in power in exchange for political favors

- **Compromise of 1877** *n.* a deal in which Democrats agreed to make Hayes president if Republicans ended Reconstruction and pulled federal troops out of the South

- **Copperhead** *n.* a negative nickname for Democrats who opposed emancipation of slaves and the draft

- **corruption** *n.* dishonesty, unlawfulness

WORDS IN CONTEXT   Follow the directions for using the Key Vocabulary words in context.

1. Explain the *15ᵗʰ Amendment.*

_____

_____

2. Write the definition of *bribery* using your own words.

_____

_____

3. Explain the *Compromise of 1877.*

_____

_____

4. Write the sentence in which the word *Copperhead* appears in the lesson.

_____

_____

5. Write the definition of *corruption.*

_____

_____

UNIT 6

CHAPTER 17 SECTION 3
The End of Reconstruction

VOCABULARY PRACTICE

KEY VOCABULARY

- **defect** *v.* to break away
- **Liberal Republicans** *n.* a group during the 1870s who believed the government had become too large and too powerful
- **literacy test** *n.* test of one's ability to read and write
- **Panic of 1873** *n.* an economic crisis triggered by bank and railroad failures
- **poll tax** *n.* a fee charged when people register to vote

THREE-COLUMN CHART Complete the chart for each of the Key Vocabulary words. Write the word's definition, and then provide a definition in your own words.

WORD	DEFINITION	IN MY OWN WORDS
defect		

UNIT 7

CHAPTER 18 SECTION 1

Gold, Silver, and Cattle

NATIONAL GEOGRAPHIC LEARNING

READING AND NOTE-TAKING

MAKE GENERALIZATIONS   Complete an Idea Diagram about the information in Section 1.1. Rewrite the introduction to the Section in your own words. Then take notes on specific details under each subheading. After you finish reading, write a generalization about Mining Boomtowns.

LESSON TITLE: _____

INTRODUCTION: _____
_____
_____

SUBHEADING: _____   SUBHEADING: _____

DETAILS:

_____
_____
_____
_____
_____

_____
_____
_____
_____
_____

GENERALIZATION: _____
_____
_____

READING AND NOTE-TAKING

IDENTIFY MAIN IDEA AND DETAILS   Use a Main Idea and Details Web to organize your notes on the cattle boom and cowboys.

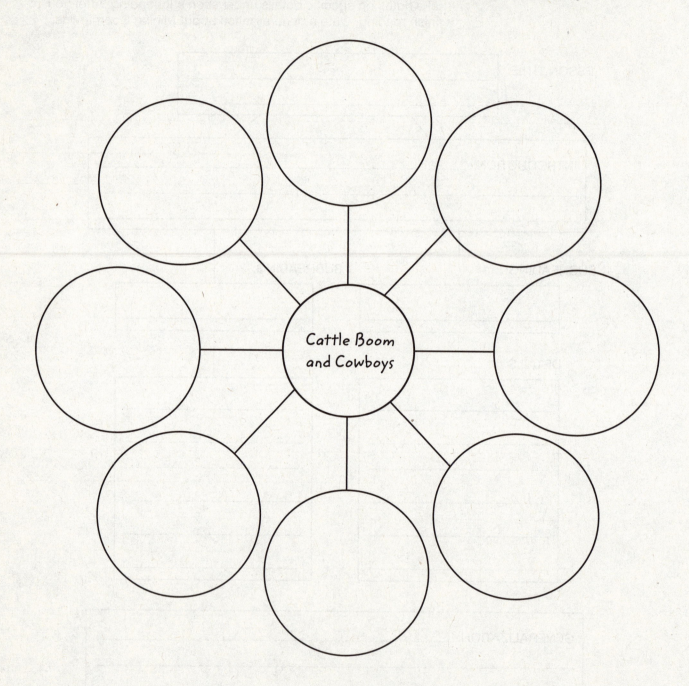

Cattle Boom and Cowboys

UNIT 7

CHAPTER 18 SECTION 2
Farm Economics and Populism

NATIONAL GEOGRAPHIC LEARNING

READING AND NOTE-TAKING

SEQUENCE EVENTS AND TAKE NOTES

As you read Section 2, take notes on details from each lesson. Then write a paragraph summarizing the information.

2.1 Farming in the West

- _____
- _____
- _____
- _____
- _____
- _____
- _____
- _____

2.2 Women and Children on the Prairie

- _____
- _____
- _____
- _____
- _____
- _____
- _____

2.3 Farmers and Populism

- _____
- _____
- _____
- _____
- _____
- _____
- _____
- _____
- _____

SUMMARIZE Write a paragraph summarizing the content from Section 2.

_____
_____
_____
_____
_____
_____
_____
_____
_____
_____
_____
_____
_____
_____
_____

CHAPTER 18 SECTION 3
Native Americans Fight to Survive

NATIONAL GEOGRAPHIC LEARNING

READING AND NOTE-TAKING

OUTLINE AND TAKE NOTES   As you read Section 3, take notes using the headings and subheadings as a starting point.

3.1 Native Americans of the Plains

A. Changing Lives on the Plains

- _____
- _____
- _____
- _____

B. The Native American Wars

- _____
- _____
- _____
- _____

3.3 Native Americans of the Northwest and Southwest

A. _____

- _____
- _____
- _____
- _____

B. _____

- _____
- _____
- _____
- _____

UNIT 7

CHAPTER 18 SECTION 3
Native Americans Fight to Survive *continued*

3.4 Wounded Knee

A. _____

- _____
- _____
- _____
- _____

B. _____

- _____
- _____
- _____
- _____

SUMMARIZE Write a paragraph summarizing the information from Section 3.

_____
_____
_____
_____
_____
_____
_____
_____
_____
_____
_____
_____
_____
_____
_____

UNIT 7 — CHAPTER 18 SECTION 1
Gold, Silver, and Cattle

VOCABULARY PRACTICE

KEY VOCABULARY

- **cattle drive** *n.* the process of moving a herd of cows and steer from one place to another, usually from ranch to railroad hub

- **entrepreneur** (ehn-treh-preh-neur) *n.* a person who starts, manages, and is responsible for a business

- **ghost town** *n.* an abandoned town that has fallen into ruin

- **hydraulic mining** *n.* a system of mining in which pressurized water is used to remove topsoil and gravel, which are then processed to draw out precious metals

WDS CHART   Complete a Word-Definition-Sentence (WDS) Chart for each Key Vocabulary word.

cattle drive

W
D   S

_____   _____
_____   _____
_____   _____

W
D   S

_____   _____
_____   _____
_____   _____

W
D   S

_____   _____
_____   _____

W
D   S

_____   _____
_____   _____

UNIT 7

CHAPTER 18 SECTION 1
Gold, Silver, and Cattle

VOCABULARY PRACTICE

KEY VOCABULARY

- **lode** (lohd) *n.* a large deposit of ore, such as silver or gold

- **placer mining** *n.* a system of mining where individual miners find gold nuggets in riverbeds, usually by panning

- **posse** (poh-see) *n.* a group organized by a sheriff to hunt down criminals or fugitives

- **stockyard** *n.* an enormous outdoor corral in which animals are penned until they can be slaughtered

FOUR-COLUMN CHART Complete the chart below for each Key Vocabulary word. In the last column, use the word in a sentence.

WORD	DEFINITION	ILLUSTRATION	SENTENCE
lode			

UNIT 7

CHAPTER 18 SECTION 2
Farm Economics and Populism

NATIONAL
GEOGRAPHIC
LEARNING

VOCABULARY PRACTICE

KEY VOCABULARY

- **bonanza farm** *n*. an enormous farm established by an investor who runs it for profit

- **cooperative** *n*. a group of farmers or others who combine their money to purchase needed products and services

- **exoduster** *n*. one of the thousands of African Americans who migrated to the Midwestern plains from the post-Civil-War South to start a new life

- **Farmers' Alliance** *n*. one of several organizations founded in the 1880s to advance political and economic concerns of farmers; similar to the Grange but more political

- **Grange** *n*. a U.S. farmers' organization founded in 1867 to provide social and economic support to agricultural families

- **migrant worker** *n*. a laborer who moves from one job to another as needed; usually a farm laborer

- **prairie** *n*. a vast area of flat land covered with tall plants

- **surplus** (SUR-plus) *n*. the amount left over, an excess

DEFINITION CLUES   Answer the questions below about the Key Vocabulary words. Read the text around the word to find the answers.

1. Who were the exodusters? _____

2. How did the farmers use the prairie? _____

3. Describe the bonanza farms. _____

    _____

4. Who were migrant workers and what did they do? _____

5. What happened when farmers had a surplus? _____

6. Who formed the Grange? Why? _____

    _____

7. How was the Farmers' Alliance different from the Grange? _____

    _____

8. What was a cooperative? _____

UNIT 7

CHAPTER 18 SECTION 2
Farm Economics and Populism

VOCABULARY PRACTICE

KEY VOCABULARY

- **creditor** *n.* a person to whom a debt is owed

- **free silver movement** *n.* a late-19th-century economic movement that promoted a monetary system based on silver in addition to gold

- **gold standard** *n.* a monetary policy requiring that the government can print only an amount of money equal to the total value of its gold reserves

- **industrialist** *n.* a person who owns and runs an industry

- **populist** *n.* a politician who claims to represent the concerns of ordinary people

- **recession** (rih-SE-shuhn) *n.* an economic downturn

WDS CHART   Complete a Word-Definition-Sentence (WDS) Chart for each Key Vocabulary word.

W _____

D _____

S _____

_____

W _____

D _____

S _____

_____

W _____

D _____

S _____

_____

W _____

D _____

S _____

_____

W _____

D _____

S _____

_____

W _____

D _____

S _____

_____

UNIT 7

CHAPTER 18 SECTION 3
Native Americans Fight to Survive

NATIONAL GEOGRAPHIC LEARNING

VOCABULARY PRACTICE

KEY VOCABULARY

- **Americanization** *n.* the act of teaching immigrants and Native Americans the mainstream culture and language of the United States with the expectation that they will adapt to and embrace it.

- **Ghost Dance** *n.* a Native-American religious movement based on a dance ritual meant to communicate with the dead and bring an end to white control of the West; began in the 1870s

- **Long Walk** *n.* the 300-mile forced walk of the Navajo from their homeland to a reservation at Bosque Redondo, New Mexico; imposed by the U.S. government in 1864

- **reservation** *n.* an area of land in the United States that is kept specifically for Native Americans to live on

I READ, I KNOW, AND SO   Use the graphic organizers below to explore your understanding of the Key Vocabulary words.

I Read	
I Know	And So

I Read	
I Know	And So

UNIT 7

CHAPTER 18 SECTION 3

Native Americans Fight to Survive *continued*

NATIONAL GEOGRAPHIC LEARNING

I Read		
I Know		And So

I Read		
I Know		And So

SUMMARY PARAGRAPH Summarize the information from Section 3 using the Key Vocabulary words.

_____

_____

_____

_____

_____

_____

_____

_____

AMERICAN VOICES
Sitting Bull
c.1831–1890

George Armstrong Custer
1839–1876

Sitting Bull, c. 1890   George Armstrong Custer, c. 1864

(l) ©Bridgeman Images; (r) ©National Archives

"No white man controls our footsteps. If we must die, we die defending our rights."
— Sitting Bull

"I regard Custer's massacre as a sacrifice of troops, brought on by Custer himself, that was wholly unnecessary." — President Ulysses S. Grant about George Armstrong Custer

Sitting Bull was a Lakota chief respected for his wisdom and military capability. George Armstrong Custer was a brash and conceited U.S. Army officer, frequently disciplined and known for reckless aggression. The two met as opponents at the bloody Battle of the Little Bighorn.

Tatanka Iyotake, also known as Sitting Bull, a Lakota Sioux chief, was born around 1831, in what is now South Dakota. He earned a reputation for intelligence, leadership, and fearlessness, even among his opponents in the U.S. Army. Sitting Bull first encountered white men in battle in 1863. For the next five years, he fought against the U.S. Army to protect his tribe's hunting lands.

George Armstrong Custer was born in Ohio on December 5, 1839, and attended the U.S. Military Academy at West Point. He gained a reputation for aggressive tactics and military disobedience. He won a few battles for the Union during the Civil War, but his tactics cost many Union soldiers their lives. After a one-year suspension for mistreating soldiers in 1868, Custer attacked a peaceful Cheyenne village, leaving 103 people dead, including women and children.

That same year, the Lakota signed a treaty with the U.S. government designating the Black Hills in South Dakota as sacred Lakota land. But when gold was discovered there in 1874, Custer's cavalry protected the miners. Sitting Bull led Lakota and Cheyenne warriors in resistance, while the U.S. Army sought to drive the Lakota onto reservations.

In June 1876, Custer and his regiment attacked a Lakota encampment. This was the Battle of the Little Bighorn, during which Sitting Bull and his men surrounded Custer's forces and killed them all, including Custer.

Sitting Bull won that battle, but the U.S. Army chased him to Canada. Years later, Sitting Bull returned to his reservation, where he died in 1890 in a gunfight as his followers tried to protect him.

HISTORICAL THINKING

ANALYZE CAUSE AND EFFECT What events led up to the Battle of the Little Bighorn?

_____

_____

UNIT 7

CHAPTER 19 SECTION 1
America Enters the Industrial Age

NATIONAL GEOGRAPHIC LEARNING

READING AND NOTE-TAKING

__CONCEPT WEBS__ As you read Sections 1.1 and 1.3, write notes about railroads and inventions in the Concept Webs below.

Railroads

_____

_____

_____

_____

_____

Inventions

_____

_____

_____

_____

__SUMMARIZE__ Write a short paragraph summarizing the information you noted about railroads and inventions.

_____

_____

_____

_____

_____

UNIT 7

CHAPTER 19 SECTION 1
America Enters the Industrial Age

NATIONAL GEOGRAPHIC LEARNING

READING AND NOTE-TAKING

SEQUENCE CHAIN   As you read Sections 1.4 and 1.5, complete the Sequence Chain with details about the growth of big business and the Gilded Age.

Sequence Chain

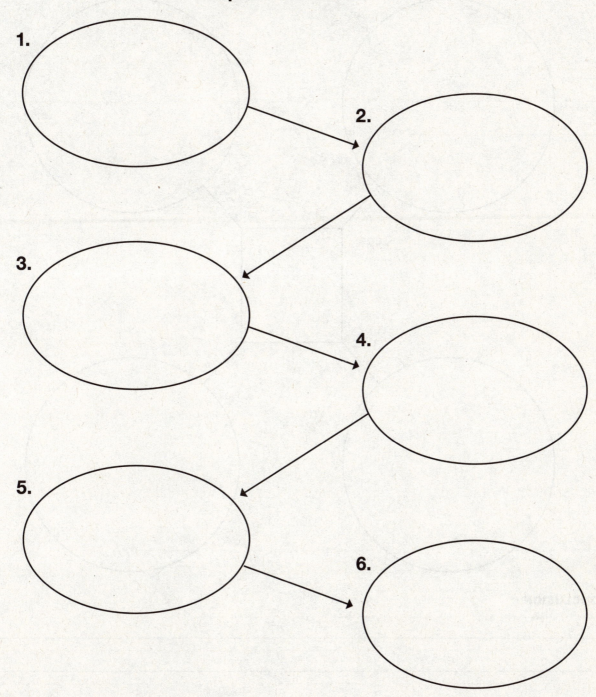

CHAPTER 19 SECTION 2
Immigration and Modern Urban Growth

NATIONAL GEOGRAPHIC LEARNING

READING AND NOTE-TAKING

DRAW CONCLUSIONS   As you read Section 2, use the Idea Web to take notes on the new immigrants. Then draw your own conclusion about immigration at this time and write it on the lines below.

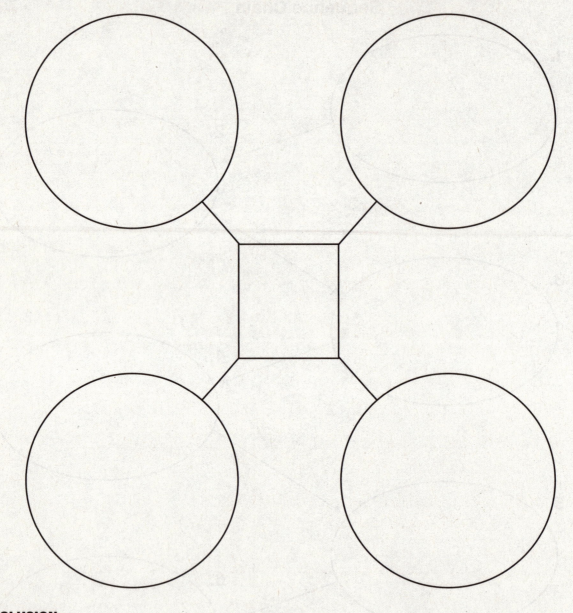

CONCLUSION

_____

_____

_____

CHAPTER 19 SECTION 2
Immigration and Modern Urban Growth

NATIONAL GEOGRAPHIC LEARNING

READING AND NOTE-TAKING

MAKE GENERALIZATIONS   Complete an Idea Diagram about the information in Section 2.3. Rewrite the introduction to the lesson in your own words. Then take notes on specific details under each subheading. After you finish reading, write a generalization about the growth of cities.

LESSON TITLE: _Cities Grow Rapidly_ _____

_____

INTRODUCTION: _____

_____

_____

SUBHEADING: _____

_____

SUBHEADING: _____

_____

DETAILS:

_____

_____

_____

_____

_____

_____

_____

_____

_____

_____

GENERALIZATION: _____

_____

_____

UNIT 7
CHAPTER 19 SECTION 3
Discrimination Against Minorities

READING AND NOTE-TAKING

IDENTIFY CAUSES AND EFFECTS Use the chart below to record causes and effects that relate to racism and segregation the United States.

Causes	Effects
industrialization, urbanization, immigration, and an economic downturn	

© National Geographic Learning, a part of Cengage Learning

UNIT 7 CHAPTER 19 SECTION 3
Discrimination Against Minorities

NATIONAL
GEOGRAPHIC
LEARNING

READING AND NOTE-TAKING

IDENTIFY SIGNIFICANCE

As you read Section 3, take notes about the actions of historical figures mentioned in the text. Then in the third column, identify why each historical figure's actions are significant.

HISTORICAL FIGURE	ACTIONS	SIGNIFICANCE
Homer Plessy		

UNIT 7

CHAPTER 19 SECTION 4
The Labor Movement

NATIONAL GEOGRAPHIC LEARNING

READING AND NOTE-TAKING

OUTLINE AND TAKE NOTES   As you read Section 4, take notes using the headings and subheadings as a starting point.

4.1 The Lives of Workers

A. Working Conditions

- _____
- _____
- _____
- _____

B. Women and Children

- _____
- _____
- _____
- _____

4.2 Rise of Labor Unions

A. _____

- _____
- _____
- _____
- _____

B. _____

- _____
- _____
- _____
- _____

© National Geographic Learning, a part of Cengage Learning

The Labor Movement *continued*

NATIONAL GEOGRAPHIC LEARNING

4.3 Labor Conflicts

A. _____

- _____
- _____
- _____
- _____

B. _____

- _____
- _____
- _____
- _____

SUMMARIZE Write a paragraph summarizing the information from Section 4.

_____
_____
_____
_____
_____
_____
_____
_____
_____
_____
_____
_____
_____
_____
_____
_____
_____

CHAPTER 19 SECTION 1
America Enters the Industrial Age

VOCABULARY PRACTICE

KEY VOCABULARY

- **Bessemer process** *n.* a steel manufacturing process that involves blowing air into molten iron to remove impurities, which results in a stronger metal

- **boom-and-bust cycle** *n.* a series of periods of economic growth followed by sudden economic downturns

- **capitalism** *n.* an economic system in which private individuals, as opposed to the government, own and profit from businesses

- **corporation** *n.* a company or group that acts legally as a single unit to run a business

- **Gilded Age** *n.* the last three decades of the 19th century, characterized by greed and corruption

- **laissez-faire** (LAH-zey-fehr) *n.* an economic policy in which a government lets businesses operate without much regulation; *laissez-faire* means "allow to" in French

- **mass culture** *n.* the set of popular values and ideas that arise from widespread access to media, music, art, and other entertainment

- **Pacific Railway Acts** *n.* two acts passed in the 1860s that gave two companies the contracts to construct a transcontinental railroad

- **patent** *n.* a document that gives the bearer exclusive rights to make and sell an invention

- **philanthropy** *n.* the financial support of a worthy or charitable cause

- **standard time** *n.* the uniform division of time among locations that lie roughly on the same line of longitude, establishing time zones

- **steel** *n.* a hard metal made from a mixture of iron and carbon

- **transcontinental railroad** *n.* a railroad that runs across a continent

- **trust** *n.* a group of corporations managed, but not directly owned, by a board

DEFINITION AND DETAILS   Study the definitions of the Key Vocabulary words above to answer the questions below and on the next page.

1. Which two words are economic systems or policies? Define them. _____

_____

_____

2. Which two words have to do with steel? Define them. _____

_____

_____

UNIT 7 **CHAPTER 19 SECTION 1**
America Enters the Industrial Age *continued*

NATIONAL
GEOGRAPHIC
LEARNING

VOCABULARY PRACTICE

3. Which two words are about railroads? Define them. _____

_____

_____

4. Which two words are about companies or groups of companies? Define them.

_____

_____

5. Which word is about protecting inventors? Define it. _____

_____

_____

6. Which word describes a historical age? _____

_____

_____

7. Which word describes an up-and-down economic period? _____

_____

8. Which word is about time zones? _____

_____

9. Which word is about the public's values and entertainment? Define it. _____

_____

_____

10. Which word describes giving money to charity? Define it. _____

_____

_____

UNIT 7

CHAPTER 19 SECTION 2
Immigration and Modern Urban Growth

NATIONAL
GEOGRAPHIC
LEARNING

VOCABULARY PRACTICE

KEY VOCABULARY

- **bedrock** *n.* solid rock that lies under loose soil

- **mutual aid society** *n.* an organization formed by members of a particular group to provide economic and other assistance to each other

- **political machine** *n.* a party organization that ran big cities, ruled by strong and often corrupt leaders who offered favors to members in exchange for votes and other support

- **refugee** (REF-yoo-gee) *n.* a person who flees to another country to escape danger or persecution

- **Social Gospel** *n.* a Protestant religious movement that stressed the importance of churches to become involved with social issues and reform

WORDS IN CONTEXT   Follow the directions for using the Key Vocabulary words in context.

1. Describe what *bedrock* is.

_____

_____

2. Write the definition of *mutual aid society* using your own words.

_____

_____

3. Explain what a *political machine* is.

_____

_____

4. Write the sentence in which the word *refugee* appears in the lesson.

_____

_____

5. Write the definition of *Social Gospel*.

_____

_____

UNIT 7 CHAPTER 19 SECTION 2
Immigration and Modern Urban Growth

NATIONAL
GEOGRAPHIC
LEARNING

VOCABULARY PRACTICE

KEY VOCABULARY

- **settlement house** *n.* a place that provides assistance to poor and immigrant residents of a community

- **skyscraper** *n.* a very tall building

- **streetcar** *n.* a vehicle on rails set in city streets that could transport many passengers at once, like a train

- **suburb** *n.* a residential area on the edge of a city or town

- **tenement** (TEHN-eh-ment) *n.* a quickly constructed apartment building; usually refers to a crowded urban dwelling for immigrants and the poor

- **urbanization** *n.* a process in which economic, industrial, and population patterns shifted from rural areas to cities

DESCRIPTIVE PARAGRAPH
Write a paragraph describing urban growth using all of the Key Vocabulary words. Begin with a topic sentence. Add information and details. Then conclude with a summary sentence.

_____

_____

_____

_____

_____

_____

_____

_____

_____

_____

_____

_____

_____

_____

_____

UNIT 7

CHAPTER 19 SECTION 3
Discrimination Against Minorities

VOCABULARY PRACTICE

KEY VOCABULARY

- **Chinese Exclusion Act** *n.* an 1882 law prohibiting Chinese workers from immigrating to the United States for a 10-year period

- **Jim Crow laws** *n.* laws created in the 1880s by southern politicians to take away the rights of African Americans

- **poll watcher** *n.* a person assigned to a polling place to guard against voting irregularities

- **self-reliance** *n.* individual independence developed through practical skills and education

WORD MAPS   Complete Word Maps for each of the four Key Vocabulary words.

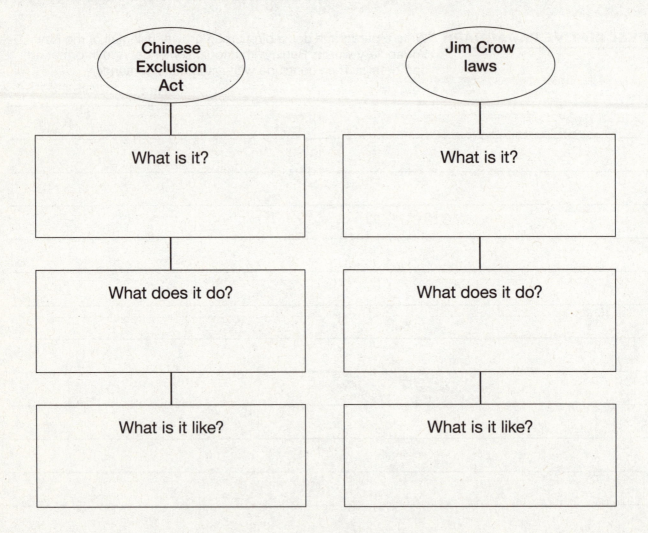

UNIT 7

CHAPTER 19 SECTION 3
Discrimination Against Minorities *continued*

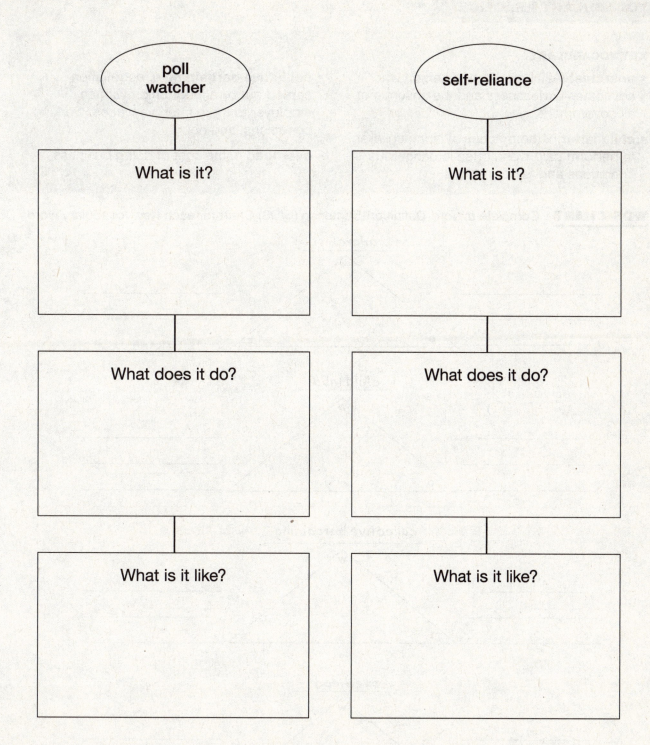

poll watcher

What is it?

What does it do?

What is it like?

self-reliance

What is it?

What does it do?

What is it like?

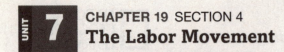

UNIT 7

CHAPTER 19 SECTION 4
The Labor Movement

NATIONAL GEOGRAPHIC LEARNING

VOCABULARY PRACTICE

KEY VOCABULARY

- **anarchist** (AHN-ark-ist) *n.* a person who advocates lawlessness and the absence of all government

- **child labor** *n.* the practice of hiring children to perform paid work, often in dangerous conditions and for low wages

- **collective bargaining** *n.* negotiation carried out by a labor union with an employer to try to improve wages, working conditions, and hours

- **overhead** *n.* the cost of doing business

WDS CHART   Complete a Word-Definition-Sentence (WDS) Chart for each Key Vocabulary word.

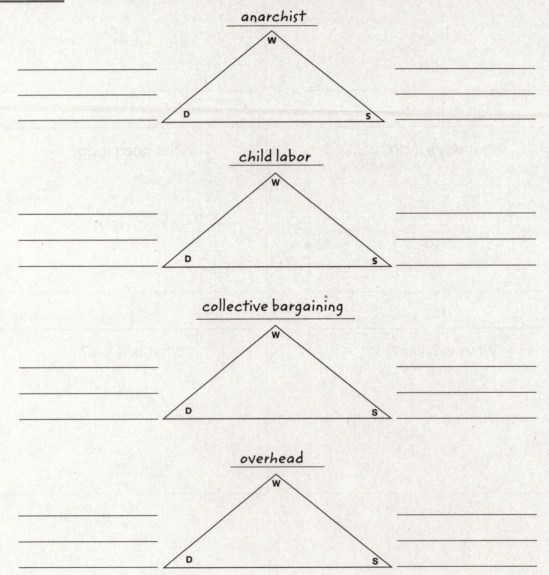

UNIT 7 — CHAPTER 19 SECTION 4
The Labor Movement

VOCABULARY PRACTICE

KEY VOCABULARY

- **robber baron** *n.* an industrial leader known for cutthroat tactics against workers and competitors

- **scab** *n.* a person willing to cross union lines to work during a strike

- **sweatshop** *n.* a factory that pays low wages, provides crowded, unsafe conditions, and requires long work hours

DEFINITION TREE Complete a Definition Tree for each Key Vocabulary word. Write the definition on the top branch and then use each word in a sentence.

robber baron

AMERICAN VOICES

Booker T. Washington
1856–1915

W.E.B. Du Bois
1868–1963

"In all things that are purely social we can be as separate as the fingers, yet one as the hand in all things essential to mutual progress."
— Booker T. Washington

"The cost of liberty is less than the price of repression." — W.E.B. Du Bois

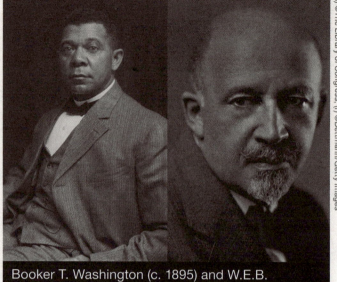

Booker T. Washington (c. 1895) and W.E.B. Du Bois (c. 1940) were civil rights leaders with widely different approaches.

African-American leaders Booker T. Washington and W.E.B. Du Bois clashed over how African Americans should work for civil rights in post–Civil War America.

Born April 5, 1856, Booker T. Washington spent his first nine years enslaved in Virginia. Following emancipation, his family moved to West Virginia where Washington worked in salt furnaces and coal mines. The hard work did not lessen his determination to get an education. Eventually, Washington attended and then taught at the Hampton Institute in Virginia.

In 1881, Washington founded a trade school for African Americans in Alabama, now known as Tuskegee Institute. Washington believed financial independence was the best route to civil rights. He promoted his "Atlanta Compromise," which said that in exchange for blacks remaining peaceful and socially separate, whites would work to improve social and economic conditions for all Americans. His nonthreatening approach to race relations gained him both white and black followers.

William Edward Burghardt Du Bois, or W.E.B. Du Bois, was born February 23, 1868, in Great Barrington, Massachusetts. He graduated from Fisk University and earned a doctorate from Harvard

University. Horrified by the racist culture of Jim Crow laws, disenfranchisement, and lynchings, Du Bois challenged Washington's ideas. He believed protest, not peaceful accommodation, was the better approach toward gaining civil rights.

Du Bois helped found the Niagara Movement in 1905. This group of African-American scholars and professionals attacked Washington's accommodation ideas. Du Bois was a founding member of the National Association for the Advancement of Colored People (NAACP). Du Bois wrote essays, poems, and books dealing with race and was often critical of white Americans.

Washington died November 14, 1915, in Alabama. Du Bois eventually became disillusioned with United States politics. He moved to Ghana, in Africa, where he died August 27, 1963.

HISTORICAL THINKING

COMPARE AND CONTRAST How did Washington's and Du Bois's views on gaining civil rights differ?

_____

_____

AMERICAN VOICES
Cornelius Vanderbilt
1794–1877

©National Archives

Cornelius Vanderbilt, a true entrepreneur, photographed c. 1860–1865

"I have always served the public to the best of my ability. Why? Because . . . it is to my interest to do so." — Cornelius Vanderbilt

Cornelius Vanderbilt, a leading American businessman, built a transportation empire out of the purchase of one ferryboat.

Cornelius Vanderbilt did not come from a wealthy family. Born May 27, 1794, on Staten Island, New York, he was the fourth of nine children. He quit school when he was 11 years old to help his father pilot a ferry back and forth from Staten Island to Manhattan. When he was 16, Vanderbilt borrowed money from his parents and bought his own ferryboat.

During the War of 1812, Vanderbilt expanded his business, purchasing more boats to help supply military outposts in New York. He gained control of transportation on the Hudson River by cutting fares and offering passengers luxuries no other shipping company could afford. He expanded his business, providing transportation between Long Island, New York; Providence, Rhode Island; and Boston, Massachusetts. Next, he created a company that carried passengers and goods from New York to San Francisco, California, by way of Nicaragua. A savvy businessperson, Vanderbilt kept his fares lower than the competition's, and by 1846, he was a millionaire.

By the middle of the 19th century, trains had become an important form of transportation. More than 9,000 miles of railroad track had been laid by 1850. Although he had been a passenger in a deadly New Jersey train derailment in 1833, Vanderbilt saw great potential in rail travel. He bought enough stock in the New York and Harlem Railroad to become its owner in 1863. Purchasing and combining several other railroad companies allowed Vanderbilt to offer, for the first time, rail transportation from New York City to Chicago,

Illinois. Vanderbilt's new empire made him the richest man in the world.

Cornelius Vanderbilt was not thought of as a philanthropist. Yet before his death on January 4, 1877, he donated a million dollars to a college in Tennessee, now known as Vanderbilt University. He left most of his millions to his eldest son and several millions to his other sons and his grandsons, but relatively little to his second wife and daughters.

HISTORICAL THINKING

DRAW CONCLUSIONS Vanderbilt built his first successful business from the money his parents gave him to buy a ferry when he was only 16. What conclusions can you draw about Vanderbilt's character from that?

_____

_____

U.S. HISTORY

AMERICAN VOICES
César Chávez
1927–1993

"It's ironic that those who till the soil, cultivate and harvest the fruits, vegetables, and other foods that fill your tables with abundance have nothing left for themselves." — César Chávez

A labor leader, civil rights activist, and founder of the National Farm Worker's Association, César Chávez devoted his life to creating a better working environment for immigrant farm workers.

César Chávez was born on March 31, 1927, in Yuma, Arizona. His father was an immigrant farmer who lost his land due to a dishonest business deal. When Chávez was 11, his family moved to California, and lived in a barrio of San Jose known as Sal Si Puedes. They earned money picking fruit and vegetables on farms, moving frequently to find work. When they could, Chávez and his siblings attended school wherever they were living at the time. In fact, Chávez and his brother went to as many as 37 different schools, some of which were integrated. They heard many racist remarks, and were often punished for speaking Spanish at school.

After graduating from eighth grade, Chávez worked as a migrant farm worker. He then served in the U.S. Navy and married Helen Fabela. Together, they had eight children. While living in San Jose, California, Chávez met two people who greatly influenced his life: Father Donald McDonnell and Fred Ross. They discussed farm workers and strikes, and they believed people who worked together could make their communities better. Chávez had read about Ghandi's nonviolent protests and understood the value of education. He joined Ross's group, the Community Service Organization, and helped improve the lives of people in many California communities. He then went on to form the National Farm Worker's Association in 1962.

César Chávez, champion of farm laborers, in 1975, the year he led a 1,000-mile march to support union elections

©CSU Archives/Everett Collection Inc./Alamy Stock Photo

Through his determined leadership and nonviolent strikes, which included hunger strikes, Chávez brought attention to the poor treatment of farm workers, their low pay, and the dangers they faced working in fields sprayed with pesticides. Chávez's 36-day Fast for Life was completed in 1988, and was continued by many prominent actors and leaders.

César Chávez died peacefully in 1993. A few days later, he was honored by fellow farm workers, labor leaders, and family members in a large celebration. In 1994, President William Clinton awarded him the Presidential Medal of Freedom for facing discrimination with courage, and improving working conditions for farm laborers in California, Texas, Arizona, and Florida.

HISTORICAL THINKING

SUMMARIZE How did Chávez contribute to the farm labor movement during his lifetime?

_____

_____

_____

UNIT 7 · CHAPTER 19 LESSON 2.5
Urban Poverty

NATIONAL GEOGRAPHIC LEARNING

DOCUMENT-BASED QUESTION

Use the questions here to help you analyze the sources and write your paragraph.

DOCUMENT ONE: from *How the Other Half Lives*, by Jacob Riis, 1890

1A Why do you think Riis call tenements "the evil offspring of public neglect and private greed"?

_____

1B Constructed Response Why do you think tenements might have been a cause of "despair" for public health officials?

_____

DOCUMENT TWO: from *The Jungle*, by Upton Sinclair, 1906

2A In this passage, what is causing the "immense volumes of smoke" that Sinclair describes?

_____

2B Constructed Response How did Chicago appear to new immigrant workers in Sinclair's novel?

_____

DOCUMENT THREE: from *Twenty Years at Hull-House*, by Jane Addams, 1910

3A For an immigrant "straight from the fields of Germany," what practicalities does Addams touch on that would have been unfamiliar?

_____

3B Constructed Response What point do you think Addams is trying to make about the circumstances poor immigrants face?

_____

SYNTHESIZE & WRITE

What challenges did the urban poor encounter during the late 19th and early 20th centuries?

Topic Sentence: _____

_____

Your Paragraph: _____

_____

_____

_____

UNIT 7

CHAPTER 20 SECTION 1
Teddy Roosevelt and Progressivism

READING AND NOTE-TAKING

SEQUENCE EVENTS As you read Section 1, complete the Sequence Chain with details about how the United States started to change beginning in the 1890s.

Sequence Chain

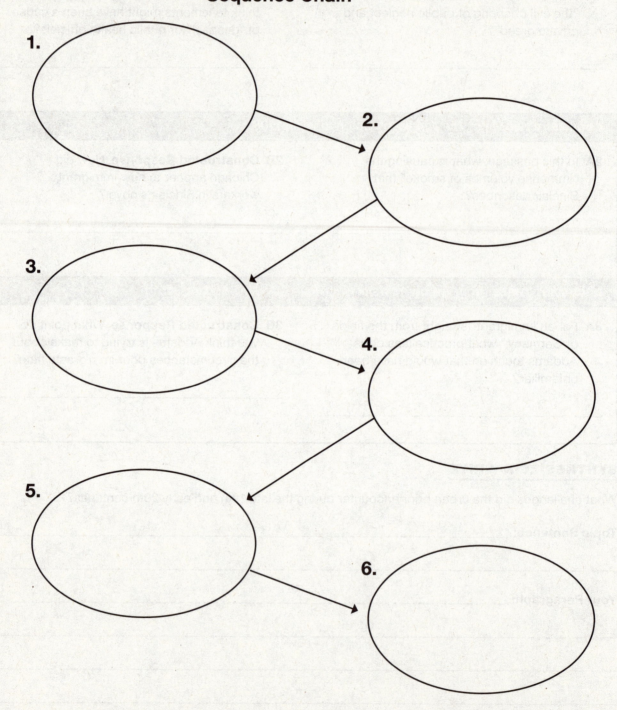

UNIT 7

CHAPTER 20 SECTION 1
Teddy Roosevelt and Progressivism *continued*

Sequence Chain

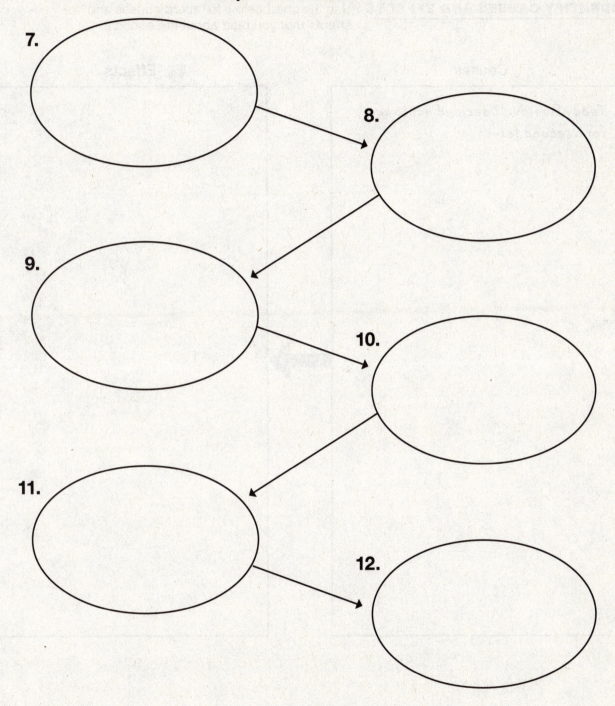

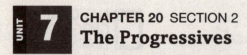

UNIT 7

CHAPTER 20 SECTION 2
The Progressives

NATIONAL GEOGRAPHIC LEARNING

READING AND NOTE-TAKING

IDENTIFY CAUSES AND EFFECTS   Use the chart below to record causes and effects that you read about in Section 2.

Causes	Effects
Teddy Roosevelt decided not to run for a second term.	

UNIT 7

CHAPTER 20 SECTION 2
The Progressives

READING AND NOTE-TAKING

IDENTIFY MAIN IDEA AND DETAILS Use a Main Idea and Details Web to organize your notes on the impact of modern technology.

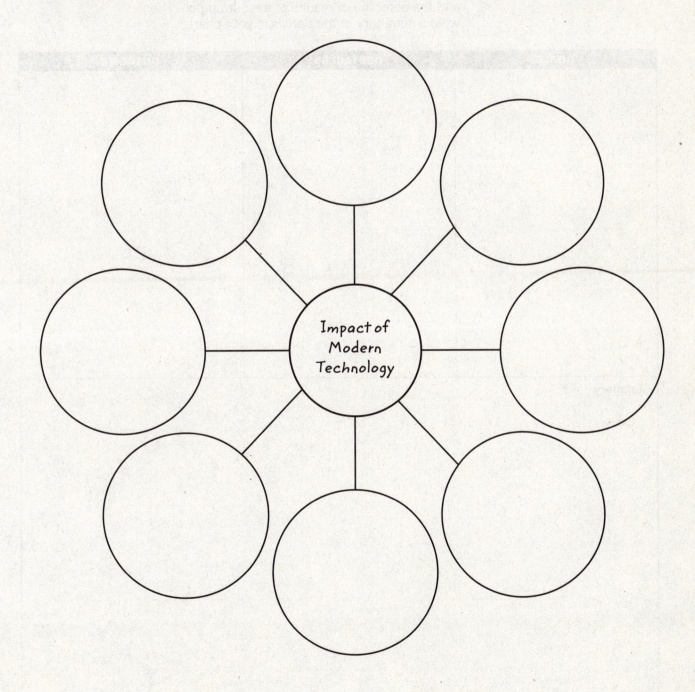

Impact of Modern Technology

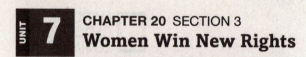

READING AND NOTE-TAKING

GOALS AND OUTCOMES As you read Section 3, record details about the goals of women, the obstacles that stood in their way, and the outcome or results of their struggles. Then write a summary of the details in your chart.

GOALS	OBSTACLES	OUTCOME

Summary

READING AND NOTE-TAKING

ANNOTATE A TIME LINE   After you read Section 3, consider the dates listed below. Review the text and identify one event for each year listed. Write a description of the event in the box provided.

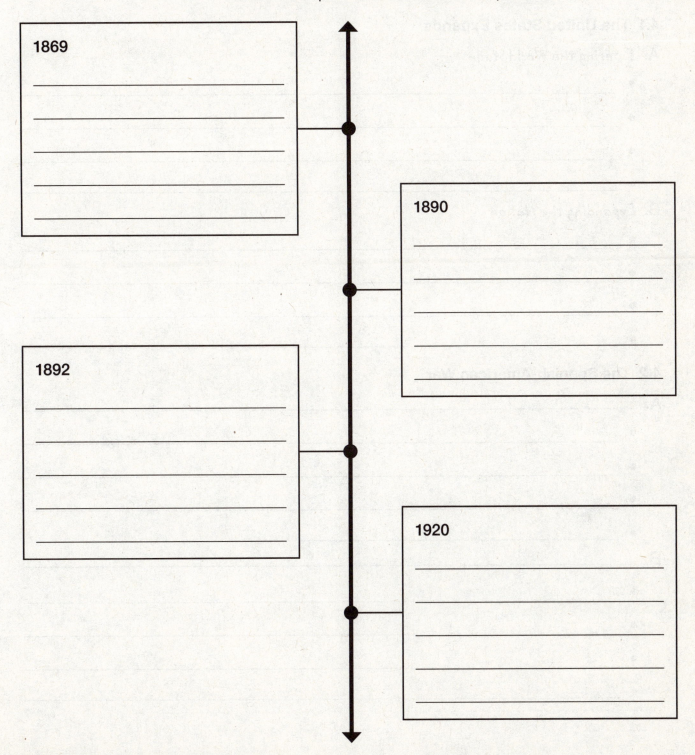

1869

1890

1892

1920

UNIT 7 CHAPTER 20 SECTION 4
America on the World Stage

READING AND NOTE-TAKING

OUTLINE AND TAKE NOTES As you read Section 4, take notes using the headings and subheadings as a starting point.

4.1 The United States Expands

A. *Entering the World Stage*

- _____
- _____
- _____
- _____

B. *Expanding the Nation*

- _____
- _____
- _____
- _____

4.2 The Spanish-American War

A. _____

- _____
- _____
- _____

B. _____

- _____
- _____
- _____
- _____

UNIT 7

CHAPTER 20 SECTION 4
America on the World Stage *continued*

NATIONAL GEOGRAPHIC LEARNING

4.3 The Filipino-American War

A. _____

- _____
- _____
- _____
- _____

B. _____

- _____
- _____
- _____
- _____

4.4 Involvement in Latin America and Asia

A. _____

- _____
- _____
- _____

B. _____

- _____
- _____
- _____
- _____

UNIT 7

CHAPTER 20 SECTION 1

Teddy Roosevelt and Progressivism

NATIONAL GEOGRAPHIC LEARNING

VOCABULARY PRACTICE

KEY VOCABULARY

- **commissioner** *n.* a government representative

- **conservation movement** *n.* a movement to promote the protection of natural resources and wildlife

- **direct primary election** *n.* an election in which members of a political party nominate candidates by a direct vote

- **initiative** (ih-NIH-shuh-tihv) *n.* a process by which regular citizens propose a law and require that fellow citizens vote on it

- **Meat Inspection Act** *n.* a 1906 law that sought to ensure the purity and safety of meat

DEFINITION CHART Complete a Definition Chart for the Key Vocabulary words. In the third column, illustrate the word. In the last column, use the word in a sentence.

WORD	DEFINITION	ILLUSTRATION	SENTENCE

UNIT 7
CHAPTER 20 SECTION 1
Teddy Roosevelt and Progressivism

VOCABULARY PRACTICE

KEY VOCABULARY

- **populism** *n.* the belief that common people, not the wealthy, should control their government

- **progressivism** *n.* a social movement that believed in equality for all people and called for people and the government to work together to bring about social change

- **Pure Food and Drug Act** *n.* a 1906 law that empowered the federal government to protect the quality, purity, and safety of foods and drugs

- **referendum** *n.* the practice of submitting a law directly to voters to accept or reject the law

- **Sherman Antitrust Act of 1890** *n.* a federal statute passed to prohibit monopolies

JOURNAL ENTRY Suppose you were living in the early 1900s. Write a journal entry explaining your opinion of the changes and ideas that are named by the Key Vocabulary words from Section 1. Use all the vocabulary words in your journal entry.

_____

_____

_____

_____

_____

_____

_____

_____

_____

_____

_____

_____

_____

_____

UNIT 7

CHAPTER 20 SECTION 2
The Progressives

NATIONAL GEOGRAPHIC LEARNING

VOCABULARY PRACTICE

KEY VOCABULARY

- **assembly line** *n.* a system in which workers stand in place as work passes from operation to operation in a direct line until the product is assembled

- **Clayton Antitrust Act** *n.* a 1914 law that described the illegality of trusts' unlawful business practices and closed the loopholes they used

- **Federal Reserve Act** *n.* the 1913 law that established the Federal Reserve Board, which oversaw 12 reserve banks; the banks would control the nation's flow of money

- **income tax** *n.* a tax on the income of an individual

FOUR-COLUMN CHART Complete the chart below for each Key Vocabulary word. In the last column, use the word in a sentence.

WORD	DEFINITION	IN YOUR OWN WORDS	SENTENCE

UNIT 7

CHAPTER 20 SECTION 2
The Progressives

NATIONAL GEOGRAPHIC LEARNING

VOCABULARY PRACTICE

KEY VOCABULARY

- **loophole** *n.* unclear language that allows people to get around laws and avoid obeying them

- **reserve bank** *n.* a bank that under the Federal Reserve Board's supervision, controls the nation's flow of money

- **scientific management** *n.* the process of studying individual people at work to determine the most efficient, most cost-effective way to do a job

DEFINITION TREE For each Key Vocabulary word, complete a Definition Tree. Write the definition on the top branch and then use each word in a sentence.

loophole

UNIT 7 — CHAPTER 20 SECTION 3
Women Win New Rights

VOCABULARY PRACTICE

KEY VOCABULARY

- **prohibition** *n*. the 18th Amendment to the Constitution banning the production, sale, importation, and transportation of liquor in the United States

- **teetotaler** (TEE-toh-tuh-lur) *n*. a person who does not drink alcoholic beverages

VOCABULARY Y-CHART Complete a Y-Chart to explore the meanings of the Key Vocabulary words *prohibition* and *teetotaler*.

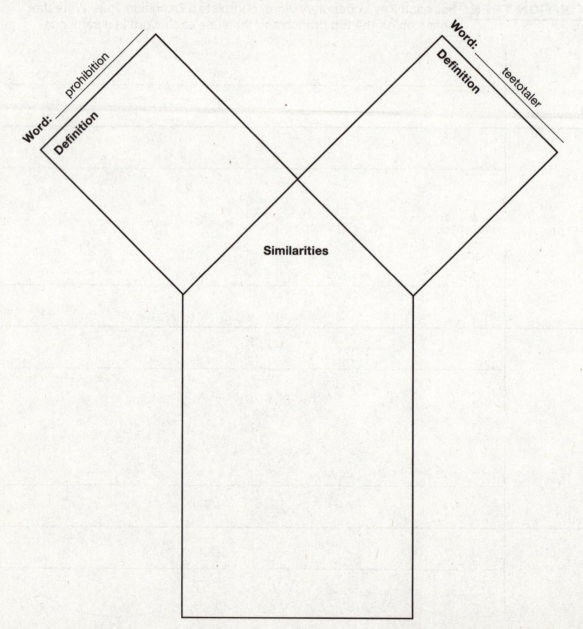

UNIT 7

CHAPTER 20 SECTION 3
Women Win New Rights

NATIONAL GEOGRAPHIC LEARNING

VOCABULARY PRACTICE

KEY VOCABULARY

- **lobbyist** *n.* a person who tries to persuade lawmakers to support particular laws and political ideas

- **social work** *n.* work aimed at improving the lives of others

- **suffragist** (SUHF-reh-jihst) *n.* a person who supports and fights for the right to vote, particularly a woman's right to vote

RELATED IDEA WEB Write one of the Key Vocabulary words inside a circle along with its definition in your own words. Then draw lines or arrows connecting the circles to show how the words are related, based on what you read in Section 3. Write your explanation of the connection next to the line or arrow.

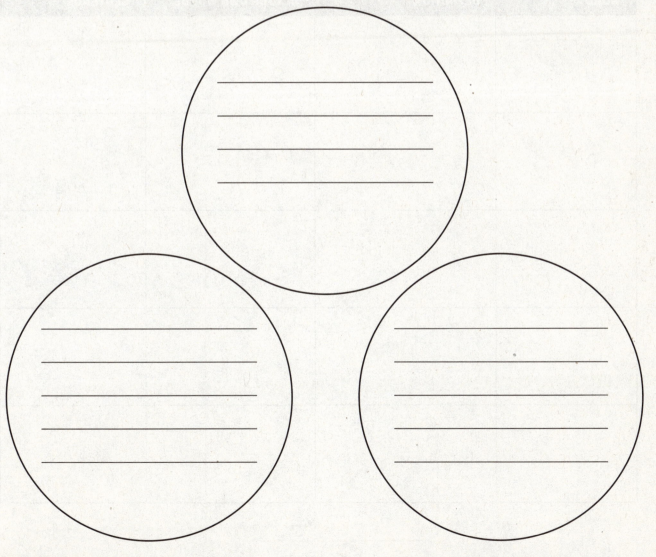

UNIT 7

CHAPTER 20 SECTION 4
America on the World Stage

VOCABULARY PRACTICE

KEY VOCABULARY

- **archipelago** (ar-keh-PEH-leh-go) *n.* a chain of islands

- **autonomy** *n.* self-rule

- **court-martial** *v.* to try a member of the armed services accused of offenses against military law

- **imperialism** *n.* a governmental system in which a stronger nation controls weaker nations or territories

- **isthmus** (IS-muhs) *n.* a narrow strip of land that connects two larger landmasses and separates two bodies of water

DEFINITION CHART   Complete the chart below for each Key Vocabulary word.
In the last column, use the word in a sentence.

WORD	DEFINITION	IN YOUR OWN WORDS	SENTENCE

UNIT 7 CHAPTER 20 SECTION 4
America on the World Stage

VOCABULARY PRACTICE

KEY VOCABULARY

- **Open Door Policy** *n.* the late 19th-century and early 20th-century policy calling for equal trading privileges for all nations with economic interests in China

- **Platt Amendment** *n.* a 1901 amendment to military legislation establishing the conditions by which the United States would withdraw from Cuba after the Spanish-American War but retain the right to intervene in Cuban affairs

- **Rough Riders** *n.* the untrained but tough group of cowboys, miners, police officers, and Native Americans who volunteered to be soldiers under the command of Theodore Roosevelt in the Spanish-American War

- **sphere of influence** *n.* a claim a country makes to be the exclusive influence on another country's political or economic activities

- **yellow journalism** *n.* a type of news reporting that exaggerates and dramatizes events, presenting readers with distorted views of the truth, in order to sell newspapers

THREE-COLUMN CHART Complete the chart for each of the five Key Vocabulary words. Write the word and its definition. Then provide a definition using your own words.

WORD	DEFINITION	IN MY OWN WORDS

AMERICAN VOICES
John Muir
1838–1914

Naturalist and Sierra Club president John Muir, c. 1909

"Only by going alone in silence, without baggage, can one truly get into the heart of the wilderness." — John Muir

Naturalist and writer John Muir championed the cause of environmental preservation and helped establish several national parks. He also founded the Sierra Club.

Born April 21, 1838, in Scotland, John Muir moved with his family to Wisconsin when he was 11 years old. John worked hard for his family, but when he had free time, he wandered the wilderness near his home. There he gained a love for the natural world.

As a young man, Muir nearly lost an eye during an industrial accident. He decided to quit his job and spend the rest of his life devoted to nature. He moved to California and traveled through Nevada, Oregon, Washington, and Alaska, savoring the wonders of the wild. During his travels, he came across large regions of land stripped completely of trees by logging companies. He saw polluted lakes and rivers and blasted hillsides left by mining companies stripping resources from the ground. He wrote newspaper articles to report what he had witnessed around the country.

Muir knew there needed to be regions of the country that no person or industry could legally exploit, or profit from. He pushed the government to create a conservation policy to protect wild lands. Muir published powerful conservation articles in *The Century* magazine. His writings helped spur Congress to create Yosemite National Park and Sequoia National Park in 1890. Muir also influenced the creation of the Petrified Forest and Grand Canyon National Park.

To continue the work he'd begun, Muir founded the Sierra Club, a group of conservationists, in 1892. He said he wanted to "do something for wildness and make the mountains glad." Soon after, Muir caught President Theodore Roosevelt's attention. In 1903, Roosevelt visited Muir in Yosemite National Park. For three days, they hiked, camped, and had campfire discussions. Muir's talks inspired Roosevelt, leading to the creation of multiple national parks and forests, bird sanctuaries, and wildlife refuges. Muir served as the Sierra Club's president until his death in 1914.

HISTORICAL THINKING

FORM AND SUPPORT OPINIONS How might the United States be different today if John Muir and others had not worked to protect wilderness areas? Use evidence from the passage to support your opinion.

_____

_____

AMERICAN VOICES
Woodrow Wilson
1856–1924

"The world must be made safe for democracy."
— Woodrow Wilson

The United States' 28th president, Woodrow Wilson, led the nation into World War I and created the League of Nations, the precursor to the United Nations.

Woodrow Wilson was born in Staunton, Virginia, on December 28, 1856. He did not learn to read until he was 10, which led many to believe he was dyslexic. With persistence, he became an excellent student. He graduated from the College of New Jersey, now Princeton University, and then studied law at the University of Virginia. He passed the bar in 1882 and returned to Princeton, where he taught for several years before becoming the university's president.

Wilson was strongly interested in studying and participating in government. In 1910, he was elected governor of New Jersey. Democratic leaders encouraged the popular governor to seek higher office. In 1912, he ran for and was elected 28th president of the United States.

In spite of complaints by some of his staff and the National Association for the Advancement of Colored People (NAACP), Wilson segregated the federal government. He claimed it was for the good of African Americans and would reduce friction between workers. He made one concession to the protests—he condemned lynching.

In 1914, World War I broke out in Europe. Having lived through the Civil War as a child, Wilson was not keen on the nation becoming involved in war again. Yet when Germany began sinking U.S. ships, he had little choice. Wilson sent U.S. troops overseas in 1917 to fight on the side of the Allies—France, Russia, and Britain—and on November 11, 1918, the war ended with an Allied victory. The devastation of the war troubled Wilson. He developed the idea for

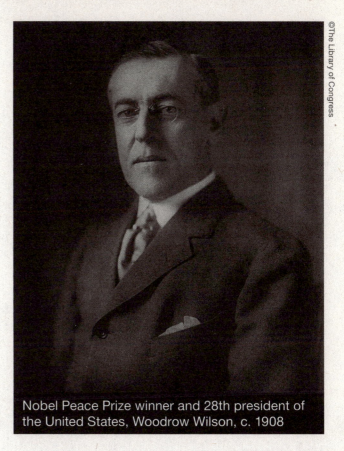

Nobel Peace Prize winner and 28th president of the United States, Woodrow Wilson, c. 1908

©The Library of Congress

the League of Nations, countries that would work together to negotiate disputes and seek peace. In 1919, Wilson won a Nobel Peace Prize for his efforts. Woodrow Wilson suffered a stroke in 1919 while still in office. He finished his second term as president in 1921 and died in 1924.

HISTORICAL THINKING

MAKE INFERENCES Why do you think Wilson's experience as a child during the Civil War made him uneasy about taking part in World War I?

_____

_____

SUMMARIZE What inspired Wilson to create the League of Nations and what was its purpose?

_____

_____

Social Studies Skills
Reading and Writing

SOCIAL STUDIES SKILLS — CHAPTER 1

Three Worlds Before 1500
READING LESSON

COMPARE AND CONTRAST

LEARNING THE STRATEGY

Suppose you were to meet someone from another part of the world. You might find that your lives have a number of similarities. For example, your new friend might also attend school every day, and hang out with friends in his or her spare time. You would also find that your lives were different in many ways, from the languages you speak to the kinds of food you eat. When you examine how things are alike, you are *comparing*. When you examine how things are different, you are *contrasting*.

A history text will often describe two or more cultures by comparing and contrasting them. When a text compares cultures, it presents information about their similarities and differences. However, when contrasting cultures, a text will present only the differences. To grasp a text's comparisons and contrasts, follow these steps.

Step 1 Determine what the subject of a passage or a paragraph is.

Step 2 In the passage, identify several specific features about the subjects that are being compared and those that are being contrasted.

Step 3 Search for clue words that indicate similarities (comparing). Common clue words include *similarly, also, in addition,* and *both.*

Step 4 Search for clue words that indicate differences (contrasting). Common clue words include *in contrast, unlike, on the other hand,* and *however.*

GUIDED MODEL

(A) A Split Between Protestants and Catholics Around the time of the Renaissance, the Catholic Church began to lose some of its power. Some members charged the church with corruption and called for reform. The gradual progression toward change within the church eventually led to the **Reformation**, a split from the Catholic Church that took place in the early 16ᵗʰ century. **(B) Martin Luther**, a German pastor and university professor, led this movement. **(D)** He believed biblical scripture was more important than the pope's authority. **(D)** He also believed that Christians achieved God's favor through faith, rather than by doing good deeds. Luther was eventually excommunicated, or expelled, from the Catholic Church for his teachings.

Followers of the Reformation became known as Protestants, **(C)** and the church split between Protestants and Catholics. Over time, many different Protestant churches, called denominations, developed, each with its own set of beliefs within the framework of Christianity.

Step 1 Determine the subject.

   (A) The subject is a split between Protestants and Catholics

Step 2 Identify the features being compared and contrasted.

   (B) The features are the beliefs of Martin Luther and the beliefs of the Catholic Church.

Step 3 Look for clue words that indicate similarities.

   SIMILARITIES (C) Both fell within the framework of Christianity.

Step 4 Look for clue words that indicate differences.

   DIFFERENCES (D) Unlike Catholics, Luther believed biblical scripture was more important than the pope's authority. He also believed Christians achieved God's favor through faith, **rather than** by doing good.

TIP A Y-Notes Chart is a useful graphic organizer for comparing two topics. List the differences of each topic in the branches, and the similarities in the straight section.

SOCIAL STUDIES SKILLS Continued

NATIONAL GEOGRAPHIC LEARNING

APPLYING THE STRATEGY

GETTING STARTED Now look at how information is compared and contrasted in Lesson 1.3, "Eastern American Cultures," in Chapter 1. As you read the lesson, use the graphic organizer below to take notes on the similarities and differences between the Mound Builders of the Midwest and eastern regions, and the people of the Woodlands. This will help you gain a deeper understanding of how region and climate affected the way people lived. Be sure to fill out the diagram in your own words. To get you started, one similarity has been filled in for you.

COOPERATIVE OPTION You may wish to work with a partner in your class to review the lesson and complete the graphic organizer.

TAKING NOTES

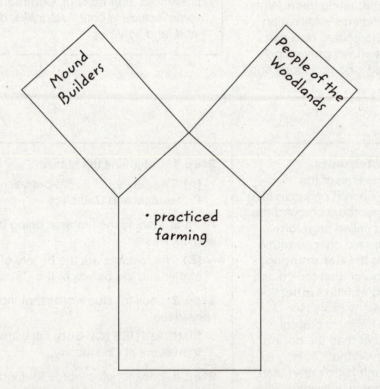

THINK AND DISCUSS

1. How were the Mound Builders and Woodlands people similar?

2. How were the Mound Builders and Woodlands people different?

3. After comparing and contrasting, what do you think was the most important difference between the Mound Builders and the Woodlands people?

 **Three Worlds Before 1500**

SOCIAL STUDIES SKILLS — CHAPTER 1

WRITING LESSON

WRITE AN ARGUMENT

LEARNING THE STRATEGY

Suppose you are participating in a class debate about the history of the kingdom of Mali. You must convince the other side that Mansa Musa was the most important of Mali's rulers. To make your case, you would write an argument. In an **argument**, you make a statement, or *claim*, about a topic or an issue.

To support your claim, you would provide reasons and evidence that show your claim to be true. Common types of evidence are facts, statistics, quotations, and examples. You would want to organize your evidence logically, and be sure it came from a credible, or believable, source.

Finally, you would have to anticipate the reader's counter-argument and write a *response* to it, explaining why it is not correct.

Step 1 Collect information and data about your topic and decide what your claim will be.

Step 2 Write at least three reasons that support your claim. For each reason, list at least one piece of evidence that backs up the reason.

Step 3 Anticipate an argument that could be made against your claim, and write a response to that argument.

Step 4 Read your draft. Try to read it from the perspective of someone who is undecided on the issue. Then revise your argument until it is as logical and persuasive as possible.

GUIDED MODEL

Mansa Musa: The Greatest of Mali's Rulers

(A) The great Sundiata Keita united Mali under one kingdom and brought peace to the land, but Mansa Musa was truly Mali's most important ruler. **(B)** One reason Mansa Musa's reign stands out is his journey to Mecca in 1324. Many rulers might have traveled on conquering missions, but Musa traveled in the service of faith and learning. **(B)** Secondly, the generosity he displayed while on his pilgrimage helped to establish Mali as a trading empire. **(B)** Finally, unlike his predecessor, Mansa Musa worked to bring knowledge and culture to his kingdom.

(C) Of course, Mansa Musa could not have ruled Mali at all, if Sundiata Keita had not founded the kingdom in the first place. However, it was Mansa Musa's leadership that brought word of Mali's wealth and power to the rest of the world.

Step 1 Decide what your claim will be.

  (A) The writer claims that Mansa Musa was Mali's most important ruler.

Step 2 Write at least three reasons that support your claim.

  (B) The writer lists three reasons that support the claim and backs up each one with one piece of evidence.

Step 3 Anticipate an argument.

  (C) The writer anticipates an objection and responds to it.

TIP An Argument Chart can help you organize your ideas and evidence. In the chart, write your viewpoints, or claims, the evidence that supports them, and possible opposing viewpoints.

SOCIAL STUDIES SKILLS Continued

NATIONAL GEOGRAPHIC LEARNING

APPLYING THE STRATEGY

GETTING STARTED Now write your own argument. In the "Connect to Your Life" section of the Chapter Review, you are asked to decide whether or not modern-day trade has the same cultural impact that it had 600 or more years ago, and write an essay outlining your argument. Use the steps explained in this lesson and in the Argument Chart below to plan your argument. Begin by filling out the Argument Chart: record your viewpoints, support, and opposing viewpoints. Then, use your notes to guide you as you draft your essay.

COOPERATIVE OPTION Work with a partner to complete an Argument Chart. Discuss your claim, the reasons and evidence you might use to support it, and how you would respond to any counter-arguments others might make. Then, fill out the chart and use it to organize your essay.

TAKING NOTES

My Claim

↓

My Reasons and Evidence

1.

2.

3.

↓

Counter-argument and My Response

THINK AND DISCUSS

1. How did you choose which reasons and evidence to use to support your claim?

2. What counter-argument did you respond to in your essay, and why?

3. What understanding about the impact of trade now and in the past did you gain by writing the argument?

Name	Class	Date

SOCIAL STUDIES SKILLS | CHAPTER 2

European Exploration of the Americas
READING LESSON

NATIONAL GEOGRAPHIC LEARNING

DRAW CONCLUSIONS

LEARNING THE STRATEGY

Suppose you find a backpack in the school library. It doesn't have a name on it, but inside it you find a towel and a pair of goggles. You can probably assume that the backpack's owner is a swimmer. Since the backpack is at school, you conclude that it belongs to someone on the swim team. You decide to bring it to the swim coach.

You probably **draw conclusions** like this all the time. Historians also draw conclusions about the past, based on artifacts, texts, and other sources. When you draw conclusions about a text, you use facts and evidence from the text in order to make a statement about its larger meaning. Drawing conclusions about a text can deepen your understanding of the text as a whole. Follow these steps to draw conclusions about a text.

> **Step 1** Read the text closely to identify the facts.
>
> **Step 2** Make educated guesses based on the facts.
>
> **Step 3** Use the educated guesses you've made to draw conclusions about the facts.

GUIDED MODEL

Queen Elizabeth I and Spain

Spain had a head start on settling North America, but England started to catch up, largely because of **Queen Elizabeth I. (A)** The Protestant queen ascended to the English throne in 1558. She saw Spain as a threat to England's independence. **(A)** Her brother-in-law, Philip II of Spain, like many Catholics, wished to see Elizabeth unseated from the throne. **(A)** He supported Mary, Queen of Scots, Elizabeth's Catholic cousin and heir to the English throne. **(A)** But after being implicated in a plot to take Elizabeth's life, Mary was arrested, tried, and beheaded for conspiracy.

Step 1 Identify the facts in the text.

FACTS (A) Elizabeth I was a Protestant queen. Her brother-in-law, Philip II of Spain was a Catholic, and many Catholics did not want Elizabeth to be queen. Philip II supported Mary, Queen of Scots, who was eventually beheaded for attempting to plot against Elizabeth's life.

Step 2 Make educated guesses based on the facts.

EDUCATED GUESSES The Spanish king opposed Elizabeth and supported Mary, Queen of Scots, so he may have supported Mary's attempt on Elizabeth's life, too.

Step 3 Use the educated guesses you've made to draw a conclusion.

CONCLUSIONS Elizabeth may have been right to see Spain as a threat to her and to England's independence.

TIP Use a diagram to organize the evidence you find in a text. The diagram can help you clarify your thinking as you draw conclusions about a text.

315

SOCIAL STUDIES SKILLS Continued

NATIONAL
GEOGRAPHIC
LEARNING

APPLYING THE STRATEGY

GETTING STARTED Now draw conclusions as you read Lesson 1.4, "Conquistadors in the North," in Chapter 2. As you read the lesson, use the graphic organizer to take notes on the evidence you find and the conclusions you draw. Drawing conclusions about the text will deepen your understanding of the challenges faced by some conquistadors in the Americas. To get you started, one piece of evidence has been filled in for you.

COOPERATIVE OPTION You may wish to work with a partner to review the lesson and complete the graphic organizer.

TAKING NOTES

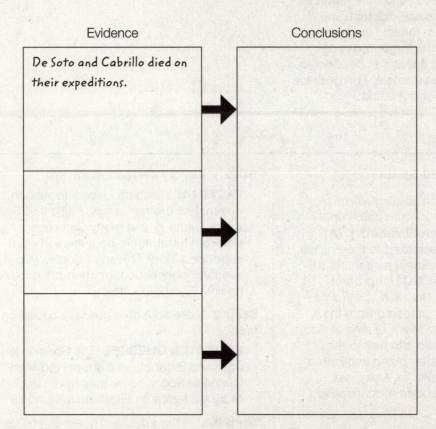

Evidence

De Soto and Cabrillo died on their expeditions.

Conclusions

THINK AND DISCUSS

1. Why might people have chosen to become conquistadors?

2. Do you think the conquistadors had realistic expectations about North America?

3. Were the conquistadors' explorations successful in any ways? Explain.

SOCIAL STUDIES SKILLS CHAPTER 2

European Exploration of the Americas
WRITING LESSON

NATIONAL GEOGRAPHIC LEARNING

WRITE AN EXPLANATION

LEARNING THE STRATEGY

When you write an **explanation**, you give readers information about a topic. You provide facts and examples to help them understand the topic more fully. To write an explanation, first select a topic. Then provide details to support your ideas. The most common types of supporting details are facts, examples, statistics, quotations, expert opinions, and personal experience.

After you have selected your supporting details, you need to arrange them in a logical order. If you are describing something that took place over a period of time, it makes sense to arrange your details chronologically, or in the order they took place. If you're writing a how-to article, you could arrange the steps sequentially: one step at a time from first to last. If you are writing about a general topic, you might group your information by category.

Step 1 Select a topic you would like to inform your readers about and gather detailed information about it.

Step 2 Write a sentence that introduces and states your topic. This is your main idea.

Step 3 Include at least three details that provide information on your topic.

Step 4 Organize your details either chronologically, step-by-step, or by category.

Step 5 Write a concluding statement about your topic that restates the main idea in a different way.

GUIDED MODEL

(A) The Triangular Trade
(B) For about 400 years, Europeans brought enslaved Africans to the Americas in chains, under a system called the Triangular Trade. **(C)** West African slave traders raided villages and brought back captured Africans, whom they sold to European traders in exchange for goods.

(D) In the next "leg" of the triangle, the enslaved captives would be forced onto ships and sailed across the Atlantic, in a horrifying journey called the Middle Passage. Many would die along the way, as a result of disease, abuse, or overcrowding.

Finally, when they arrived in the Americas the captured people would again be sold—this time in exchange for goods from the Americas, bound for Europe. **(E)** From the 1500s to the 1800s, millions of people were torn from their homelands in this way; many of them would never be free again.

Step 1 Select a topic.

　(A) The topic is the international slave trade sometimes called the Triangular Trade.

Step 2 Write a sentence that introduces and states your topic.

　(B) This sentence states the topic.

Step 3 Include at least three details that provide information on your topic.

　(C) The writer includes details about the topic.

Step 4 Organize your details either chronologically, step-by-step, or by category.

　(D) The writer organizes the details step-by-step.

Step 5 Write a concluding sentence.

　(E) The writer concludes by stating the main idea again but in a different way.

　TIP Use a graphic organizer to plan and organize your explanation. For example, if you are going to explain how two or things are connected, consider organizing your ideas in a table.

SOCIAL STUDIES SKILLS Continued

NATIONAL GEOGRAPHIC LEARNING

APPLYING THE STRATEGY

GETTING STARTED Now write your own explanation. In the "Connect to Your Life" section in the Chapter Review, you are asked to write a paragraph explaining a connection between a time when you first experienced something new and a European sailor's first encounter with some Native Americans. Use the steps explained in this lesson and in the graphic organizer below to plan your explanation. The graphic will help you organize the details that connect your experience to that of the sailor. After you have organized your information, use your notes to help you draft your paragraph.

COOPERATIVE OPTION After you have written your draft, show it to a partner in your class and ask for suggestions on ways to improve it. You may also offer suggestions for your partner's draft. Remember to be positive and constructive.

TAKING NOTES

	Sailor's Experience	My Experience	Connections
Detail 1			
Detail 2			
Detail 3			

THINK AND DISCUSS

1. How did you decide which of your own experiences to describe?

2. Does your experience have more similarities to the sailor's experience, or more differences?

3. What understanding about the experiences of European explorers in the Americas did you gain by writing this explanation?

SOCIAL STUDIES SKILLS **CHAPTER 3** **The Thirteen Colonies**
READING LESSON

NATIONAL GEOGRAPHIC LEARNING

MAKE INFERENCES

LEARNING THE STRATEGY

Think about a time you tried to find something you had lost. You may have thought about the last time you had the object with you and retraced your steps in search of it. Or perhaps you searched, based on your habits, in all the places you might have put the object. You used what you knew about yourself to help you figure out where the thing might be.

In a similar way, historians use what they already know to **make inferences** about, or to figure out the meaning of, past events. This process helps historians analyze events. Follow these steps to make inferences and figure out the meaning of a text.

Step 1 Read the text looking for facts and ideas.

Step 2 Think about what the writer does not say but wants you to understand. Ask yourself: *How do these facts connect with what I already know? How does this information help me understand the text?*

Step 3 Reread the text and use what you know to make an inference.

GUIDED MODEL

Uncovering Jamestown

About all William Kelso had to go on were some historical accounts and documents, including a roughly drawn Spanish map from 1608 showing the triangular James Fort. **(A)** But he also knew that the only aboveground ruins that had survived in Jamestown were parts of a church tower. **(B)** Kelso reasoned that the settlers would have built the fort near the church, so he began there.

Step 1 Identify facts stated in the text.

FACT (A) Kelso knew that parts of a church tower were the only surviving aboveground ruins in Jamestown.

Step 2 Think about what the writer does not say but wants you to understand.

UNSTATED (B) The writer doesn't explain why Kelso thought the settlers would have built their fort near the church, but I know that religion was important in England, where the settlers were from.

Step 3 Make an inference.

INFERENCE Kelso looked for the fort near the church tower because he knew that religion was an important part of the settlers' lives and guessed they would place buildings related to other important aspects nearby.

TIP Use an Inference Equation chart to keep track of inferences. Write down what the text says in the first column. Write down what you already know in the second column. Write your inferences in the third column. Keep in mind that you can base inferences on information from visuals, as well as on facts or opinions from the text.

SOCIAL STUDIES SKILLS Continued

NATIONAL
GEOGRAPHIC
LEARNING

APPLYING THE STRATEGY

GETTING STARTED Now make inferences as you read Lesson 1.1, "Colonizing Virginia," in Chapter 3. As you read the lesson, use the graphic organizer below to take notes on the inferences you make. Making inferences about the text will help you better understand how Virginia's first colonists finally achieved success in their new home. One row is filled in to help you get started.

COOPERATIVE OPTION You may wish to work with a partner in your class to review the lesson and complete the graphic organizer.

TAKING NOTES

What Text Says +	What I Know =	Inference
The settlers were interested in searching for gold.	Early explorers found gold in the Americas.	The settlers expected to find gold in Virginia.

THINK AND DISCUSS

1. What does the fact that the settlers searched for gold rather than planting crops suggest that they and the Virginia Company saw as the main reason for settling Jamestown?

2. Why did many of Jamestown's settlers die from diseases?

3. How did the geography of Jamestown support the eventual success of the colony?

SOCIAL STUDIES SKILLS — CHAPTER 3

The Thirteen Colonies
WRITING LESSON

NATIONAL GEOGRAPHIC LEARNING

WRITE AN INFORMATIVE TEXT

LEARNING THE STRATEGY

When you write an informative text, you tell readers about a topic in an objective way. In other words, you inform readers without interjecting your own opinions. Suppose you want to write an informative text about the life of a colonist. You would begin by introducing the topic. For example, you might say, "John Alden's life story provides a typical example of the hardships and triumphs of the early colonists."

Next, include specific details to support the main idea. For example, you might note that John Alden survived the voyage to America and the difficult first winter after his arrival. You would continue to support the main idea by providing other examples. Finally, you would end the your informative text with a concluding sentence that summarizes or restates the main idea in a different way.

Step 1 Select a topic you would like to inform your readers about and gather detailed information about it.

Step 2 Write a sentence that introduces and states your topic. This is your main idea.

Step 3 Include at least three details that provide information on your topic.

Step 4 Write a conclusion that restates the main idea in a different way.

GUIDED MODEL

(A) John Alden Biographical Sketch
(B) John Alden's life story provides a typical example of the hardships and triumphs of the early colonists. **(C)** Hired as a cooper, or barrel maker, aboard the *Mayflower*, Alden endured the difficult voyage to America.

(C) Alden survived the terrible first winter in Plymouth, during which many other colonists, including the entire family of his future wife Priscilla Mullins, died. Alden and Mullins married around 1623 and eventually had ten children.

(C) Alden became a prominent member of the Massachusetts government, serving as deputy governor and treasurer. **(C)** He also helped found the town of Duxbury, where he built a house. He owned several parcels of land there that he later distributed to his children.

(D) Learning about Alden's life helps people understand how early colonists overcame challenges and founded successful colonies in America.

Step 1 Select a topic.
  (A) The topic is John Alden.

Step 2 Write a sentence that introduces and states the main idea.
  (B) This sentence states the main idea.

Step 3 Include at least three details that provide information on your topic.
  (C) The writer includes details on the topic.

Step 4 Write a concluding sentence.
  (D) The writer concludes by stating the main idea again but in a different way.

TIP When you research, gather more information than you need. Then choose the most interesting information to include in your text.

SOCIAL STUDIES SKILLS Continued

APPLYING THE STRATEGY

GETTING STARTED Now write your own informative text. In the "Connect to Your Life" section of the Chapter Review, you are asked to write a paragraph that connects colonists who came to America with a present-day group of people who moved to a new place by analyzing reasons why each group moved. Use the graphic organizer below to plan your informative text. The graphic organizer will help you organize your notes. After you have completed the graphic organizer, use the steps explained in this lesson to write your draft.

COOPERATIVE OPTION Exchange completed drafts with a partner in your class. Offer each other suggestions on ways to improve the drafts. Remember to be positive and constructive.

TAKING NOTES

GROUPS	REASONS FOR MOVING

THINK AND DISCUSS

1. How did you decide which group of present-day people to connect to the colonists?

2. How did you determine the reasons why that group moved to a new place?

3. What insights about the reasons people leave their homelands did you gain by writing this paragraph?

SOCIAL STUDIES SKILLS | **CHAPTER 4** | **Colonial Development**
READING LESSON

NATIONAL GEOGRAPHIC LEARNING

IDENTIFY MAIN IDEAS AND DETAILS

LEARNING THE STRATEGY

Suppose you want to tell a friend about a movie you saw recently. You would probably describe the central idea of the movie and add a few important or especially interesting details.

In a text, the **main idea** is the most important or central idea. Main ideas are in everything you read: paragraphs, passages, chapters, and books. Sometimes the main idea is conveyed in a sentence, but other times it may just be implied. The **supporting details** are facts that support the main idea. If the main idea is implied, the supporting details give clues about what the main idea is. Identifying a main idea and its supporting details will help you understand a text more fully. It may also help you identify the author's purpose or point of view. To find the main idea and details of a paragraph, follow these steps.

Step 1 Look for the main idea in the first and last sentences of a paragraph. If the main idea is not clearly stated, look for details that give you clues about what the main idea is.

Step 2 Find the supporting details in the paragraph. These are facts, statistics, ideas, examples, quotations, and other specific items that clarify the main idea. If the main idea is in the first sentence, the supporting details follow it. If the main idea is stated in the last sentence, the supporting details come before it.

GUIDED MODEL

Backcountry Farmers

(A) Backcountry farmers learned to be self-sufficient. **(B)** They used one of the most plentiful natural resources of this region—timber—to build simple log cabins. **(B)** They hunted and raised enough crops and livestock to feed their families. **(B)** Women in the backcountry worked in the home, the fields, and the wild. Many of them carried guns. **(B)** Also, unlike many people in the Southern Colonies, most of the immigrants living in the backcountry didn't rely on slaves.

Step 1 Find the main idea in the first or last sentence.

   MAIN IDEA (A) Backcountry farmers learned to be self-sufficient.

Step 2 Find the supporting details in the paragraph.

   DETAIL (B) They used timber to build log cabins.

   DETAIL (B) They hunted and raised food for their families.

   DETAIL (B) Women of the backcountry worked.

   DETAIL (B) Backcountry immigrants did not rely on slaves.

   TIP Look for clues that indicate how a text presents information. For example, the word *unlike* indicates a comparison.

SOCIAL STUDIES SKILLS Continued

APPLYING THE STRATEGY

GETTING STARTED Now identify the main idea and the supporting details in Lesson 4.3, "Rights in England and the Colonies." Read the last paragraph under "Colonial Assemblies" and use the graphic organizer below to record its main idea and supporting details. This will help you gain a deeper understanding of the relationship between England and the colonies. To get you started, the main idea is filled in.

COOPERATIVE OPTION You may wish to work with a partner in your class to review the paragraph and complete the graphic organizer.

TAKING NOTES

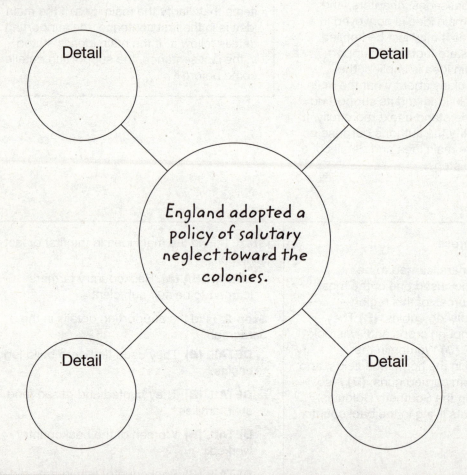

Detail

Detail

England adopted a policy of salutary neglect toward the colonies.

Detail

Detail

THINK AND DISCUSS

1. What information do the details give to support the main idea of the text?

2. How do the details of the text help you understand the meaning of the term *salutary neglect*?

3. What aspects of the details reveal the colonists' views about England's policy of salutary neglect?

SOCIAL STUDIES SKILLS | **CHAPTER 4** | **Colonial Development**
WRITING LESSON

NATIONAL GEOGRAPHIC LEARNING

WRITE A NARRATIVE

LEARNING THE STRATEGY

A historical **narrative** is an account or story of events or experiences. Narratives may be fictional, or made up, or they may be based on facts supported by evidence from informational texts.

All narratives share certain characteristics, including a specific setting, or time and place. The narration of experiences or events usually follows a logical sequence, which provides clear and coherent writing. When they are appropriate to the style and purpose of the narrative, descriptive details, including sensory details that appeal to sight, sound, touch, taste, and smell, can help bring events and people to life for the audience.

Before writing a narrative, decide which point of view to use. Most narratives are written from a first-person or a third-person point of view.

Step 1 Identify the topic of your narrative and gather facts about its events, people, and places,

Step 2 Determine the setting and point of view of your narrative.

Step 3 Recount events in logical sequence.

Step 4 Use descriptive details to help bring your narrative to life.

GUIDED MODEL

(A) Arrival in Philadelphia, 1750
(B) After a long and treacherous voyage, our ship arrived at Philadelphia in the spring of 1750. The sights and sounds of the harbor were overwhelming. Colorful flags of trade ships from Holland, England, Spain, and the West Indies fluttered from their tall masts as their captains shouted orders to unload cargoes of spices, rum, linens, and fine porcelains. Sailors spoke to each other in languages I did not understand as they loaded barrels of flour, corn, and tobacco onto outgoing ships headed for distant ports.

(C) Broad streets laid out in a regular grid made it easy to explore the city that would be my new home. I counted several churches and meeting houses where people could worship as they pleased. I saw a library, a hospital, and even a fire company, which consisted of volunteers who put out fires in the city!

(D) Tall, brick rowhouses lined the street I was seeking. In my excitement at finding the place where I would live, I nearly stumbled as my boots sank into the muddy, unpaved road. No place is without problems! Yet it seemed incredible that in only 80 years Philadelphia had risen from a wilderness to become a prosperous city.

Step 1 Identify the topic of your narrative.

  (A) The writer is narrating an immigrant's arrival in the colonies.

Step 2 Determine the setting and point of view of your narrative.

  (B) The narrative is set in Philadelphia in 1750. The writer is using a first-person point of view.

Step 3 Recount events in a logical sequence.

  (C) The writer guides readers through the city in a logical sequence.

Step 4 Use descriptive details to help bring your narrative to life.

  (D) The writer uses sensory details to describe the sights and sounds of the city as well as the feeling of walking through mud.

  TIP Use an outline to help you organize the ideas in your narrative and produce clear and coherent writing.

SOCIAL STUDIES SKILLS Continued

NATIONAL GEOGRAPHIC LEARNING

APPLYING THE STRATEGY

GETTING STARTED Now write your own narrative. In the "Connect to Your Life" section of the Chapter Review, you are asked to write a paragraph connecting a modern student's experiences of moving to a new place with a colonist's experience. Use the steps explained in this lesson and the graphic organizer below to develop your narrative. Begin by creating an outline to plan your narrative. Write down key ideas after the Roman numerals in the outline. Write details after the letters. Draw evidence from informational texts to support the historical aspects of your narrative. Follow your outline as you draft your narrative. Be sure to choose descriptive details that help bring your writing to life.

COOPERATIVE OPTION After you have written your draft, exchange it with a partner in your class. Offer each other suggestions to improve the drafts. Remember to be positive and constructive.

TAKING NOTES

I. _____

    A. _____

    B. _____

II. _____

    A. _____

    B. _____

III. _____

    A. _____

    B. _____

THINK AND DISCUSS

1. How did using an outline help you create a clear and coherent narrative?

2. How did you use evidence from informational texts to support the ideas in your narrative?

3. How did your choice of point of view affect your narrative?

SOCIAL STUDIES SKILLS — CHAPTER 5

The Road to Revolution
READING LESSON

NATIONAL GEOGRAPHIC LEARNING

ANALYZE CAUSE AND EFFECT

LEARNING THE STRATEGY

Think about what happens when you heat a pot of water. The water boils. These events show **cause and effect**. Heating the water is a cause. A **cause** is an event, action, or condition that makes something else happen. The action of heating the water causes the water to boil. The water boiling is the effect of heating the water. An **effect** is an event that results from a cause.

Historians analyze cause and effect to figure out why events happened. They consider how an event led to changes over time. One cause can create several effects, or one effect may have more than one cause. A cause may be an event or an action. It may also be a condition, or a state of being. Follow these steps to figure out cause-and-effect relationships.

Step 1 Determine the cause of an event. Look for clue words that show cause, such as *because*, *due to*, *since*, and *therefore*.

Step 2 Determine the effect that results from the cause. Look for clue words such as *led to*, *consequently*, and *as a result*.

Step 3 Look for a chain of causes and effects. An effect may be the cause of another action or event.

GUIDED MODEL

PROBLEMS ARISE

(A) Concerned about the high cost of the French and Indian War, **(B)** the king was eager to limit contact between the Native Americans and the colonists in order to keep the peace.

(C) As you have read, the king issued a law requiring colonists to stay east of a line drawn on a map along the crest of the Appalachian Mountains. This law was called the Proclamation of 1763. Settlers in the western areas objected to the proclamation. They felt the king was restricting their freedom to expand colonial territories westward.

(C) Soon, colonists along the eastern coast also found themselves frustrated by laws they found oppressive. After the war, many British soldiers were moved into port cities such as New York and Boston to help enforce laws. In 1765, the British Parliament passed the Quartering Act. The Quartering Act required colonists to provide housing for British soldiers. If a city did not have barracks to house the soldiers, the men were housed in local inns, homes, and stables, or vacant houses or barns.

Step 1 Determine the Cause

CAUSE (A) The cause is the French and Indian War.

Step 2 Determine the Effect

EFFECT (B) The British increased control over the colonies.

Step 3 Look for a chain of causes and effects

CAUSES/EFFECTS (C) Because of the war, the British Empire found itself in debt. This led to the desire to increase control over the colonies. The passage of the Proclamation of 1763, the Sugar Act, and the Quartering Act caused frustration to grow throughout the colonies.

TIP Test whether events have a cause-and-effect relationship by using this construction: "Because [insert cause], [insert effect] happened." If the construction does not work, one event did not lead to the other.

SOCIAL STUDIES SKILLS Continued

NATIONAL GEOGRAPHIC LEARNING

APPLYING THE STRATEGY

GETTING STARTED Now practice analyzing cause and effect in Lesson 2.1, "The Townshend Acts" and "The Colonists React" in Chapter 5. Use your analysis of cause and effect to deepen your understanding of the effects of the Townshend Acts. Use the graphic organizer below to take notes on the text. One square is filled in for you to help you get started.

COOPERATIVE OPTION You may wish to work with a partner in your class to review the lesson and complete the graphic organizer.

TAKING NOTES

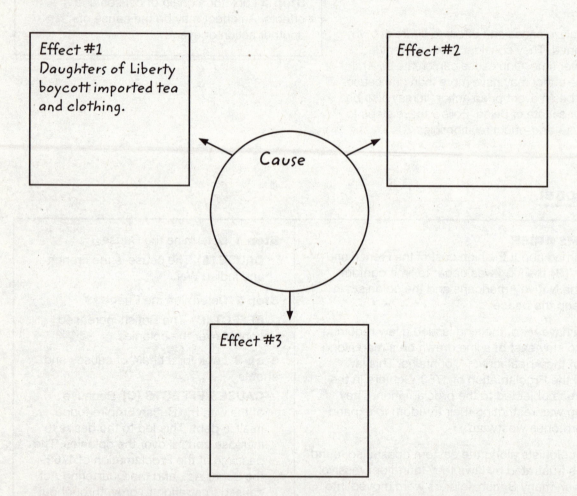

Effect #1
Daughters of Liberty boycott imported tea and clothing.

Effect #2

Cause

Effect #3

THINK AND DISCUSS

1. Why were the Townshend Acts upsetting to the colonists?

2. What influenced the colonists to protest?

3. How did the Great Awakening push the colonists toward rebellion and independence?

SOCIAL STUDIES SKILLS | **CHAPTER 5** | **The Road to Revolution**
WRITING LESSON

WRITE A NARRATIVE

LEARNING THE STRATEGY

A history text usually contains **narrative** accounts of events. A narrative is an account, or story of events or experiences. Narratives may be fictional, or made up, or they may be factual.

All narratives share certain characteristics, including a specific setting, or time and place. The events in a narrative usually follow a logical sequence, or order. Descriptive details, such as sensory details, help bring events and people to life. Sensory details are details that appeal to sight, sound, touch, taste, and smell.

Before writing a narrative, you should decide what point of view you will use. Most narratives are written from either a first-person or third-person point of view.

To write a historical narrative, follow these steps.

> **Step 1** Identify the topic of your narrative and gather facts about its events, people, and places.
>
> **Step 2** Determine the setting and point of view of your narrative.
>
> **Step 3** Recount events in a logical sequence.
>
> **Step 4** Use descriptive details to help bring your narrative to life.

GUIDED MODEL

(A) The Day of the Tea Party

(B) Life isn't easy under the tyrant King George: first there was the Proclamation of 1763, then the Sugar and Currency Acts, and now the Tea Act—the worst of them all. The patriotic people are fed up and tonight, the Sons of Liberty will get their revenge.

(C) Earlier, as I made my way down the street, the signs of protest were everywhere; **(D)** the salt stained wooden boats floated in the harbor and were filled with the tea which we refused to allow to be unloaded. This tea would be our target.

When I arrived home just before nightfall, I disguised myself in the costume of a Native American and **(D)** put a small tomahawk in my belt. Then I made my way down to the harbor where I met the rest of the group. We boarded the three ships and made our way to the crates of tea.

(D) All night, we smashed the crates and dumped the contents into the freezing cold water. As we worked, a crowd of people gathered alongside the harbor and cheered us on. The other cargo we left alone because we were sending a message: the people of Boston won't stand for taxation without representation.

Step 1 Identify the topic of your narrative.

   (A) The writer is narrating what happened on the day of the Boston Tea Party

Step 2 Determine the setting and point of view of your narrative.

   (B) The narrative is set in Boston during the time of the American Revolution. The writer is using a first-person point of view.

Step 3 Recount events in a logical sequence.

   (C) The writer takes readers through the trader's day in a logical sequence.

Step 4 Use descriptive details to help bring your narrative to life.

   (D) The writer uses sensory details to describe what the narrator felt, the ships looked like, and what the protestor wore.

   TIP Use an outline to help you organize the events of your narrative and write them in a logical order.

SOCIAL STUDIES SKILLS Continued

NATIONAL GEOGRAPHIC LEARNING

APPLYING THE STRATEGY

GETTING STARTED Now write your own narrative. In the "Connect to Your Life" section of the Chapter Review, you were asked to write a narrative connecting a recent event to the events of the time period leading up to the Declaration of Independence. Now use the steps explained in this lesson and the graphic organizer below to develop a narrative describing an event from the chapter from the perspective of a person who lived at that time. Begin by creating an outline to plan your narrative. Write down key ideas after the roman numerals in the outline. Write down details after the letters in the outline. Be sure to choose descriptive details that help bring your narrative to life. Follow your outline as you draft your narrative.

COOPERATIVE OPTION After you have written your draft, show it to a partner in your class and invite his or her suggestions on ways to improve the draft. You can also offer suggestions for your partner's draft. Remember to be positive and constructive.

TAKING NOTES

I. _____

    A. _____

    B. _____

II. _____

    A. _____

    B. _____

III. _____

    A. _____

    B. _____

THINK AND DISCUSS

1. How is a first person eyewitness account different from what you read in a standard history book?

2. Which details added the most important information to your narrative?

3. How did researching and writing your narrative shape your opinion about life during the time leading up to the American Revolution?

SOCIAL STUDIES SKILLS | **CHAPTER 6**

The American Revolution
READING LESSON

NATIONAL GEOGRAPHIC LEARNING

FORM AND SUPPORT OPINIONS

LEARNING THE STRATEGY

Think about a movie you have seen recently. Did you think it was a good movie? Why or why not? When you **form an opinion**, you determine and assess the significance, importance, or quality of something. Unlike facts, opinions can't be proven or disproven. However, it is important to **support** your opinions with examples, facts, and explanations.

Historians use facts, statistics, and examples to tell about people and events from the past. Sometimes, a historian will also express an opinion or a judgment about his or her subjects. Readers must be careful to tell the difference between facts and opinions in a text. Readers must ask themselves whether a statement can be proven, or whether it expresses an unprovable judgment. Follow these steps to form and support an opinion about a text.

Step 1 Read the passage. Look for reliable information about the subject, including facts, statistics, and quotations.

Step 2 Form your own opinion about the subject.

Step 3 Find facts to support your opinion.

GUIDED MODEL

(A) Women in the American Revolution
(A) Mary Ludwig Hays McCauley carried water to cool off the soldiers and the hot cannon her husband was firing during battle. This earned her the nickname Molly Pitcher. **(B)** She also worked with her husband to fire the cannon. **(A)** **(B)** Other women served in combat during the war. One of them was Margaret Corbin, who is buried and honored with a monument at the United States Military Academy at West Point, New York.

(A) Anna Smith Strong was a member of a spy ring on the coast of New York. She used a code based on how she hung out her laundry to let other members of the ring know when a messenger with information was arriving.

Step 1 Read the passage. Look for reliable information about the subject.

   SUBJECT (A) Women in the American Revolution

   (A) Important information about the subject: "Molly Pitcher" helped her husband and other soldiers on the battlefield. Some women served in combat; others worked as spies.

Step 2 Form your own opinion about the subject.
My opinion: Colonial women were comfortable working alongside men.

Step 3 Find facts to support your opinion.

   (B) Women such as Mary Ludwig Hayes McCauley, Margaret Corbin, and Anna Smith Strong worked alongside men to make a difference—just as women do today.

TIP To distinguish facts from opinions, ask yourself: can this be proved? If it cannot be proved, because it expresses a feeling or a judgment, then it is an opinion. You can use a diagram such as a chart to keep track of the facts and examples that support your opinions.

SOCIAL STUDIES SKILLS Continued

NATIONAL
GEOGRAPHIC
LEARNING

APPLYING THE STRATEGY

GETTING STARTED Now practice forming and supporting your own opinions as you read Lesson 3.2, "The Tide Turns," in Chapter 6. As you read the lesson, use the graphic organizer below to record your opinions about the people and events described in the text. In the right-hand column, record the evidence that supports your opinions. Remember: if you cannot find evidence to support an opinion, you must revise it. An example has been provided to help you get started.

TAKING NOTES

Opinion	Evidence
The Continental Army's replacement of Horatio Gates was the most important factor in turning the tide of the war.	• Gates's replacement, Nathanael Greene, changed the army's southern strategy.

HISTORICAL THINKING

1. In your opinion, what was the most important decision Nathanael Greene made as commander of the Continental Army's southern troops?

2. What evidence supports your opinion about Greene's decisions?

3. In your opinion, how should the Patriots have treated Loyalists who surrendered? Explain, using supporting evidence from the text.

 **The American Revolution**
WRITING LESSON

WRITE AN EXPLANATION

LEARNING THE STRATEGY

When you write an **explanation**, you give readers information about a topic. You provide facts and examples to help them understand the topic more fully. To write an explanation, first select a topic. Introduce your topic to your readers clearly, telling them what they can expect to learn about it in your writing. Then, provide details and evidence to support your ideas.

To help your readers understand your ideas, you first need to arrange them in a logical order. The order you choose will depend on your purpose for writing. For example, if you are describing something that took place over a period of time, it makes sense to arrange your details chronologically. If you are writing about a general topic, you might group your information by category. Use transitions to compare (*similarly, also, in addition*), contrast (*on the other hand, in contrast*), and connect (*first, then, afterward*) your ideas.

Step 1 Select a topic you would like to inform your readers about and gather detailed information about it.

Step 2 Write a sentence that introduces and states your topic. This is your main idea.

Step 3 Include at least three details that provide information on your topic.

Step 4 Organize your details either chronologically, step-by-step, or by category.

Step 5 Write a concluding sentence about your topic that restates the main idea in a different way.

GUIDED MODEL

(A) Trenton and Yorktown: British Errors, American Victories
(B) At the battles of Trenton and Yorktown, however, the Americans also owed their victories to something else: the British Army's mistakes.

(C) When George Washington's troops sailed across the Delaware River on Christmas Day, 1776, their enemies in Trenton should have been ready for them. The Hessian commander ignored those warnings, however, and the Continental troops defeated the British.

(D) Similarly, at the Battle of Yorktown, miscalculations led to a British defeat. Unlike the commander at Trenton, Lord Cornwallis was prepared for an American attack. Unfortunately, he also chose an unfortunate location for his camp.

(E) The Americans could not have won these battles if they had not also been brave and skilled fighters.

Step 1 Select a topic.
  (A) the battles of Trenton and Yorktown
Step 2 Write a sentence that introduces and states your topic.
  (B) This sentence introduces the topic.
Step 3 Include at least three details that provide information on your topic.
  (C) The writer includes details about the topic.
Step 4 Organize your details either chronologically, step-by-step, or by category.
  (D) The writer organizes the details by category to connect, compare, and contrast ideas.
Step 5 Write a concluding sentence.
  (E) The writer concludes by stating the main idea again but in a different way.

TIP Whether you are writing about events, categories, or people, you can use a graphic organizer to help you.

SOCIAL STUDIES SKILLS Continued

NATIONAL GEOGRAPHIC LEARNING

APPLYING THE STRATEGY

GETTING STARTED Now write your own explanation. In the "Connect to Your Life" section in the Chapter Review, you are asked to write a paragraph explaining why two individuals from the American Revolution are heroes. Use the steps explained in this lesson and the graphic organizer below to plan your explanation. The outline will help you organize your introduction, your ideas about each individual, the evidence from the text that supports each idea, and your concluding sentence. After you have finished organizing your information, draft your paragraph.

COOPERATIVE OPTION When you have written your draft, show it to a partner in your class and invite his or her suggestions on how to improve it. You can also offer suggestions for your partner's first draft. Remember to be positive and constructive.

TAKING NOTES

Explanation Outline

Topic Sentence:

↓

Detail 1:
Detail 2:
Detail 3:

↓

Concluding Sentence:

HISTORICAL THINKING

1. How did you choose your subjects for this explanation?

2. How were your two subjects similar and how were they different?

3. What did you learn about different ways to show heroism from writing this explanation?

SOCIAL STUDIES SKILLS FROM FEDERATION TO CONSTITUTION
READING LESSON

DETERMINE CHRONOLOGY

LEARNING THE STRATEGY

Think of a time you described an event or conversation to a friend. You probably described things that happened or things people said in the order they occurred. You started at the beginning and continued to the end. When you relate events in the order in which they occurred in time, you **determine chronology**. Thinking about events in sequence, or time order, helps you understand how they relate to each other.

Historians often determine chronology to tell how a civilization developed or to describe the reign of a ruler. Identifying the time order of historic events can help you understand how the events are related. Follow these steps to determine chronology.

Step 1 Look for clue words and phrases that suggest time order. Clue words include the names of months and days or words such as *before, after, finally, a year later,* or *lasted.*

Step 2 Look for dates in the text and match them to events.

GUIDED MODEL

(A) The Northwest Territory
Operating under the Articles of Confederation, Congress passed a series of **ordinances**, or laws, for settling the western lands. These ordinances established an orderly system for transferring federally owned land into private holdings, townships, and states. **(A)** The first ordinance, passed in **(B)** 1784, divided the territory into a small number of self-governing districts that could later become states.

(A) The second ordinance was the **(B) Ordinance of 1785**. It called for surveying and organizing districts into townships. The townships would be further divided into lots that the government would sell at a minimum of $1 per acre. Each township also had to set aside land for a school.

(A) Finally, the **(B)** Northwest **Ordinance of 1787** renamed the land the Northwest Territory.

Step 1 Look for clue words and phrases that suggest time order

   Time Clues (A) *The first, The second, Finally*

Step 2 Look for specific dates in the text

   Be sure to read the text carefully. Historians may not always list the dates in time order. As you read, it is important to match the event with its date.

   Dates **(B)**

   1784: first land ordinance
   1785: Ordinance of 1785
   1787: Northwest Ordinance of 1787

TIP As you read, you can create a timeline to track the time order of the events discussed in the text. A timeline is a visual tool that is used to sequence events. Timelines often read from left to right, listing events from the earliest to the latest.

SOCIAL STUDIES SKILLS Continued

APPLYING THE STRATEGY

GETTING STARTED Now sequence events as you read Lesson 3.1, "Federalists and Antifederalists," in Chapter 7. Sequencing events will help you better understand the process by which the Constitution was ratified by the states. As you read the lesson, use the timeline graphic organizer below to sequence events. List the earliest event in the first box on the left and the latest event in the last box on the right. Remember to use both clue words and dates to determine the time order of events. The first box is filled in to help you get started.

COOPERATIVE OPTION You may wish to work with a partner in your class to review the lesson and complete the graphic organizer.

TAKING NOTES

Timeline

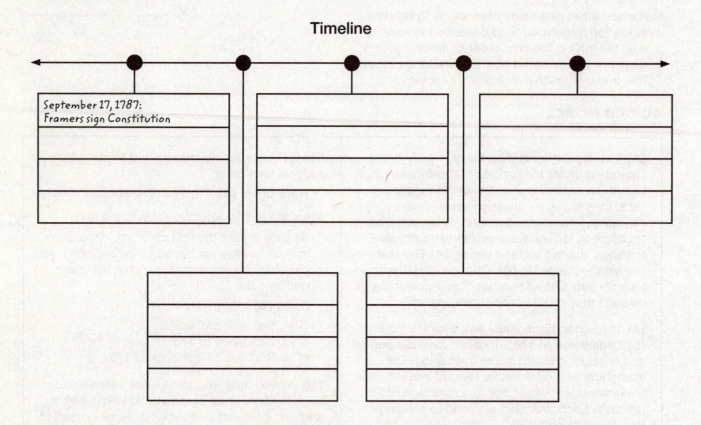

September 17, 1787:
Framers sign Constitution

HISTORICAL THINKING

1. What event made Mercy Otis Warren argue for a Bill of Rights? When did this event occur?

2. Who contributed to *The Federalist* and when was it published?

3. Put these events in order: *The Federalist* is published, The Bill of Rights is added to the Constitution, Framers sign Constitution.

SOCIAL STUDIES SKILLS — CHAPTER 7

FROM CONFEDERATION TO CONSTITUTION
WRITING LESSON

WRITE AN EXPLANATION

LEARNING THE STRATEGY

A history text usually contains **narrative** accounts of events. A narrative is an account or story of events or experiences. Narratives may be fictional, or made up, or they may be factual.

All narratives share certain characteristics, including a specific setting, or time and place. The events in a narrative usually follow a logical sequence, or order. Descriptive details, such as sensory details, help bring events and people to life. Sensory details are details that appeal to sight, sound, touch, taste, and smell.

Before writing a narrative, you should decide what point of view you will use. Most narratives are written from either a first-person or third-person point of view.

To write a historical narrative, follow these steps.

> **Step 1** Identify the topic of your narrative and gather facts about its events, people, and places.
>
> **Step 2** Determine the setting and point of view of your narrative.
>
> **Step 3** Recount events in a logical sequence.
>
> **Step 4** Use descriptive details to help bring your narrative to life.

GUIDED MODEL

(A) Daniel Shays is Coming
Dear Diary,

(B) As I look out my window, and see that vile "army" of Daniel Shays approach, I can't help but think of better times.

In the beginning, we were all so hopeful. The Articles of Confederation would be a fine form of government, we thought **(C)** when we ratified them in 1778.

The Articles offered more freedom to the common people than any in history. **(C)** And, if that were not enough, with the ordinances of 1784, 1785, and 1787, we offered more land than any common person could ever imagine.

(C) But now, how do they repay us? **(D)** Hundreds of these so-called Regulators try to crowd into the small courthouse, blocking the judges from doing their work. I pray General Lincoln's militia arrives quickly. If not, I fear order will never be restored.

Step 1 Identify the topic of your narrative.

  (A) The writer is narrating events which occur during Shays's Rebellion.

Step 2 Determine the setting and point of view of your narrative.

  (B) The narrative is set in America before the signing of the Constitution, during Shay's Rebellion. The writer is using a first-person point of view and thinking back to a better time.

Step 3 Recount events in a logical sequence.

  (C) The writer takes readers through several historical events during the time period in a logical sequence.

Step 4 Use descriptive details to help bring your narrative to life.

  (D) The writer uses sensory details to describe the action of the militia and the fear of the narrator.

TIP Use an outline to help you organize the events of your narrative and write them in a logical order.

SOCIAL STUDIES SKILLS Continued

APPLYING THE STRATEGY

GETTING STARTED Now write your own narrative. In the "Connect to Your Life" section of the Chapter Review, you are asked to write a paragraph connecting one of the First Amendment rights to your life as an American today. Use the steps explained in this lesson and the graphic organizer below to develop your narrative. Begin by choosing the topic, the particular freedom that has played a role in your life or the life of someone you know. Then determine the setting of your narrative and the point of view you will use. Next, create an outline to help you tell your narrative in a logical order. Write the key ideas or events of your narrative after the Roman numerals in the outline. Write details after the letters in the outline. Be sure to choose descriptive and sensory details that help bring your narrative to life. Follow your outline as you draft your narrative.

COOPERATIVE OPTION After you have written your draft, show it to a partner in your class and invite his or her suggestions on ways to improve the draft. You can also offer suggestions for your partner's draft. Remember to be positive and constructive.

TAKING NOTES

I. _____

   A. _____

   B. _____

II. _____

   A. _____

   B. _____

III. _____

   A. _____

   B. _____

HISTORICAL THINKING

1. How did adding specific details strengthen your narrative?

2. How did researching and writing your narrative help you understand the importance of First Amendment rights?

3. Examine some of the other rights guaranteed to Americans in the first ten amendments. Have any of them played an important role in your life?

 **GROWING PAINS IN THE NEW REPUBLIC**
SOCIAL STUDIES **SKILLS** CHAPTER **8** READING LESSON

NATIONAL GEOGRAPHIC LEARNING

IDENTIFYING PROBLEMS AND SOLUTIONS

LEARNING THE STRATEGY

Throughout history, people have faced problems and learned how to solve them. When you **identify problems**, you find the difficulties people faced. When you identify **solutions**, you learn how people tried to fix their problems. Follow these steps to identify problems and solutions.

Step 1 Read the text and determine what problem or problems people faced.

Step 2 Determine what caused the problems. There may be multiple causes.

Step 3 Identify the solutions people used to resolve, or fix, the problems.

Step 4 Determine if the solution succeeded. Ask yourself, "Was the problem solved?"

GUIDED MODEL

Creating the Court
(A) In addition to building the Cabinet, Washington and Congress created a court system. The Constitution established a Supreme Court as the nation's highest court. **(B)** But it left the question of how many justices would sit on the Court to Congress and didn't specify what its powers would be. **(C)** So, in 1789, Congress passed the Federal Judiciary Act. It called for the Supreme Court to have six justices—one Chief Justice and five associate justices. **(D)** Today, eight associate justices sit on the court. The Chief Justice presides over the judicial branch of the U.S. government as well as over the Supreme Court itself. John Jay became the country's first Chief Justice.

Step 1 Read the passage and determine what problem people faced.

  Problem (A) Washington and Congress needed to create a court system.

Causes (B) The Constitution was not specific about the makeup and powers of the court.

Step 3 Identify the solutions people used to resolve the problem.

Solutions (C) Congress passed a law that gave more specific instructions.

Step 4 Determine if the solution succeeded.

Success? (D) Yes. Today's Supreme Court is similar to the one established in 1789.

TIP A chart is a useful tool for recording information about a problem and a solution. Organize your chart to have separate rows for a description of the problem, its causes, the solutions, and the success of the solutions.

SOCIAL STUDIES SKILLS Continued

APPLYING THE STRATEGY

GETTING STARTED Now turn to Lesson 2.4 "The Parties in Conflict." Read the "Adams vs. Jefferson" passage. Identify the problems and solutions using a chart like the one below. The first box is filled in to help you get started. TIP: You can find some of the causes of the problem in "The French Revolution" passage of Lesson 2.2, "Competition for Territory and the French Revolution."

COOPERATIVE OPTION You may wish to work with a partner in your class to review the lesson and complete the graphic organizer.

TAKING NOTES

What was the problem?	Remaining neutral in foreign conflict was difficult for the United States.
What were the causes?	
What was the solution?	
Did the solution work?	

HISTORICAL THINKING

1. Why did John Adams attempt to negotiate with France?

2. How did Congress and the people of the United States respond to the XYZ Affair?

3. Was the United States successful in its goal of remaining neutral in foreign conflicts? Why or why not?

SOCIAL STUDIES SKILLS CHAPTER 8 — GROWING PAINS IN THE NEW REPUBLIC
WRITING LESSON

NATIONAL GEOGRAPHIC LEARNING

WRITE AN EXPLANATION

LEARNING THE STRATEGY

When you write an **explanation**, you give readers information about a topic. You provide facts and examples so they will understand the topic more fully. To write an explanation, first select a topic. Then provide details to support your facts. The most common types of supporting details are facts, examples, statistics, quotations, expert opinions, and personal experience.

After you select your details, you need to arrange them in a logical order. If you are describing something that happened over time, it makes sense to present your details chronologically, in the order that they happened. If you're writing a how-to article, you can present the steps sequentially, one step at a time from first to last. If you are writing about a general topic, you could group your information by category.

To write an explanation, follow these steps.

Step 1 Select a topic you would like to inform your readers about and gather detailed information about it.

Step 2 Write a sentence that introduces and states your topic. This is your main idea.

Step 3 Include at least three details that provide information on your topic.

Step 4 Organize your details either chronologically, step-by-step, or by category.

Step 5 Write a concluding sentence about your topic that restates the main idea in a different way.

GUIDED MODEL

(A) The Alien and Sedition Acts
(B) Tthe Alien and Sedition Acts are two of the most controversial laws ever passed in the United States.

(D) One major problem was that the laws limited free speech. **(C)** The law was a way to limit opposition by restricting what citizens and journalists could say.

(D) Secondly, the laws served the political purposes of the Federalists. **(C)** Thus the laws, by placing strict limits on immigration were aimed at preventing Democratic-Republicans from gaining new voters.

(D) Finally, the laws were fiercely opposed by many in the government. **(C)** Thomas Jefferson, who was Vice President, went so far as to argue that they were unconstitutional.

(E) Limiting constitutional rights, targeting political opponents, and causing members of the government to protest were all factors in the controversy over the Alien and Sedition Acts.

Step 1 Select a topic.

    (A) The topic is the Alien and Sedition Acts

Step 2 Write a sentence that introduces and states your topic.

    (B) This sentence states the main idea about the topic.

Step 3 Include at least three details that provide information on your topic.

    (C) The writer includes details on the topic.

Step 4 Organize your details.

    (D) The writer organizes the details by category. The categories include the fact that the laws: 1) limited free speech, 2) were political, and 3) were opposed by some in the government.

Step 5 Write a concluding sentence.

    (E) The writer concludes by stating the main idea again but in a different way.

TIP Put the most exciting or interesting detail about your topic last for the most impact.

© National Geographic Learning, a part of Cengage Learning

SOCIAL STUDIES SKILLS Continued

APPLYING THE STRATEGY

GETTING STARTED Now write your own explanation. In the "Connect to Your Life" section of the Chapter Review, you are asked to write a paragraph explaining how the election of 1796—the first one with political parties involved—is similar to and different from a recent election. Use the steps explained in this lesson and the graphic organizer below to plan your explanation. The graphic organizer will help you clearly state your topic and organize details about your topic into different categories. For this explanation, you should identify three categories in which you can explain how the elections were similar or different. Each of these categories should include supporting details. For example, "Number of Political Parties" could function as one of your categories. After you have organized your information, write your draft.

COOPERATIVE OPTION After you have written your draft, show it to a partner in your class and invite his or her suggestions on ways to improve the draft. You can also offer suggestions for your partner's draft. Remember to be positive and constructive.

TAKING NOTES

Topic Sentence		

Detail	Detail	Detail
Number of Political Parties		

Concluding Sentence		

HISTORICAL THINKING

1. How did you decide around which categories to use to organize your explanation?

2. What challenges did you face in coming up with supporting details to support your explanation?

3. Do you think it was possible for the two parties in the 1796 election to compromise? Why or Why not?

SOCIAL STUDIES SKILLS

CHAPTER 9

The Jefferson Years
READING LESSON

NATIONAL GEOGRAPHIC LEARNING

ANALYZE CAUSE AND EFFECT

LEARNING THE STRATEGY

Think about what happens when you heat a pot of water. The water boils. These events show **cause** and **effect**. Heating the water is a cause. A **cause** is an event, action, or condition that makes something else happen. The action of heating the water causes the water to boil. The water boiling is the **effect** of heating the water. An effect is an event that results from a cause.

Historians analyze cause and effect to figure out why events happened. They consider how an event led to changes over time. One cause can create several effects, or one effect may have more than one cause. A cause may be an event or an action. It may also be a condition, or a state of being. Follow these steps to figure out cause-and-effect relationships.

Step 1 Determine the cause of an event. Look for clue words that show cause, such as *because, due to, since*, and *therefore*.

Step 2 Determine the effect that results from the cause. Look for clue words such as *led to, consequently,* and *as a result*.

Step 3 Look for a chain of causes and effects. An effect may be the cause of another action or event.

GUIDED MODEL

Tecumseh's Idea
While the United States was trying to maintain neutrality in the war in Europe, trouble was developing at home. **(A)** American expansion into the Northwest Territory had **(B)** increased conflict with Native American nations. **(B)** Shawnee chief **Tecumseh** (tuh-KUM-suh), in particular, began to speak out against the destruction of native cultures and economies. He also criticized Native American leaders who sold their land to the United States.

(C) To present a united front against the United States, Tecumseh visited Native American tribes and spoke to them about forming a confederation, or alliance. In 1809, while Tecumseh traveled the country, the U.S. government negotiated the Treaty of Fort Wayne with several other tribes. The Native American leaders who signed the agreement sold 2.9 million acres of their land to the government for a fraction of a penny per acre. This type of "deal" was just what Tecumseh had been trying to prevent. **(C)** The treaty was the last straw and inspired many more Native American groups to join Tecumseh's cause.

Step 1 Determine the Cause.

  CAUSE (A) The cause was American expansion into the Northwest Territory

Step 2 Determine the Effect

  EFFECT (B) The immediate effect was to increase conflict with Native Americans, especially the Shawnee chief Tecumseh.

Step 3 Look for a chain of causes and effects

  CAUSES/EFFECTS (C) Tecumseh's opposition led the U.S. government to negotiate the Treaty of Fort Wayne with other tribes. This lopsided agreement, in turn, led more Native American groups to join with Tecumseh.

TIP Test whether events have a cause-and-effect relationship by using this construction: "Because [insert cause], [insert effect] happened." If the construction does not work, one event did not lead to the other.

SOCIAL STUDIES SKILLS Continued

**NATIONAL
GEOGRAPHIC
LEARNING**

APPLYING THE STRATEGY

GETTING STARTED Now practice analyzing cause and effect. Turn to Lesson 3.1, "Neutrality or War?" in Chapter 9. Use your analysis of cause and effect to deepen your understanding of the section titled, "Cutting Off Trade." Use the graphic organizer below to take notes on the text. Recall that each cause you find may have more than one effect. Two squares are filled in to help you get started.

COOPERATIVE OPTION You may wish to work with a partner in your class to review the section and complete the graphic organizer.

TAKING NOTES

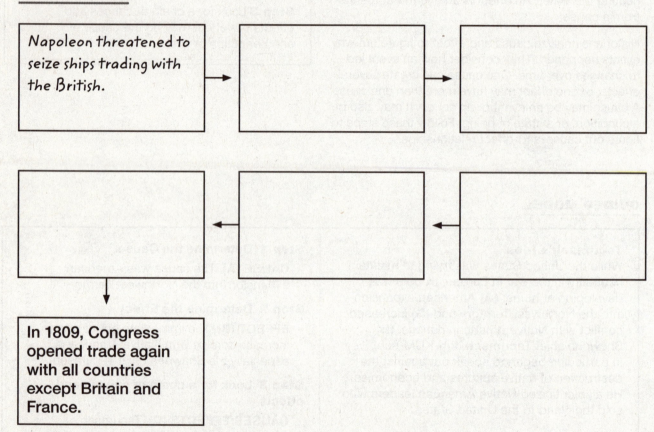

Napoleon threatened to seize ships trading with the British.

In 1809, Congress opened trade again with all countries except Britain and France.

HISTORICAL THINKING

1. What effect did Napoleon's threat to seize ships have on the United States?

2. Why did many New Englanders oppose the Embargo Act?

3. Do you think the Non-Importation Act and Embargo Act were effective in accomplishing their goals?

SOCIAL STUDIES SKILLS   CHAPTER 9

The Jefferson Years
WRITING LESSON

NATIONAL GEOGRAPHIC LEARNING

WRITE A NARRATIVE

LEARNING THE STRATEGY

A history text usually contains **narrative** accounts of events. A narrative is an account or story of events or experiences. Narratives may be fictional, or made up, or they may be factual.

All narratives share certain characteristics, including a specific setting, or time and place. The events in a narrative usually follow a logical sequence, or order. Descriptive details, such as sensory details, help bring events and people to life. Sensory details are details that appeal to sight, sound, touch, taste, and smell.

Before writing a narrative, you should decide what point of view you will use. Most narratives are written from either a first-person or third-person point of view.

To write a historical narrative, follow these steps.

Step 1 Identify the topic of your narrative and gather facts about its events, people, and places.

Step 2 Determine the setting and point of view of your narrative.

Step 3 Recount events in a logical sequence.

Step 4 Use descriptive details to help bring your narrative to life.

GUIDED MODEL

(A) Lincoln Meets King
(B) The White House meeting between Abraham Lincoln and Martin Luther King, Jr. was a pleasant one. **(C)** King began by thanking Lincoln for the important work he did ending the terrible institution of slavery. **(D)** Lincoln tipped his large dark hat and replied that he was sorry it had taken so long.

(C) The most interesting part of the meeting was when Lincoln and King discussed their regrets.

(D) "What keeps me awake at night," said Lincoln, stroking his beard, "is the Civil War. There was so much needless death. If only it could have been avoided."

(C) "I have regrets too," said King. "The Civil Rights movement was also plagued by violence. Although I always preached nonviolence, my wish did not always come true."

Both Abraham Lincoln and Martin Luther King, Jr. worked to bring racial justice and equality to the United States. Although both lived during periods of turmoil and violence, their actions and influence led to important progress.

Step 1 Identify the topic of your narrative.

   (A) The writer is narrating a fictional meeting between Abraham Lincoln and Martin Luther King, Jr.

Step 2 Determine the setting and point of view of your narrative.

   (B) The narrative states the location is the White House and uses a third-person point of view.

Step 3 Recount events in a logical sequence.

   (C) The writer first describes the conversation that took place between the two figures and then concludes with a comparison.

Step 4 Use descriptive details to help bring your narrative to life.

   (D) The writer describes the details of Lincoln's hat tip and beard stroking.

TIP Use a graphic organizer to help you organize the events of your narrative and write them in a logical order.

SOCIAL STUDIES SKILLS Continued

NATIONAL GEOGRAPHIC LEARNING

APPLYING THE STRATEGY

GETTING STARTED Now write your own narrative. In the "Connect to Your Life" section of the Chapter Review, you are asked to write a narrative imagining a meeting between a historical figure and a well-known person living today. Use the steps explained in this lesson and the graphic organizer below to develop your narrative. Begin by choosing the two people and the setting for your narrative. Then, plan a logical series of events. Include in your notes descriptive details that you can use to bring your narrative to life. Follow your outline as you draft your narrative.

COOPERATIVE OPTION After you have written your draft, show it to a partner in your class and invite his or her suggestions on ways to improve the draft. You can also offer suggestions for your partner's draft. Remember to be positive and constructive.

TAKING NOTES

People	Setting

Beginning

Middle
1.
2.
3.
4.

End

HISTORICAL THINKING

1. How did imagining the meeting between a historical figure and someone well-known now make history more relevant to your life?

2. How did you use dialogue to show similarities and differences between your historical and modern-day figures?

3. Why is it important to use descriptive details when writing a narrative?

SOCIAL STUDIES SKILLS

CHAPTER 10

Expansion and Growth
READING LESSON

NATIONAL GEOGRAPHIC LEARNING

DRAW CONCLUSIONS

LEARNING THE STRATEGY

Imagine that you have just come across a type of insect that you've never seen before. You'd probably want to know what it is and whether it's dangerous. To find out, you might gather evidence: for example, you could look up what kinds of insects live in your area. Then you might look at their pictures to see if any of them look similar to the one you found. From this evidence, you could make an educated guess that what you found was, say, a golden ground beetle. Since this beetle is not harmful, you conclude that the insect you found was safe to touch.

You probably **draw conclusions** like this all the time. Historians also draw conclusions about the past, based on artifacts, texts, and other sources. When you draw conclusions about a text, you use facts and evidence from the text in order to make a statement about its larger meaning. Drawing conclusions about a text can deepen your understanding of the text as a whole. Follow these steps to draw conclusions about a text.

Step 1 Read the text closely to gather evidence.

Step 2 Make educated guesses based on the evidence.

Step 3 Use the educated guesses you've made to draw a conclusion.

GUIDED MODEL

The Erie Canal
Americans built a system of constructed waterways called canals that allowed boats and ships to travel inland to move goods. **(A)** The largest of them, the Erie Canal, connected the Hudson River to the Great Lakes. It cut through 363 miles of land in upstate New York and linked New York City to growing cities like Buffalo, Cleveland, Detroit, and Chicago.

(A) After the Erie Canal was finished, farmers in Ohio, Illinois, Indiana, and other states in the Midwest could ship their grain much more cheaply and quickly to the East. Before the canal, farmers had to pay $100 per wagon to ship their produce. By using the canal, it was only $20. Instead of 20 days, the journey took just eight.

Step 1 Read the text closely to gather evidence.

  EVIDENCE (A) The Erie Canal was the largest canal of a national system.

  EVIDENCE (A) With the canal, farmers could ship goods to the East more quickly and cheaply.

Step 2 Make educated guesses based on the evidence.

  EDUCATED GUESSES Many growing cities needed a way to ship their goods.

Step 3 Use the educated guesses you've made to draw a conclusion.

  CONCLUSION New York City must have been one of the largest and most important markets in the United States at the time.

  TIP A graphic organizer such as a diagram can help you clarify your thinking. Then use educated guesses to draw your conclusions.

SOCIAL STUDIES SKILLS Continued

APPLYING THE STRATEGY

GETTING STARTED Now practice drawing conclusions as you read Lesson 3.2, "Increasing Regional Tensions," in Chapter 10. As you read the lesson, use a Conclusions Diagram to take notes on the evidence you find and the conclusions you draw. Drawing conclusions about the text will deepen your understanding of the conflicts regarding the admissions of new states brought about by the issue of slavery. To get you started, one piece of evidence has been filled in for you.

COOPERATIVE OPTION You may wish to work with a partner in your class to review the lesson and complete the graphic organizer.

TAKING NOTES

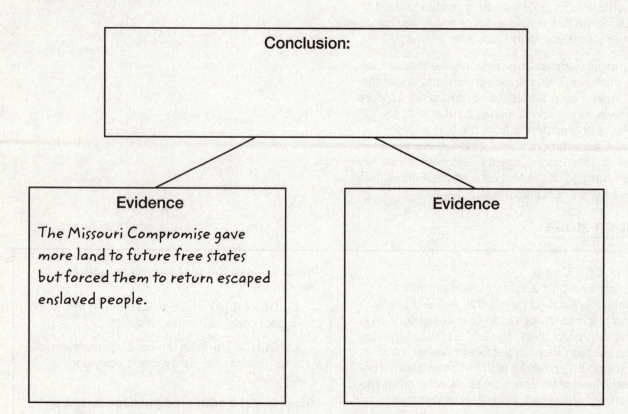

Conclusion:

Evidence

The Missouri Compromise gave more land to future free states but forced them to return escaped enslaved people.

Evidence

HISTORICAL THINKING

1. Why was the Missouri Compromise important?

2. What was the unorganized territory?

3. Explain sectionalism.

SOCIAL STUDIES SKILLS **CHAPTER 10** Expansion and Growth
WRITING LESSON

NATIONAL GEOGRAPHIC LEARNING

WRITE A NARRATIVE

LEARNING THE STRATEGY

A history text often contains **narrative** accounts of events. A narrative is an account of or a story about events or experiences. Narratives can be fictional, or made up, or they may be factual.

All narratives share certain characteristics, including a specific setting, or time and place. The events in a narrative often follow a logical sequence, or order. They include an interesting conclusion, or ending, that follows naturally from the rest of the story. Descriptive details, such as sensory details, help bring events and people to life. In a narrative about a historical person or event, you will also want to include details such as relevant facts, or quotations from the historical figures involved.

Before writing a narrative, you should decide which point of view you should use. Most narratives are written in either the first-person or third-person point of view.

Follow these steps to write a historical narrative.

Step 1 Identify the topic of your narrative and gather facts about its events, people, and places.

Step 2 Determine the setting and point of view of your narrative.

Step 3 Recount events in a logical sequence.

Step 4 Use descriptive details to bring your narrative to life.

GUIDED MODEL

(A) My Life in the Lowell Mills
The morning bell is ringing, as it rings each and every day at 5:45. First shift is about to begin. **(B)** Can it really be only three weeks since I left our farm and came here to Lowell? It feels like a lifetime.

(B) I wash quickly, and dress even more quickly. The factory fines "operatives," as we are called, who arrive late. I scurry to my place at the looms. Cotton fluff and dust float in the hot, still air like snowflakes.

(C) My massive loom settles into a loud, clacking rhythm. Hours tick by, and the work seems endless. Miss Harriet Farley says this is why we earn such good money. At 4:00, there is a sudden cry. Amelia has hurt herself on her machine.

(C) At last, the shift is over! I dread tomorrow morning, when that bell will ring again.

Step 1 Identify the topic of your narrative.

(A) The writer is narrating events in the life of a Lowell mill worker.

Step 2 Determine the setting and point of view of your narrative.

(B) The narrative is set in Lowell, Massachusetts, in a textile factory. It uses a first person point of view.

Step 3 Recount events in a logical sequence.

(C) The writer takes readers through the mill worker's day in chronological order.

Step 4 Use descriptive details to bring your narrative to life.

(D) The writer uses sensory details to show readers a clear picture of the factory.

TIP You can use a graphic organizer such as a Story Map to help you organize your narrative's characters, settings, events, and conclusion.

SOCIAL STUDIES SKILLS Continued

APPLYING THE STRATEGY

GETTING STARTED Now write your own narrative. In the "Connect to Your Life" section of the Chapter Review, you are asked to write a narrative connecting your own experience with new technology to that of someone in the early- to mid-1800s. Follow the steps explained in the lesson, and use the graphic organizer below to create a logical order for the events of your narrative. Include relevant details in your story map, and follow your map as you draft your narrative. Remember: since you are writing a narrative about historical events, you will want to research your characters, settings, and descriptive details.

COOPERATIVE OPTION After you have written your draft, show it to a partner in your class and invite her or him to make suggestions on ways to improve it. You can also offer suggestions for your partner's draft. Remember that your comments should be positive and constructive.

TAKING NOTES

Beginning

↓

Middle
1.   3.
2.   4.

↓

End

HISTORICAL THINKING

1. How did the conclusion of your narrative help connect your experiences and those of a person in the early- to mid-1800s?

2. What historical details did you include to add important information to your narrative?

3. How did researching and writing your narrative help you understand the impact of new technologies on the people of the early- to mid-1800s?

SOCIAL STUDIES SKILLS CHAPTER 11
THE AGE OF JACKSON
READING LESSON

NATIONAL GEOGRAPHIC LEARNING

COMPARE AND CONTRAST

LEARNING THE STRATEGY

Have you ever traded similar items, like bicycles, with a friend? Or maybe you have borrowed a friend's phone because yours was not working. If you have, you might have found that while the two items had many things in common, they also had a few differences. When you examine how things are alike, you **compare** them. When you examine how things are different, you **contrast** them.

A history text will often compare and contrast two ideas, individuals, groups, or events. When a text compares, it presents information about their similarities and differences. When a text contrasts, it presents the differences. To better understand when a text is comparing and contrasting, follow these steps.

Step 1 Determine what the subject of a passage or a paragraph is.

Step 2 In the passage, identify several specific features about the subject that are being compared and those that are being contrasted.

Step 3 Search for clue words that indicate similarities (comparing). Common clue words include *similarly*, also, *in addition*, and *both*.

Step 4 Search for clue words that indicate differences (contrasting). Common clue words include *in contrast*, *unlike*, *on the other hand*, and *however*.

GUIDED MODEL

(A) The Whig Party

(A) In 1834, senators Clay and Webster had formed a new political party, which they called the **Whig Party** after a British political group that had criticized the monarchy.

(B) Clay, Webster, and other opponents of Andrew Jackson chose the name because they believed Jackson had exceeded his powers as president. In fact, they often referred to him as "King Andrew."

(D) Unlike the Democrats, who supported an agrarian society, the Whigs promoted business and the expansion of industry.

Step 1 Determine the subject.

  (A) The subject is the Whig Party.

Step 2 Identify the features being compared and contrasted.

  (B) The features being compared and contrasted are the policies of the Whig Party and those of Andrew Jackson's party.

Step 3 Look for clue words that indicate similarities.

  (C) SIMILARITIES

  There are no clue words in this passage that indicate similarities.

Step 4 Look for clue words that indicate differences.

  (D) DIFFERENCES

  Unlike the Democrats, who supported an agrarian society, the Whigs promoted business and the expansion of industry.

  TIP

  A Y-Chart is a useful graphic organizer for comparing and contrasting two topics. List the differences between each topic in each of the branches, and their similarities in the base.

SOCIAL STUDIES SKILLS Continued

APPLYING THE STRATEGY

GETTING STARTED Now look at how information is compared and contrasted in Lesson 1.1, "Expanding Democracy," in Chapter 11. As you read the lesson, use the graphic organizer below to take notes on the similarities and differences between the elections of 1824 and 1828. This will help you gain a deeper understanding of how the American political landscape changed during that time period.

COOPERATIVE OPTION You may wish to work with a partner in your class to review the lesson and complete the graphic organizer.

TAKING NOTES

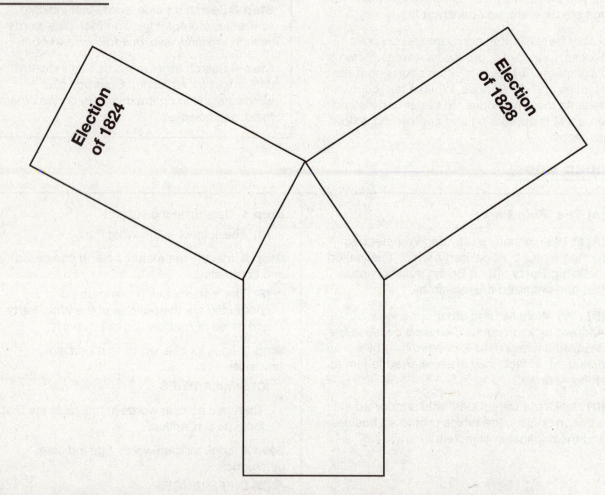

HISTORICAL THINKING

1. How were the presidential elections of 1824 and 1828 similar?

2. How were the presidential elections of 1824 and 1828 different?

3. After comparing and contrasting these two elections, how do you think the expansion of voting rights affected the election?

SOCIAL STUDIES SKILLS — CHAPTER 11

THE AGE OF JACKSON
WRITING LESSON

NATIONAL GEOGRAPHIC LEARNING

WRITE AN EXPLANATION

When you write an **explanation**, you give readers information about a topic. You provide facts and examples to help them understand the topic more fully. To write an explanation, first select a topic. Then provide details to support your explanation of the topic. The most common types of supporting details are facts, examples, statistics, quotations, expert opinions, and personal experience.

After you have selected your supporting details, arrange them in a logical order. If you are describing something that took place over a period of time, it makes sense to arrange your details chronologically, or in the order they took place. If you're writing a how-to essay, you could arrange the steps sequentially: one step at a time from first to last. If you are writing about a general topic, you might group your information by category.

To write an explanation, follow these steps.

Step 1 Select a topic you would like to inform your readers about and gather detailed information about it.

Step 2 Write a sentence that introduces and states your topic. This is your main idea.

Step 3 Include at least three details that provide information on your topic.

Step 4 Organize your details either chronologically, step-by-step, or by category.

Step 5 Write a concluding statement about your topic that restates the main idea in a different way.

GUIDED MODEL

(A) President Jackson vs. the Supreme Court
(B)) In the 1830s, a battle between Native Americans and white settlers turned into a battle between the president and the Supreme Court. **(C)** Native American groups at the time were looking for ways to remain in their homelands. **(C)** White settlers, meanwhile, were looking for ways to move the Native American groups out, to lands west of the Mississippi.

(D) To do this, the government first passed the Indian Removal Act, but the Cherokee fought back against it. Then, the Cherokee brought their case to the Supreme Court. The Supreme Court took their side in the case, and declared the Indian Removal Act unconstitutional. Rather than obey the court's ruling, however, Jackson sent troops to remove the Cherokee from their lands and send them to Indian Territory. **(E)** In doing so, he exposed a division between the presidency and the judiciary.

Step 1 Select a topic.

(A) The topic is a conflict between the president and the Supreme Court.

Step 2 Write a sentence that introduces and states your topic.

  (B) The writer states the topic in the first sentence.

Step 3 Include at least three details that provide information on your topic.

  (C) The writer includes details about how the conflict between the president and Supreme court developed.

Step 4 Organize your details either chronologically, step-by-step, or by category.

  (D) The writer organizes the details chronologically.

Step 5 Write a concluding sentence.

  (E) The writer concludes by stating the main idea again but in a different way.

SOCIAL STUDIES SKILLS Continued

APPLYING THE STRATEGY

GETTING STARTED Now write your own explanation. In the "Connect to Your Life" section in the Chapter Review, you are asked to write a paragraph using your own experience to explain how two of the opposing groups discussed in the chapter could overcome their dispute. Use the steps explained in this lesson to plan your explanation. After you have organized your details, draft your paragraph, including a conclusion that restates your main idea.

COOPERATIVE OPTION After you have written your draft, show it to a partner in your class and ask for suggestions on ways to improve it. You may also offer suggestions for your partner's draft. Remember to be positive and constructive.

TAKING NOTES

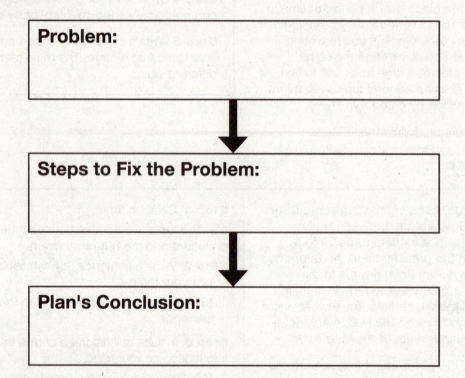

Problem:

↓

Steps to Fix the Problem:

↓

Plan's Conclusion:

HISTORICAL THINKING

1. Which groups and conflict did you choose to write about, and why?

2. What experience from your own life helped you figure out a solution to their conflict?

3. What did you learn about these groups and their conflict while writing this paragraph?

SOCIAL STUDIES SKILLS

CHAPTER 12

MANIFEST DESTINY
READING LESSON

IDENTIFY MAIN IDEAS AND DETAILS

LEARNING THE STRATEGY

Think about an experience you had recently that you would like to share with a friend. You want to tell the most important thing that happened, but you also want to add details that will help your friend better understand your experience. You may decide to tell the main event first and then supply details, or you may use the details to build up to the main event.

When you read, look for the **main idea**, the most important idea in the text. It will help you identify the author's purpose or point of view. The main idea may be expressed in a sentence, or it may just be implied. The **supporting details** in a text are the facts that support the main idea or give clues about it. Supporting details may help you understand the meaning of vocabulary in a text. Identifying the main idea and its supporting details will help you understand a text more fully. To find the main idea and details in a paragraph, follow these steps.

Step 1 Look for the main idea in the first and last sentences of a paragraph. If the main is not clearly stated, look for details that give you clues about what the main idea is.

Step 2 Find the supporting details in the paragraph. These are facts, statistics, ideas, examples, quotations, and other specific items that clarify the main idea. If the main idea is in the first sentence, the supporting details follow it. If the main idea is stated in the last sentence, the supporting details come before it.

GUIDED MODEL

Land Grants and Settlers
(A) The Mexican government also gave land grants to American farmers and merchants. **(B)** One American merchant received permission to form a colony even before Mexican independence. **(B)** In 1820, Moses Austin persuaded the Spanish governor to allow him to bring a few hundred families to settle in Tejas. He died a year later, before he could carry out his plan, but his son, **Stephen F. Austin**, inherited the land grant. **(B)** Austin moved 300 families into southeastern Tejas, establishing the territory's first legal American settlement. **(B)** A rush of other American immigrants soon followed.

Step 1 Find the main idea in the first or last sentence.

  (A) MAIN IDEA: The Mexican government gave land grants to Americans.

Step 2 Find the supporting details in the paragraph.

  (B) DETAIL: An American merchant received permission to form a colony.

  (B) DETAIL: Moses Austin planned to bring families to settle in Tejas.

  (B) DETAIL: Stephen Austin carried out the plan to start an American settlement in Tejas.

  (B) DETAIL: Many other American immigrants followed.

TIP In addition to supporting a main idea, details may also help you determine the chronological order of historical events. Use dates, as well as words or phrases such as *a year later* or *soon followed*, to figure out the sequence of events.

SOCIAL STUDIES SKILLS Continued

NATIONAL GEOGRAPHIC LEARNING

APPLYING THE STRATEGY

GETTING STARTED Now identify the main idea and supporting details in Lesson 1.1, "The Pull of the West." Read the third paragraph under "Opening the West" and use the graphic organizer below to record its main idea and supporting details. This will help you gain a deeper understanding of the role of mountain men in opening the West. To get you started, one of the supporting details is filled in.

COOPERATIVE OPTION You may wish to work with a partner in your class to review the lesson and complete the graphic organizer.

TAKING NOTES

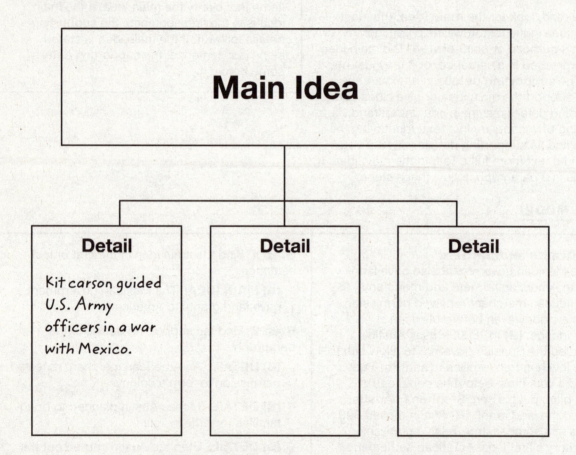

Main Idea

Detail

Kit carson guided U.S. Army officers in a war with Mexico.

Detail

Detail

HISTORICAL THINKING

1. How do the details support the main idea of the text?

2. How do the details help you determine chronological order?

3. What aspects of the text reveal the author's point of view?

SOCIAL STUDIES SKILLS | CHAPTER 12 | MANIFEST DESTINY WRITING LESSON

NATIONAL GEOGRAPHIC LEARNING

WRITE AN ARGUMENT

LEARNING THE STRATEGY

Suppose you want to write an editorial for your school newspaper to convince readers that the United States was wrong to pursue the idea of manifest destiny. You would write an **argument**, which is a case you make about an issue.

How would you go about making your argument? You would probably start with a summary of the issue and then state your position. This statement is called a *claim*. Making a claim is not enough, however. You need to provide reasons and evidence to support your claim. Evidence may include facts, statistics, quotations, and examples. Finally, you have to anticipate a reader's counter-argument. Anticipating a counter-argument is called a *response*.

To write an argument, follow these steps.

Step 1 Collect information and data about your topic and decide what your claim will be.

Step 2 Write at least three reasons that support your claim. For each reason, list at least one piece of evidence that backs up the reason.

Step 3 Anticipate an argument that could be made against your claim, and write a response to that argument.

Step 4 Read your draft. Try to read it from the perspective of someone who is undecided on the issue. Then revise your argument until it is as logical and persuasive as possible.

GUIDED MODEL

Why Manifest Destiny was Wrong
(A) The idea that the United States had a manifest destiny, or undeniable right, to expand its territory was wrong for many reasons. **(B)** The term *manifest destiny* became a popular excuse for taking over lands that rightly belonged to people who lived on them long before immigrants arrived on this continent. **(B)** The westward advance of American settlers brought disease and death to Native Americans, as well as to the settlers. **(B)** Territorial expansion led to war with Mexico and conflict with Great Britain. **(B)** It also caused division within the country over the prospect of expanding slavery.

(C) Some people argue that God intended Americans to take over the continent. However, based on the human rights abuses, war, and deaths caused by expanding nation, a more logical conclusion is that those who believed God had shown them a manifest destiny were tragically mistaken.

Step 1 Decide what your claim will be.

  (A) The writer claims that territorial expansion was wrong.

Step 2 Write at least three reasons that support your claim.

  (B) The writer lists four reasons that support the claim, based on historical evidence.

Step 3 Anticipate an argument.

  (C) The writer anticipates an argument and responds to it.

  TIP An Argument Chart can help you organize your ideas. Use an Argument Chart to list your viewpoint, your supporting details, and any opposing viewpoints you anticipate.

SOCIAL STUDIES SKILLS Continued

NATIONAL
GEOGRAPHIC
LEARNING

APPLYING THE STRATEGY

GETTING STARTED Now write your own argument. In the "Connect to Your Life" section of the Chapter Review, you are asked to identify one present-day frontier that you would like to explore and write a paragraph that presents an argument for exploring it. Use the steps explained in this lesson and the Argument Chart below to plan your argument. Begin by filling out the chart, recording your claim, support, an argument against your claim, and your response to this counter-argument. Then use your notes from the chart to help you draft your paragraph.

COOPERATIVE OPTION After you have written a first draft, invite a classmate to provide suggestions to improve your argument. You can also provide suggestions to improve your partner's first draft. Be sure all comments are positive and constructive.

TAKING NOTES

CLAIM		
REASONS AND EVIDENCE	**REASONS AND EVIDENCE**	**REASONS AND EVIDENCE**
COUNTER-ARGUMENT AND RESPONSE		

HISTORICAL THINKING

1. Which support for your argument do you think is strongest? Why?

2. How did considering a counter-argument strengthen your argument?

3. What understanding about exploring new frontiers did you gain by writing your argument?

SOCIAL STUDIES SKILLS | **CHAPTER 13** | **THE CHANGING AMERICAN IDENTITY**
READING LESSON

SYNTHESIZE

LEARNING THE STRATEGY

When you read, you take in information, details, clues, and concepts. When you **synthesize**, you combine all of that information to form an overall understanding of what you have read.

To synthesize, you determine what information is the most important. Once you have identified the most important facts, you find explanations for them and fit them in with what you already know. To synthesize, follow these steps.

Step 1 Look for solid, factual evidence.

Step 2 Look for explanations that connect facts.

Step 3 Think about what you have experienced or already know about the topic.

Step 4 Use evidence, explanations, and your prior knowledge to form a general understanding of what you have read.

GUIDED MODEL

Immigrant Neighborhoods
(B) When they arrived in the United States, British and Irish immigrants wanted to **assimilate**, or become part of, their new country. But they also held onto their culture and traditions. **(A)** In the neighborhoods where they lived close to each other, they formed groups and clubs and attended community dances, meals, and church services together. Preserving and maintaining many of their customs and traditions offered a relief from the strain of assimilation.

Step 1 Look for factual evidence.

(A) FACT British and Irish immigrants lived close together in neighborhoods and held community, club, and church events together.

Step 2 Look for explanations that connect facts.

(B) EXPLANATION British and Irish immigrants wanted to assimilate but also to keep their culture.

Step 3 Think about what you already know.

PRIOR KNOWLEDGE *I know immigrants faced challenges fitting into American life. I know that, even today, some city neighborhoods still have a predominant culture and hold community cultural events.*

Step 4 Use evidence, explanations, and your prior knowledge to form a general understanding of what you have read.

SYNTHESIS Living in neighborhoods where they could maintain their traditions helped immigrants hold onto parts of their own cultures while assimilating into their new country.

TIP Synthesis occurs when you extract the most important information from a text and give it personal meaning. Using a graphic organizer will help you see the connections between what you read and what you already know.

SOCIAL STUDIES SKILLS Continued

APPLYING THE STRATEGY

GETTING STARTED Now turn to Lesson 2.2, "Educating and Advocating." Read the first paragraph under "Reforming Institutions" and use the graphic organizer to list a fact, three explanations for it, and your prior knowledge related to the topic. Then, on the lines below the organizer, write a brief synthesis statement about the treatment of mental illness in the early 1800s. To get you started, a fact is filled in.

COOPERATIVE OPTION You may wish to work with a partner in your class to review the lesson and complete the graphic organizer.

TAKING NOTES

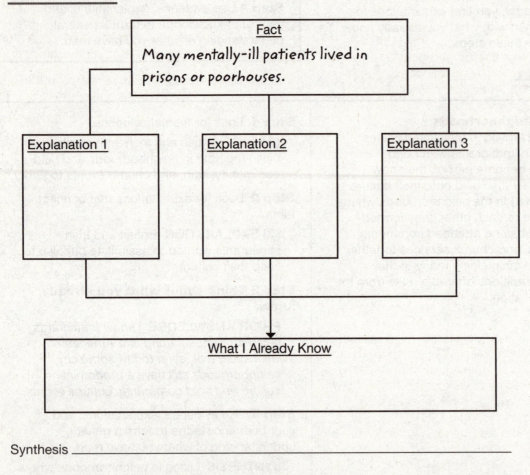

Fact
Many mentally-ill patients lived in prisons or poorhouses.

Explanation 1

Explanation 2

Explanation 3

What I Already Know

Synthesis _____

_____

HISTORICAL THINKING

1. How do the explanations connect to one another and to the fact?

2. What did you already know about the topic?

3. How does synthesizing help you understand what you read?

SOCIAL STUDIES SKILLS | CHAPTER 13 | THE CHANGING AMERICAN IDENTITY — WRITING LESSON

NATIONAL GEOGRAPHIC LEARNING

WRITE AN EXPLANATION

LEARNING THE STRATEGY

When you write an **explanation**, you give readers information about a topic. You provide facts and examples so they will understand the topic more fully. To write an explanation, first select a topic. Write a sentence that introduces or states your topic. This is your main idea. Then gather details to support your main idea. Details may include facts, examples, statistics, quotations, expert opinions, and personal experience.

After you select your details, you need to arrange them in a logical order. If you are writing about something that happened over time, you may present details chronologically, in the order they happened. If you are writing a how-to article, present the details sequentially, one step at a time from first to last. If you are writing about a general topic, group details by category.

To write an explanation, follow these steps.

Step 1 Select a topic you would like to inform your readers about and gather detailed information about it.

Step 2 Write a sentence that introduces and states your topic. This is your main idea.

Step 3 Include at least three details that provide information on your topic.

Step 4 Organize your details either chronologically, step-by-step, or by category.

Step 5 Write a concluding sentence about your topic that restates the main idea in a different way.

GUIDED MODEL

(A) Mount Holyoke College
(B) Mount Holyoke College represents a dream that succeeded in spite of challenges. **(C)** When Mary Lyon founded Mount Holyoke Female Seminary in 1837, the country was in an economic depression. **(C)** Lyon raised the necessary funds by gaining the support of male leaders and by traveling many miles by stagecoach to solicit contributions. **(C)** She lived by her advice to Mount Holyoke students: "Go where no one else will go. Do what no one else will do." **(D)** Graduates who met that challenge include Frances Perkins (1902), the first female member of a presidential cabinet, and Gabrielle Gregg (2008), the first MTV Twitter Jockey. **(E)** After overcoming early challenges, Mary Lyon's dream of empowering women through education is now a reality at Mount Holyoke College.

Step 1 Select a topic.
   (A) The topic is Mount Holyoke College

Step 2 Write a sentence that introduces and states your topic.
   (B) The writer's first sentence states the topic and main idea.

Step 3 Include at least three details that provide information on your topic.
   (C) The writer includes details on the challenges and success of the college.

Step 4 Organize your details.
   (D) The writer organizes the details into two major categories: challenges and the successes. The details about successful graduates are organized chronologically.

Step 5 Write a concluding sentence.
   (E) The writer concludes by restating the main idea in a different way.

SOCIAL STUDIES SKILLS Continued

NATIONAL GEOGRAPHIC LEARNING

APPLYING THE STRATEGY

GETTING STARTED Now write your own explanation. In the "Connect to Your Life" section of the Chapter Review, you are asked to write an explanation of how a cause you support today is linked to reform movements of the past. Use the steps explained in this lesson and the graphic organizer below to plan your explanation. The graphic will help you clearly state your main idea and list three details to support it. After you have organized your information, write your draft.

COOPERATIVE OPTION After you have written your draft, show it to a partner in your class and invite suggestions of ways to improve the draft. You can also offer suggestions to improve your partner's draft. Remember to be positive and constructive.

TAKING NOTES

TOPIC:

INTRODUCTION _____

DETAILS:

CONCLUSION: _____

HISTORICAL THINKING

1. How did you choose your topic?

2. What challenges did you face in finding and organizing the supporting details?

3. How did writing the explanation help you connect today's reforms with those of the past?

SOCIAL STUDIES SKILLS **CHAPTER 14**

A BROKEN NATION 1846-1861
READING LESSON

NATIONAL GEOGRAPHIC LEARNING

IDENTIFY MAIN IDEAS AND DETAILS

LEARNING THE STRATEGY

Imagine you need to tell a friend what a class lesson that happened on a day the friend was absent. How would you go about telling your friend about the lesson? You would decide on the most important point of the lesson and then add details to explain the main point.

The **main idea** is the key idea in a text. This makes it the most important idea in a text. Main ideas are in paragraphs, chapters, sections, and books. Sometimes the main idea is a sentence or two, and supporting details are facts that support the main idea. Other times the main idea is implied, and in those cases the **supporting details** give clues about the main idea. Identifying the main idea and the supporting details will help you understand a text more fully. It may also help you make connections between texts or chapters. To find the main idea and details of a paragraph, follow these steps.

Step 1 Look for the main idea in the first and last sentences of a paragraph. If the main idea is not clearly stated, look for details that give you clues about what the main idea is.

Step 2 Find the supporting details in the paragraph. These are facts, statistics, ideas, examples, quotations, and other specific items that clarify the main idea. If the main idea is in the first sentence, the supporting details follow it. If the main idea is stated in the last sentence, the supporting details come before it.

GUIDED MODEL

The Fugitive Slave Act
One of the most controversial parts of the Compromise of 1850 was the Fugitive Slave Act. **(A)** The act strengthened an earlier Fugitive Slave Act passed by Congress in 1783 by enforcing greater penalties on runaways and those who aided them. **(B)** Under this harsh, new act, federal marshals, or law enforcers who worked for the U.S. government, could force ordinary citizens to help capture runaway slaves. **(B)** Anyone who helped a slave escape faced penalties, **(B)** as did any marshal who failed to enforce the law. **(B)** Further, the law denied accused fugitives the right to a trial by jury.

Step 1 Find the main idea in the first or last sentences.

  (A) MAIN IDEA The 1850 Fugitive Slave Act strengthened the 1783 Fugitive Slave Act by increasing penalties on escapees and people who helped them.

Step 2 Find supporting details in the paragraph.

  (B) DETAIL Law enforcers, called federal marshals, could make any citizen to help them capture runaway slaves.

  (B) DETAIL Anyone who aided an escape faced penalties.

  (B) DETAIL Marshals who didn't enforce the law risked penalties.

  (B) DETAIL Captured runaways did not have the right to a jury trial under this law.

TIP When the main idea isn't stated in the first or last sentence, you have to find the implied main idea. Look at the details in the paragraph and ask yourself what they have in common. The connection between them is the implied main idea.

SOCIAL STUDIES SKILLS Continued

NATIONAL GEOGRAPHIC LEARNING

APPLYING THE STRATEGY

GETTING STARTED Now identify the main idea and the supporting details in Lesson 3.1, "The Election of 1860." Read the last paragraph under "The Nomination of Lincoln" and use the graphic organizer below to record its main idea and supporting details. This will help you understand the connection between Lincoln's election and the country's divisions. To get you started, the main idea is filled in.

COOPERATIVE OPTION You may wish to work with a partner in your class to review the lesson and complete the graphic organizer.

TAKING NOTES

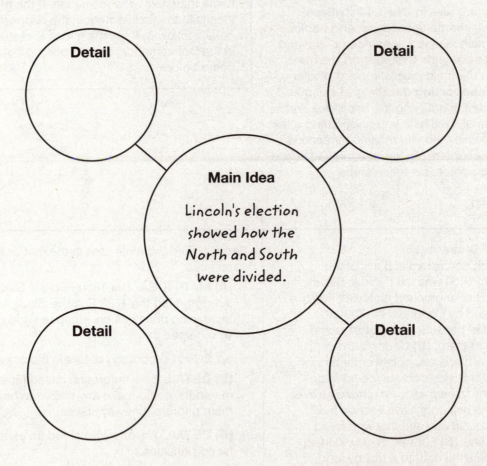

Detail

Detail

Main Idea

Lincoln's election showed how the North and South were divided.

Detail

Detail

HISTORICAL THINKING

1. What information do the details give to support the main idea of the text?

2. What conclusion can you draw from this paragraph about the South's view of Lincoln?

3. How does the main idea connect the details in the paragraph?

SOCIAL STUDIES SKILLS **CHAPTER 14** **A BROKEN NATION 1846-1861**
READING LESSON

WRITE AN INFORMATIVE TEXT

LEARNING THE STRATEGY

When you write an **informative text**, you tell readers about a topic in an objective way. In other words, you inform readers without interjecting your own opinions. Suppose you want to write an informative text about racism and slavery in the United States in the mid-1800s. You would begin by introducing the topic and main idea. For example, you might say, "Slaves in the mid-1800s in the United States experienced racism in daily life and through the nation's laws."

Next, include specific details to support the main idea. For example, you might explain that slave owners and many white Americans, especially in the South, believed African Americans were inferior to whites. You would continue to support the main idea by providing other details and examples. Finally, you would end your informative text with a concluding statement that summarizes or restates the main idea in a different way.

To write an informative text follow these steps.

Step 1 Select a topic you would like to inform your readers about and gather detailed information about it.

Step 2 Write a sentence that introduces and states your topic. This is your main idea.

Step 3 Include at least three details that provide information on your topic.

Step 4 Write a conclusion that restates the main idea in a different way.

GUIDED MODEL

(A) Racism and Slavery
In the mid 1800s, many whites believed that whites were better than African Americans, a view called racism. **(B)** Slavery in the United States existed because of widespread racism.
   (C) Some slave owners used racist ideas to explain the slave institution. These owners believed African Americans were inferior to whites, so the owners said the slaves needed to be under the care of plantation holders. **(C)** Racism was also used to justify the fear and brutality many owners used to ensure the obedience of slaves. For example, owners explained that they whipped slaves because the slaves need to be taught moral behavior. **(C)** The laws that allowed slavery were also based on racism. In the Dred Scott decision, for example, the judge ruled that slaves were personal property of their owners rather than human citizens like white people. **(D)** The widespread racism of slave owners and lawmakers enabled the institution of slavery in the United States.

Step 1 Select a topic
   (A) The topic is racism and slavery

Step 2 Write a sentence that introduces and states the main idea.
   (B) The writer states the main idea in the last sentence of the introductory paragraph.

Step 3 Include at least three details that provide information on your topic.
   (C) The writer includes details to show racism in the views and behavior of slave owners and in laws regarding slavery.

Step 4 Write a concluding sentence.
   (D) The writer concludes by stating the main idea again but in a different way.

   TIP

   Group your details according to a logical pattern. For example, group them by topic as this author does.

SOCIAL STUDIES SKILLS Continued

NATIONAL
GEOGRAPHIC
LEARNING

APPLYING THE STRATEGY

GETTING STARTED Now write your own informative test. In the "Connect to Your Life" section of the Chapter Review, you are asked to write an informative paragraph about an issue today that divides the country similar to the way the issue of slavery divided the United States in the 1800s. Use the graphic organizer below to plan your informative text. The graphic organizer will help you organize your notes. After you have completed the graphic organizer, use the steps explained in this lesson to write your draft.

COOPERATIVE OPTION Exchange completed drafts with a partner in your class. Offer each other suggestions on ways to improve the drafts. Remember to be positive and constructive.

TAKING NOTES

```
┌─────────────────────────────────────┐
│ Main Idea:                          │
│                                     │
│                                     │
└─────────────────────────────────────┘
                 │
                 ▼
┌─────────────────────────────────────┐
│ Supporting Detail 1:                │
│                                     │
├─────────────────────────────────────┤
│ Supporting Detail 2:                │
│                                     │
├─────────────────────────────────────┤
│ Supporting Detail 3:                │
│                                     │
└─────────────────────────────────────┘
                 │
                 ▼
┌─────────────────────────────────────┐
│ Conclusion Restating Main Idea:     │
│                                     │
│                                     │
└─────────────────────────────────────┘
```

HISTORICAL THINKING

1. How did you decide which issue to write about?

2. How did you choose details to support your informative main idea without inserting your own opinions?

3. What insights did you gain by writing this paragraph about how your issue or another issue, such as slavery, can divide a country?

SOCIAL STUDIES SKILLS CHAPTER **15**

Beginnings of War 1861–1862
READING LESSON

NATIONAL GEOGRAPHIC LEARNING

SUMMARIZE

LEARNING THE STRATEGY

Suppose a friend had to miss a class you are both taking. If friend asked what happened during the class, you would not repeat every word that was said. Instead, you might tell your friend the topic and some highlights of class discussion. You would make sure to include important information, such as the instructor's announcement of an upcoming assignment or test. You would summarize the class your friend missed.

When you **summarize** a text, you restate the text in your own words and shorten it. A summary includes only the main idea and the most important information and details. You can summarize a paragraph, a chapter, or a whole book. To summarize, follow these steps.

Step 1 Read the text looking for the most important information. Watch for topic sentences that provide the main ideas.

Step 2 Restate each main idea in your own words.

Step 3 Write your summary of the text using your own words and including only the most important information.

GUIDED MODEL

(A) A NEW KIND OF WAR
(A) With improvements to both rifles and larger cannons, soldiers increasingly resorted to trench warfare during the Civil War. Opposing armies dug lines of trenches, or ditches, roughly parallel to each other. The trenches gave soldiers both a vantage point from which to fire and a place to shelter from incoming rounds of ammunition. **(A)** Advances in naval technology also brought changes to warfare at sea. Before, ordinary wooden ships were vulnerable to cannon and rifle fire. New ironclad ships, or ships plated with thick metal, could withstand this heavy artillery.

Step 1 Read the text looking for the most important information. Watch for topic sentences that provide the main ideas.

(A) TOPIC SENTENCES
Topic sentences state the main ideas about changes in warfare on land and at sea.

Step 2 Restate each main idea in your own words.

RESTATED MAIN IDEA
Deadlier guns and cannons led soldiers to use more trench warfare in the Civil War.

RESTATED MAIN IDEA
New technology led to ironclad ships that held up better that wooden ship had under gun and cannon fire.

Step 3 Write your summary of the text using your own words and including only the most important information.

SUMMARY: Changes in technology led to changes in warfare during the Civil War. On land, deadlier guns and cannons increased soldiers' use of trenches, from which they could shoot with some protection from incoming fire. At sea, new ironclad ships held up better than wooden ships had under gun and cannon fire.

SOCIAL STUDIES SKILLS Continued

NATIONAL GEOGRAPHIC LEARNING

APPLYING THE STRATEGY

GETTING STARTED Now summarize a paragraph from Lesson 1.2, "An Early Confederate Victory." Read the last paragraph under "Preparing for War" and use the graphic organizer below to record its main idea and supporting details. Your completed organizer will help you summarize the information. To get you started, the Main Idea is filled in.

COOPERATIVE OPTION You may wish to work with a partner in your class to review the lesson and complete the graphic organizer.

TAKING NOTES

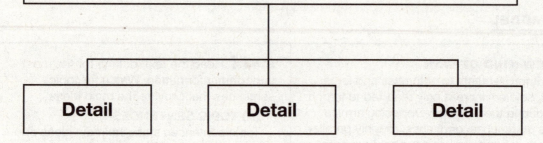

Main Idea

Shared hometowns or ethnicities linked many groups of soldiers who enlisted on both sides at the start of the Civil War.

| Detail | Detail | Detail |

HISTORICAL THINKING

1. Which unimportant details did you leave out of your summary?

2. What do the details you included in your summary reveal about the main idea of the paragraph?

3. How did summarizing the text help you understand the meaning of the term *mobilization*?

SOCIAL STUDIES SKILLS

CHAPTER 15

Beginnings of War 1861-1862
WRITING LESSON

WRITE AN ARGUMENT

LEARNING THE STRATEGY

Suppose you want to convince your classmates that George McClellan was an ineffective general during the Civil War. To persuade them, you would write an **argument**, which is a case that you make about an issue.

As you begin your argument, you make a *claim*, or statement of your position on the issue. Then, you must provide reasons and evidence to support your claim. Common types of evidence are facts, statistics, quotations, and examples. Your evidence needs to come from credible, or believable, sources. Finally, you have to anticipate a counter-argument that readers will make and write a response to it, explaining why the counter-argument is not correct.

Step 1 Collect information and data about your topic and decide what your claim will be.

Step 2 Write at least three reasons that support your claim. For each reason, list at least one piece of evidence that backs up the reason.

Step 3 Anticipate an argument that could be made against your claim, and write a response to that argument.

Step 4 Read your draft. Try to read it from the perspective of someone who is undecided on the issue. Then revise your argument until it is as logical and persuasive as possible.

GUIDED MODEL

Overly-cautious George B. McClellan: An Ineffective Civil War General
(A) We often think being careful is a good thing, but during the Civil War, being too cautious actually made Union general George B. McClellan ineffective. **(B)** The first reason McClellan's caution made him ineffective was because it led him to worry that his troops were outnumbered. **(B)** A second reason McClelland's caution made him ineffective was because it made him unwilling to lose large numbers of troops in battle. **(B)** Finally, McClellan's caution slowed down his decision making. Later in 1862, when McClellan chanced upon Lee's battle plans he cautiously delayed acting on this information. McClellan's delay gave Lee's forces time to combine and attack Union soldiers at Antietam, in the single bloodiest battle of the Civil War. **(C)** Some might say that General McClellan contributed greatly to the Civil War, especially since the Union is viewed to have won the Battle of Antietam. However, if McClellan acted sooner, rather than cautiously delay, the 23,000 deaths at Antietam might have been prevented and the entire Civil War might have been shorter. McClellan's excess caution clearly made him a less effective general.

Step 1 Decide what your claim will be.

   (A) The writer claims that being overly cautious made George B. McClellan an ineffective Civil War general.

Step 2 Write at least three reasons that support your claim

   (B) The writer describe three reasons why McClellan's caution made him ineffective and includes statistics, expert opinion, and facts as evidence to support the reasons.

Step 3 Anticipate an argument.

   (C) The writer anticipates and responds to an objection from readers who do not accept the claim of McClellan's ineffectiveness.

TIP
A graphic organizer can help you plan your argument by showing how your reasons and evidence relate to your claim and how you will address a counter-argument.

SOCIAL STUDIES SKILLS Continued

APPLYING THE STRATEGY

GETTING STARTED Now write your own argument. In the "Connect to Your Life" section of the Chapter Review, you are asked to write a paragraph in which you make an argument for or against conflict. Follow the steps explained in this lesson. You can use an Argument Planner graphic organizer to record your claim, evidence, and counter-argument. Then use your completed graphic organizer to guide you as you draft your paragraph.

COOPERATIVE OPTION After you have finished taking notes, you may wish to work with a partner before you draft your paragraph. Offer each other suggestions for improving your claims, the reasons and evidence you plan to use to support them, and your responses to counter-arguments.

TAKING NOTES

CLAIM		
REASONS AND EVIDENCE	**REASONS AND EVIDENCE**	**REASONS AND EVIDENCE**
COUNTER-ARGUMENT AND RESPONSE		

HISTORICAL THINKING

1. How did you choose which reasons and evidence to use to support your claim?

2. What counter-argument did you respond to in your paragraph, and why?

3. What understanding about conflict did you gain by writing this argument?

SOCIAL STUDIES SKILLS | **CHAPTER 16**

Reading Lesson
TURNING POINTS OF THE WAR
1863-1865

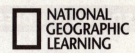

ANALYZE LANGUAGE USE

LEARNING THE STRATEGY

When you talk about your schoolwork with your friends, you may say or hear things like, "That test was a piece of cake". This statement uses *metaphor*. A metaphor is a kind of *figurative language*, words or phrases used in a way that goes beyond their literal, or dictionary, meaning. Other types of figurative language that make comparisons are similes and personification.

Writers use figurative language to make their writing more interesting and to offer comparisons that may help readers understand things in a different way. Good readers **analyze language use** to determine not only the literal meaning of words and phrases the writer uses, but also their figurative meaning.

To analyze language use when an author uses figurative language, follow these steps.

Step 1 Identify examples of figurative language.

Step 2 Analyze the comparison to understand its meaning.

Step 3 Determine how word choice indicates the author's purpose.

GUIDED MODEL

Frederick Douglass In 1832, Douglass was sent to work on a plantation, where he was regularly beaten and given little to eat. **(A)** In his own words, he was "broken in body, soul, and spirit" as "the dark night of slavery closed in upon me." Eventually, he returned to Baltimore to work in the shipyards, from where he made his escape in 1838 by fleeing to New York City. From there, he went to New Bedford, Massachusetts, where he settled and worked as a laborer.

Step 1 Identify examples of figurative language.

  (A) This sentence includes figurative language.

Step 2 Analyze the comparison to understand its meaning.

Slavery is compared to a "dark night."

Darkness and night are often associated with evil or hopelessness.

Slavery was considered by many as an evil institution because it hurt human beings.

Step 3 Determine how word choice indicates the author's purpose.

Douglass compares slavery to a "dark night" to help readers understand that he was the victim of an evil institution.

TIP As you read, take notes in a chart where you can identify figurative language, analyze the meaning of the comparison, and determine author's purpose.

SOCIAL STUDIES SKILLS Continued

NATIONAL GEOGRAPHIC LEARNING

APPLYING THE STRATEGY

GETTING STARTED Now try analyzing language use in Lesson 1.2, "Frederick Douglass: 1818-1895." As you read the lesson, use the graphic organizer below to take notes on the figurative language you read. To get you started, one example of figurative language has already been filled in for you in the first box. Follow the steps to analyze language use, then write in the smaller circles the meaning and author's purpose for using the figurative language.

COOPERATIVE OPTION You may wish to work with a partner in your class to complete the graphic organizer. Then look for other examples of figurative language or descriptive words that evoke comparison or deeper meaning.

TAKING NOTES

Analyze Figurative Language Use

Figurative Language

"We need the storm, the whirlwind, the earthquake." –Frederick Douglass.

↓

My Analysis

↓

Author's Purpose

HISTORICAL THINKING

1. What does Frederick Douglass compare the storm, whirlwind, and earthquake to?

2. What does Douglass mean when he says we need these natural occurrences?

3. Why do you think Douglass used these words in his speech?

© National Geographic Learning, a part of Cengage Learning

SOCIAL STUDIES SKILLS | **CHAPTER 16**

Writing Lesson
TURNING POINTS OF THE WAR
1863-1865

NATIONAL GEOGRAPHIC LEARNING

WRITE A NARRATIVE

LEARNING THE STRATEGY

A history text usually contains **narrative** accounts of events. A narrative is an account or story of events or experiences. Narratives may be fictional, or made up, or they may be factual. To write a historical narrative, you must understand the events, people, and places you plan to write about.

All narratives share certain characteristics, including a specific setting, or time or place. The events in a narrative usually follow a logical sequence, or order. Descriptive details, such as sensory details, help bring events and people to life. Before writing a narrative, you should decide what point of view, or perspective, you will use. Most narratives are written from either a first-person or third-person point of view.

To write a narrative, follow these steps.

Step 1 Identify the topic of your narrative and gather facts about its events, people, and places.

Step 2 Determine the setting and point of view of your narrative.

Step 3 Recount events in a logical sequence.

Step 4 Use descriptive details to help bring your narrative to life.

GUIDED MODEL

(A) A Day in My Life with the 54th Regiment
(B) The sun will rise soon in South Carolina, and I am camped with my fellow African-American soldiers of the 54th regiment. **(C)** I awake from sleep in a "dog tent," a large square of cloth buttoned over sticks. **(D)** My back aches on the cool, damp ground. Thank goodness the weather is mild, or we would freeze on this hard earth. At 5 a.m. the bugler will play reveille, and we will dress and go to roll call.

(C) After assembling, we eat. **(D)** My mouth waters imagining the smoke of cook fires. I look forward to my skillygalle, grease soaking cornmeal, for breakfast. For "dinner call" at noon, I will eat hard tack and drink water that tastes rusted from my tin cup. The day will be filled with drills, and if we are lucky, maybe a game of cards before "tattoo" call, which is the signal to go to our tents for sleep.

I remind myself that I fight for my brothers and sisters who toil under the brutality of slavery.

Step 1 Identify the topic of your narrative.

   (A) The writer is narrating events in the life of an African-American soldier.

Step 2 Determine setting and point of view.

   (B) The narrative is set at the regiment's camp in South Carolina. It uses first person point of view.

Step 3 Recount events in a logical sequence.

   (C) The writer takes readers through the soldier's day in chronological order.

Step 4 Use descriptive details to help bring your narrative to life.

   (D) Sensory details include the following: "back aches," "cool, damp ground," "hard earth," and "tastes rusted from my tin cup." The writer also uses historical terms, such as "skillygalle" and "tattoo call" that add interest to the descriptive details.

TIP You can use a graphic organizer, such as a Story Map, to help you organize the order of events.

SOCIAL STUDIES SKILLS Continued

APPLYING THE STRATEGY

GETTING STARTED Now write your own narrative. In the "Connect to Your Life" section of the Chapter Review, you are asked to write a narrative. After you choose and gather information about your topics—a turning point in your life that you will connect to a cause or consequence of the Civil War—use the steps and in this lesson to help you plan your narrative. Choose the setting of the turning point you'll describe and the point of view you'll use. You can use the Story Map to make notes about the order in which you'll present events and details that will bring your narrative to life. Use your notes to help you write. Be sure to include two or three vocabulary terms from the chapter in your narrative and to end your narrative by making it clear how your turning point connects to the Civil War.

COOPERATIVE OPTION After you have written your draft, show it to a partner in your class and invite his or her suggestions on ways to improve the draft. You can also offer suggestions for your partner's draft. Remember to be positive and constructive in your comments.

TAKING NOTES

Story Map

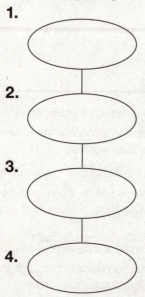

1.

2.

3.

4.

HISTORICAL THINKING

1. What historical details did you include to add important information to your narrative?

2. How did researching and writing your narrative help you better understand the Civil War?

3. How did thinking about turning points during the Civil War alongside turning points in your own life make history more relevant to your life?

Reading Lesson

RECONSTRUCTION AND THE NEW SOUTH

CHAPTER 17

DRAW CONCLUSIONS

LEARNING THE STRATEGY

Imagine you needed to buy a new computer. Which one should you buy? You would probably ask your friends and family members, look for deals, read reviews, and go the store and try a few out. This would allow you to make educated guess about which computer to purchase.

Historians do the same thing with history. They use texts, artifacts, and other sources to **draw conclusions** about the past. Drawing conclusions about a text can help you figure out the author's purpose and point of view. It can also deepen your understanding of the text's content. Follow these steps to draw conclusions about a text.

> **Step 1** Identify facts stated in the text
>
> **Step 2** Make educated guesses based on these facts
>
> **Step 3** Use the educated guesses you have made to draw a conclusion

GUIDED MODEL

Andrew Johnson Takes Over

Johnson had been an unusual choice as Lincoln's vice president. **(A)** He was a southerner from Tennessee who had served in Congress as a Democrat. **(A)** But he was definitely pro-Union, a stance fueled by his dislike for wealthy southern planters. **(A)** When Tennessee seceded, he remained in the U.S. Senate. Lincoln later appointed Johnson as Military Governor of Tennessee. During the Civil War, a military governor was charged with reestablishing the government of a southern state conquered by the Union Army.

When the 1864 election rolled around, the Republicans chose Johnson to run as Lincoln's vice president based on his loyalty to the Union. **(A)** But Johnson didn't support equal rights for African Americans. **(A)** Like most southern whites, he was deeply prejudiced, which offended many Republicans.

Step 1 Identify facts in the text

FACTS (A) Andrew Johnson was a Southern Democrat who was pro-Union. He was prejudiced against African Americans and did not support equal rights. This made Northerners suspicious of him.

Step 2 Make educated guesses based on the facts.

Andrew Johnson was likely to have problems bringing Southerners, Northerners, and African Americans together after the Civil War.

Step 3 Use the educated guesses you have made to draw conclusions.

If Abraham Lincoln had not died, Reconstruction would have gone more smoothly, as he had greater support from Northerners and African Americans than Andrew Johnson had.

TIP Use a diagram to organize the facts you have identified and the conclusions you have drawn. A diagram can help you clarify your thinking.

© National Geographic Learning, a part of Cengage Learning

SOCIAL STUDIES SKILLS Continued

NATIONAL GEOGRAPHIC LEARNING

APPLYING THE STRATEGY

GETTING STARTED Now draw conclusions as you read Lesson 2.1, "Free African Americans Gain a Voice" in Chapter 17. As you read the section of the lesson titled, "Taking Public Office," use the graphic organizer below to take notes on the evidence you find and the conclusions you draw. Drawing conclusions about the text will deepen your understanding of the impact of Radical Reconstruction on the political influence of African Americans. To get you started, one piece of evidence has been filled in for you.

COOPERATIVE OPTION You may wish to work with a partner in your class to review the lesson and complete the graphic organizer.

TAKING NOTES

Evidence and Conclusion

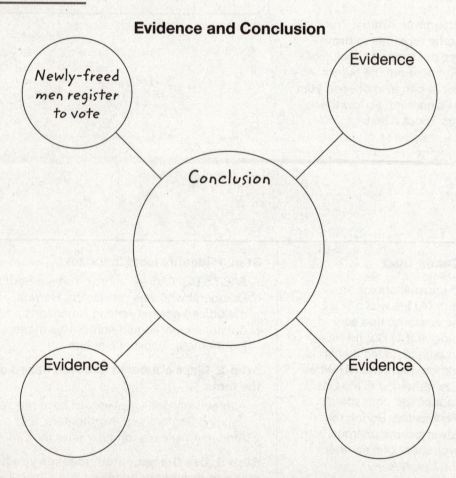

HISTORICAL THINKING

1. What influence did African Americans have in state governments during this period?

2. What influence did African Americans have in the national government during this period?

3. What conclusion can you draw about the effectiveness of Radical Reconstruction for African Americans?

Writing Lesson

SOCIAL STUDIES SKILLS — CHAPTER 17

RECONSTRUCTION AND THE NEW SOUTH

NATIONAL GEOGRAPHIC LEARNING

WRITE AN EXPOSITORY PARAGRAPH

LEARNING THE STRATEGY

Communicating information and ideas through writing is called **expository** writing. Expository paragraphs and essays often explain an idea, tell how something works, or give information about an event or issue.

To write an expository paragraph, first select a topic. Be sure your topic is not too broad. For example, the entire history of Reconstruction could not be explained in one paragraph. Instead, narrow your topic to cover a specific aspect of Reconstruction. Once you've narrowed your topic, write a sentence that introduces it. This is your main idea. Then include details that support your main idea, and determine the best way to organize them. Last, conclude with a sentence that restates the main idea.

To write an expository paragraph, follow these steps.

Step 1 Select a topic you would like to inform your readers about and gather detailed information about it.

Step 2 Write a sentence that introduces and states your topic. This is your main idea.

Step 3 Include at least three details that provide information on your topic.

Step 4 Write a concluding statement about your topic that restates the main idea in a different way.

GUIDED MODEL

(A) African American Education Under Reconstruction
(B) After the Civil War, newly freed African Americans gained educational opportunities that had not existed under slavery. (C) During slavery, in states such as Georgia, it was illegal for enslaved African Americans to learn to read. However, with the end of slavery, came the end of these discriminatory laws. (C) In addition, established in 1865, the Freedmen's Bureau setup around 3,000 schools in former slave states. (C) A combination of southern African Americans, southern whites, and northerners taught in these classrooms. Unlike in many schools of the time, these teachers were often highly qualified, having attended colleges such as Oberlin, Dartmouth, and Yale. (D) Because of the new educational opportunities, by the end of Reconstruction, over 150,000 black students had attended a school within the South.

Step 1 Select a topic.

   (A) The topic is African American education during Reconstruction.

Step 2 Write a sentence that introduces and states your topic.

   (B) This sentence introduces the topic.

Step 3 Include at least three details that provide information on your topic.

   (C) The writer includes details about the new legal freedoms, schools, and teachers.

Step 4 Write a concluding sentence.

   (D) The writer concludes by stating the main idea again but in a different way.

   TIP A graphic organizer can help you brainstorm ideas. It can also help you collect possible details to support your main idea.

SOCIAL STUDIES SKILLS Continued

NATIONAL GEOGRAPHIC LEARNING

APPLYING THE STRATEGY

GETTING STARTED Now write your own expository paragraph. In the "Connect to Your Life" section in the Chapter Review, you are asked to write a paragraph explaining how your education has helped you enjoy a favorite activity. Use the steps explained in this lesson and the graphic organizer below to plan your writing. Begin by writing a statement in the Main Idea box that names your activity. Then come up with three details that explain how education has helped you enjoy your activity. After you have organized your information, use your notes to help you write your paragraph. Remember to restate your main idea in your concluding sentence.

COOPERATIVE OPTION After you have written your draft, show it to a partner in your class and invite his or her suggestions on ways to improve the draft. You can also offer suggestions for your partner's draft. Remember to be positive and constructive.

TAKING NOTES

Main-Idea Diagram

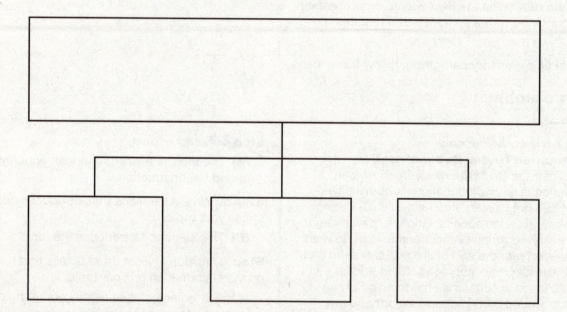

HISTORICAL THINKING:

1. How did you choose your main idea for this expository paragraph?

2. Which details were the hardest to come up with? The easiest? Why?

3. What understanding did you gain about the importance of education from this assignment?

SOCIAL STUDIES SKILLS

CHAPTER 18 Reading Lesson
WESTWARD MOVEMENT

NATIONAL GEOGRAPHIC LEARNING

CATEGORIZE

LEARNING THE STRATEGY

Do you keep your papers for the different subjects you study in different folders? Or perhaps keep your equipment for different sports in different places? If you do, you are categorizing your stuff. When you **categorize**, you sort things into groups, or categories. Almost anything can be categorized, including objects, ideas, people, and information. Categorizing is important because it helps you understand different aspects of a topic and remember information better. To categorize, follow these steps.

Step 1 Read the title and text and ask yourself what the passage is about so you can determine how the information can be categorized.

Step 2 Look for clue words to help you categorize information.

Step 3 Decide what the categories will be.

Step 4 Sort the information from the text into the categories.

GUIDED MODEL

(A) The Lives of Prairie Children

(B) In the first half of the 19th century, school was not mandatory in the United States, but most parents wanted their children to get at least a basic

(B) education. Many prairie communities built one-room schoolhouses in central locations. To attend, most children walked several miles each way. Early schools had dirt floors and were heated by a coal or wood fire. Children brought their lunches from home and used the same dipper to drink water from a community bucket. An outhouse stood behind the building; there was no indoor plumbing for bathrooms.

Even though education was important for prairie children, their **(B)** work on the homestead was considered more valuable than schoolwork. Starting about age four, children had many **(B)** chores to do and little free time to play. Because families made most of what they ate, children were expected to help milk cows, churn butter, and care for a vegetable garden to help their families survive.

Step 1 Read the title and text and ask yourself what the passage is about so you can determine how the information can be categorized.
 TOPIC (A) The Lives of Prairie Children

Step 2 Look for clue words to help you categorize information.
 CLUE WORDS (B) *school, education, work, chores*

Step 3 Decide what the categories will be
 THE CATEGORIES school and home

Step 4 Sort the information into the categories
 TIP Determining how a text presents information can help you decide what the categories will be. This text compares prairie children's lives at school and at home.

SOCIAL STUDIES SKILLS Continued

APPLYING THE STRATEGY

GETTING STARTED Now turn to Lesson 3.4, "Wounded Knee," and read the text under "More Unsuccessful Policies." Categorize the policies to help you organize the information and understand the ways government policies affected Native Americans. Use the graphic organizer below to categorize the information. To get you started, one of the categories has been filled in.

COOPERATIVE OPTION You may wish to work with a partner in your class to review the lesson and complete the graphic organizer.

TAKING NOTES

Inference Equation Chart

Categories of Government Policies	
Cultural policies	

HISTORICAL THINKING:

1. How does the text present information?

2. How are the categories related to the way the text is presented?

3. How does categorizing help you understand why the policies were ineffective?

SOCIAL STUDIES SKILLS — CHAPTER 18 — Writing Lesson
WESTWARD MOVEMENT

WRITE AN ARGUMENT

LEARNING THE STRATEGY

Suppose you are a populist candidate in the 1890s who wants to convince voters to accept your views. To make your case, you would write a speech to present your **argument**. An argument is a case that you make about an issue. You would probably start with a summary of the issues and then state your position on the issue. This statement is called a *claim*.

To support your claim, you would provide reasons and evidence, such as facts, statistics, quotations, or examples. Finally, you have to anticipate an opponent's counter-argument and write a *response* that shows why the counter-argument is incorrect.

To write a speech that presents an argument, follow these steps.

Step 1 Collect information and data about your topic and decide what your claim will be.

Step 2 Write at least three reasons that support your claim. For each reason, list at least one piece of evidence that backs up the reason.

Step 3 Anticipate an argument that could be made against your claim, and write a response to that argument.

Step 4 Read your draft. Try to read it from the perspective of someone who is undecided on the issue. Then revise your argument until it is as logical and persuasive as possible.

GUIDED MODEL

Support the Populist Party
(A) The Populist Party represents farmers and we will put more money in your pocket! How? **(B)** First, we will help you take back land from the railroad companies that you can use to grow more crops to sell. **(B)** Next, we will demand that the government put more paper money in circulation. This will raise the prices for your crops. **(B)** In addition, we support the free silver movement, which will increase the money supply and will also inflate prices. **(C)** To those who support the gold standard, we point out that as the value of the dollar goes up, the price of goods goes down. As a result, hardworking American farmers must produce more just to maintain the same level of income. If you are looking for an end to your financial problems, support the Populist Party.

Step 1 Decide what your claim will be.

  (A) The author claims that the Populist Party will raise crop prices so farmers have more money.

Step 2 Present at least three reasons that support your claim.

  (B) The speaker lists three reasons that support the claim and backs up each one with one piece of evidence.

Step 3 Anticipate an argument.

  (C) The speaker anticipates a counter-argument and responds to it.

  TIP Using an Argument Chart can help you organize your ideas. In an Argument Chart, you list your viewpoint, your supporting details, and any opposing arguments you anticipate.

SOCIAL STUDIES SKILLS Continued

APPLYING THE STRATEGY

GETTING STARTED Now write your own argument. In the "Connect to Your Life" section of the Chapter Review, you are asked to choose two groups of people who clashed over land in the West and write a paragraph in which you present an argument in favor of one side. Use the steps explained in this lesson and the Argument Chart below to plan your argument. Begin by filling out the chart, recording your viewpoint, your support, and opposing viewpoints. Then use your notes to help you draft your paragraph.

COOPERATIVE OPTION After you have written a first draft, invite a classmate to provide suggestions to improve your argument. You can also provide suggestions to improve your partner's first draft. Remember to be positive and constructive.

TAKING NOTES

Argument Chart

Viewpoint	Support	Opposing Viewpoint

HISTORICAL THINKING:

1. How did you decide which group to support in your argument?

2. Which evidence do you think provided the strongest support to your claim? Why?

3. How did anticipating a counter-argument help you understand clashes over land in the American West?

SOCIAL STUDIES SKILLS | **CHAPTER 19**

Reading Lesson
INDUSTRIALIZATION AND IMMIGRATION 1860-1914

NATIONAL GEOGRAPHIC LEARNING

IDENTIFY MAIN IDEAS AND DETAILS

LEARNING THE STRATEGY

Imagine you want to tell a friend about a good book you read recently. You would probably want to tell your friend the most important point of the book. You would probably also add some key details to help your friend experience and understand the book. You may decide to tell the main event first and then supply details, or you may use the details to build up to the main point.

When you read, look for the **main idea**, or the most important idea in a text. Main ideas are in everything you read: paragraphs, chapters, sections, and books. Sometimes the main idea is stated in a sentence or two, and **supporting details** are facts that support the main idea. Other times the main idea is implied, and in those cases the supporting details will also provide clues to help you figure out the main idea. Identifying the main idea and

supporting details can help you understand a text better. To find the main idea and details of a paragraph, follow these steps.

Step 1 Look for the main idea in the first and last sentences of a paragraph. If the main is not clearly stated, look for details that give you clues about what the main idea is.

Step 2 Find the supporting details in the paragraph. These are facts, statistics, ideas, examples, quotations, and other specific items that clarify the main idea. If the main idea is in the first sentence, the supporting details follow it. If the main idea is stated in the last sentence, the supporting details come before it.

GUIDED MODEL

Disadvantages of Railroads
(A) The railroads did not benefit everyone, though. **(B)** Train tracks cut through Native American land and hunting grounds. Small towns popped up quickly along the tracks. As a result, **(B)** the government took more Native American land to satisfy the increasing desire for property. **(B)** The natural environment suffered. Hunters came by train to kill buffalo for sport, even though Native Americans depended upon the animals for survival. **(B)** The blasting of mountains and chopping down of trees required to lay the tracks changed the landscape forever.

Step 1 Find the main idea in the first or last sentence.

(A) MAIN IDEA The railroads did not benefit everyone.

Step 2 Find the supporting details in the paragraph.

(B) DETAIL The train tracks disturbed Native American land.

(B) DETAIL The government took more Native American land in order to build towns near the railroad tracks.

(B) DETAIL The buffalo population decreased because of hunters traveling by train to hunt buffalo.

(B) DETAIL Trees were cut down, and mountains were tunneled, changing the natural environment.

TIP Use a main idea diagram to identify and organize the main idea and details. A main idea diagram can help you see how the supporting details relate to the main idea.

1 of 4 U.S. HISTORY

© National Geographic Learning, a part of Cengage Learning

SOCIAL STUDIES SKILLS Continued

APPLYING THE STRATEGY

GETTING STARTED Now identify the main idea and supporting details in Lesson 1.3, "The Age of Invention." Read the third paragraph under "New Industries, New Inventions" and use the graphic organizer below to record the main idea and supporting details. This will help you gain deeper understanding of the inventions springing from electric lights. To get you started, one of the supporting details is filled in.

COOPERATIVE OPTION You may wish to work with a partner in your class to review the lesson and complete the graphic organizer.

TAKING NOTES

Main-Idea Diagram

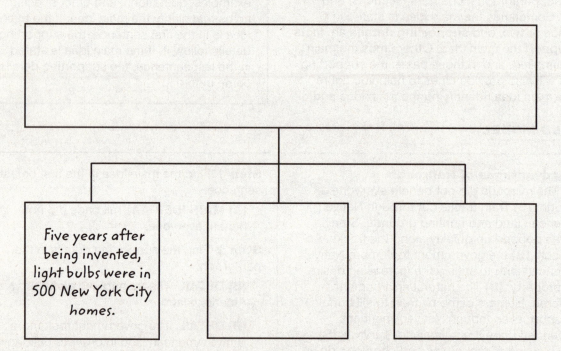

Five years after being invented, light bulbs were in 500 New York City homes.

HISTORICAL THINKING:

1. Where did you find the main idea of this paragraph?

2. Where did you find the supporting details in the paragraph?

3. How do the details in the paragraph support the main idea?

SOCIAL STUDIES SKILLS

CHAPTER 19

Writing Lesson
INDUSTRIALIZATION AND IMMIGRATION 1860-1914

WRITE AN INFORMATIVE TEXT

LEARNING THE STRATEGY

When you write an **informative text**, you tell readers about a topic in an objective way. In other words, you inform readers without interjecting your own opinions. Suppose you want to write an informative text about the community contributions of Jane Addams. You would begin by introducing the topic. For example, you might say, "Jane Addams provided services at Hull House to help immigrants and poor people."

Next, include specific details to support the main idea. For example, you might note that one main area of service at Hull House was education. You would continue to support the main idea by providing other details. Finally, you would end the informative text with a concluding sentence that summarizes or restates the main idea in a different way.

To write an informative text, follow these steps.

Step 1 Select a topic you would like to inform your readers about and gather detailed information about it.

Step 2 Write a sentence that introduces and states your topic. This is your main idea.

Step 3 Include at least three details that provide information on your topic.

Step 4 Write a conclusion that restates the main idea in a different way.

GUIDED MODEL

(A) Community Contributions of Jane Addams
(B) Jane Addams provided a range of services to help immigrants and poor people at Hull House. **(C)** Education was the primary service. Addams and Ellen Gates Starr originally opened the Hull House in 1889 as a kindergarten. Eventually, they provided elementary and high school classes, as well as college and evening courses for adults. English classes were especially important. **(C)** Hull House also supported working parents by providing infant daycare. **(C)** Addams also provided services and facilities at Hull House that helped to build community among people in the neighborhood. They sponsored a variety of clubs. They also built a gymnasium and playground, and offered meeting rooms for local groups. **(D)** Education, support for workers, and community building were among the valuable ways Addams served its poor and immigrant neighbors and visitors to Hull House.

Step 1 Select a topic
  (A) The topic is the community contributions of Jane Addams.

Step 2 Write a sentence that introduces and states the main idea.
  (B) This sentence states the main idea.

Step 3 Include at least three details that provide information on your topic.
  (C) The writer includes details on the educational, worker support, and community-building services Addams offered to support the main idea.

Step 4 Write a concluding sentence.
  (D) The writer concludes by stating the main idea again but in a different way.

TIP When you research, gather more information than you need. Then choose the most interesting information to include in your text.

SOCIAL STUDIES SKILLS Continued

NATIONAL
GEOGRAPHIC
LEARNING

APPLYING THE STRATEGY

GETTING STARTED Now write your own informative text. In the "Connect to Your Life" section of the Chapter Review, you are asked to write a paragraph that tells about the admirable traits of a person from the chapter and how you try to mirror those same traits in your own actions. Use the graphic organizer below to plan your informative text. Write the name of the person you choose in the middle, and fill in the traits you find admirable about the person on the surrounding lines. Use your notes to help you write your paragraph. Include textual evidence from the chapter that supports your ideas about the person, along with two or three vocabulary terms from the chapter.

COOPERATIVE OPTION Exchange completed drafts with a partner in your class. Offer each other suggestions on ways to improve the drafts. Remember to be positive and constructive.

TAKING NOTES

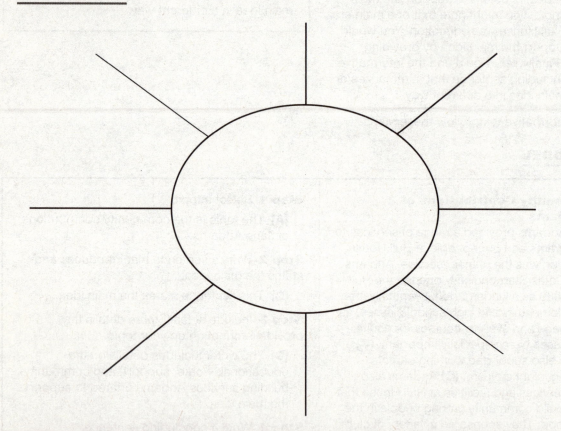

HISTORICAL THINKING:

1. How did you decide which person from the chapter you would connect to your life?

2. Did any research or closer reading for textual evidence help you understand the historical person in a more meaningful way?

3. What insights did you have about yourself after writing this informative text?

SOCIAL STUDIES SKILLS | **CHAPTER 20** | Reading Lesson
THE PROGRESSIVE ERA 1890-1920

NATIONAL GEOGRAPHIC LEARNING

SYNTHESIZE

LEARNING THE STRATEGY

When you learn new information in a classroom lesson, you take in details, clues, and concepts. You may also have prior knowledge on topics that relate to the lesson. When you combine the evidence and explanations in the lesson with what you already know, you **synthesize**, or combine data to form an overall understanding. To synthesize what you read, follow these steps.

Step 1 Look for solid, factual evidence.

Step 2 Look for explanations that connect facts.

Step 3 Think about what you have experienced or know about a topic.

Step 4 Use evidence, explanations, and your prior knowledge to form a general understanding of what you have read.

GUIDED MODEL

Women and Education

(A) The beginning of the 20th century also witnessed more American women than ever attending and graduating from high school. Some even earned a college education, but mostly in fields considered appropriate for women, such as elementary education. **(B)** Women had few educational opportunities in fields such as law, medicine, and higher education, which were considered subjects only suitable for men. But a few pioneering women fought to overcome that way of thinking. **(A)** Ellen Spencer Mussey and Emma Gillett had managed to become attorneys, but they knew how difficult it was for most women to study law and earn a degree in it. **(B)** So, in 1898, after a woman approached Mussey about studying law with her, Mussey and Gillett decided to take action. They founded the Washington School of Law in Washington D.C. Although the college also admitted men, its primary focus was educating women in the law. Today, it is part of American University.

Step 1 Look for solid, factual evidence.

(A) FACTS More American women than ever graduated from high school at the beginning of the 20th century.

(A) FACTS Ellen Spencer Mussey and Emma Gillet had become lawyers.

Step 2 Look for explanations that connect facts.

(B) EXPLANATION Some women wanted to fight the thinking that only men could study law, medicine, and higher education.

(B) EXPLANATION Mussey and Gillett founded the Washington School of Law.

Step 3 Think about what you have experienced or know about a topic.

I know that women had struggles breaking into certain fields.

Step 4 Form a general understanding of what you have read.

At the beginning of the 20th century more women were becoming educated, but higher education, and fields like medicine and law were considered appropriate only for men. In 1898, Mussey and Gillett broke through this expectation.

TIP Once you have identified the most important facts, organize them, find explanations for them, and fit them in with what you already know.

SOCIAL STUDIES SKILLS Continued

APPLYING THE STRATEGY

GETTING STARTED Now turn to Lesson 4.2, "The Spanish-American War." Read the second paragraph under "A World Power" and use the graphic organizer to list a fact, three explanations for it, and your prior knowledge related to the topic. Then on the lines below the organizer, write a brief synthesis statement about fighting during the Spanish-American War.

COOPERATIVE OPTION You may wish to work with a partner in your class to review the lesson and complete the graphic organizer.

TAKING NOTES

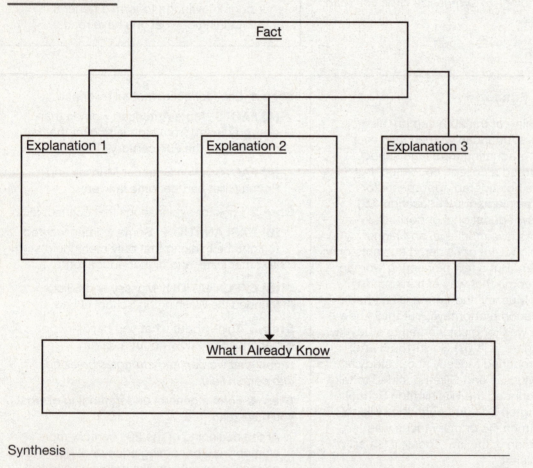

Synthesis _____

_____

HISTORICAL THINKING:

1. How do the explanations connect to one another and to the fact?

2. What did you already know about the topic?

3. How does synthesizing help you understand what you read?

SOCIAL STUDIES SKILLS — CHAPTER 20

Writing Lesson
THE PROGRESSIVE ERA

WRITE AN EXPOSITORY PARAGRAPH

LEARNING THE STRATEGY

Communicating information and ideas through writing is called **expository writing**. Expository paragraphs and essays often explain an idea, tell how something works, or give information about an event or issue.

To write an expository paragraph, first select a topic. Be sure your topic is not too broad. For example, the entire history of Theodore Roosevelt's presidency could not be explained in a paragraph. Instead, narrow your topic to cover a specific aspect of his presidency. Once you've narrowed your topic, write a sentence that introduces it. This is your main idea. Then include details that support your main idea, and determine the best way to organize them. Last, conclude with a sentence that restates the main idea.

To write and expository paragraph, follow these steps.

Step 1 Select a topic you would like to inform your readers about and gather detailed information about it.

Step 2 Write a sentence that introduces and states your topic. This is your main idea.

Step 3 Include at least three details that provide information on your topic.

Step 4 Write a concluding sentence that restates your main idea in a different way.

GUIDED MODEL

(A) Conservation Under Theodore Roosevelt
(B) As president, Theodore Roosevelt created organizations that preserved land and wildlife. **(C)** Roosevelt started the United States Forest Service in 1901. This service protected 230 million acres of public land. **(C)** The National Park System thrived under Roosevelt and beyond. Even after his presidency, in 1916, he helped preserve public lands by establishing twenty-three of the thirty-five park sites created by the National Park Service. **(C)** Also during his presidency, Roosevelt started the Federal Bird Reserve, which protected birds. Across the nation, he created fifty-one reserves for birds. Over time these refuges protected other wildlife, too, and became today's United States Fish and Wildlife Service. **(D)** Without the conservation efforts and policies of Theodore Roosevelt, the United States would not have so many public lands dedicated to wildlife preservation and protection.

Step 1 Select a topic.
  (A) The topic is conservation under Theodore Roosevelt.

Step 2 Write a sentence that introduces and states your topic.
  (B) This sentence states the main idea.

Step 3 Include at least three details that provide information on your topic.
  (C) This detail is about Roosevelt's establishment of the United States Forest Service.

  (C) This detail is about Roosevelt's efforts to support the park systems on a national level.

  (C) This detail is about Roosevelt's creation of the Federal Bird Reserve.

Step 4 Write a concluding sentence that restates your main idea in a different way.
  (D) The writer concludes by stating the main idea again but in a different way.

  TIP Idea Diagrams help writers brainstorm and organize ideas. They are ideal tools to use to collect possible details to support a main idea or topic.

SOCIAL STUDIES SKILLS Continued

NATIONAL GEOGRAPHIC LEARNING

APPLYING THE STRATEGY

GETTING STARTED Now write your own expository paragraph. In the "Connect to Your Life" section of the Chapter Review, you are asked to compare the media of the Progressive Era with today's media. Use the steps explained in this lesson and the graphic organizer below to plan your writing. Fill in details about the media of the Progressive Era, and fill in details about today's media. Then fill in details of how the two are the same. After you have organized your information, write your paragraph.

COOPERATIVE OPTION Exchange completed drafts with a partner in your class. Offer each other suggestions on ways to improve the drafts. Remember to be positive and constructive.

TAKING NOTES

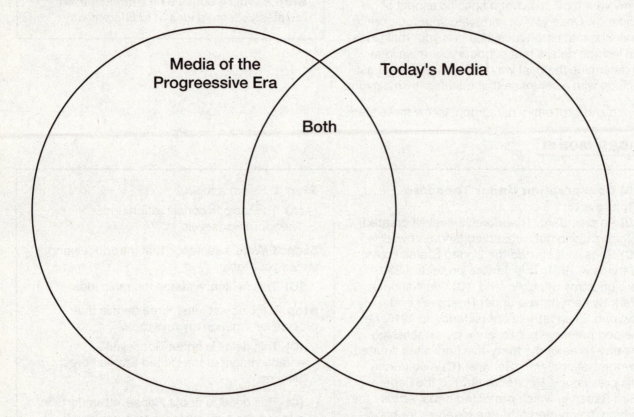

Media of the Progreessive Era

Today's Media

Both

HISTORICAL THINKING:

1. Describe the media of the Progressive Era.

2. How is the media of the Progressive Era similar to today's media?

3. What insights about the spread of information did you gain by writing this paragraph?